FAITHFULNESS

The Ministry Writings of
C. John and Gretchen Steer

Autumn Ridge Church
Rochester, Minnesota
AutumnRidgeChurch.org
2007

Mission

The mission of Autumn Ridge Church is captured in the words:

Loving God. Serving people.

When Jesus was asked, "Of all the commandments, which is the most important?" he replied:

> . . . *'Love the Lord your God with all your heart and with all your soul and with all your mind and with all your strength.' The second is this: 'Love your neighbor as yourself.' There is no commandment greater than these. (Mark 12:29-31)*

Acknowledgments

The authors and editors joyfully acknowledge the support and encouragement of many whose contributions propelled this project.

The thoughtful writings of scholars, theologians, professors, teachers and Bible commentators influenced important aspects of this collection. Further inspiration came from the congregations served by the authors.

The editors particularly acknowledge the comments, encouragement support and prayers of Laura Maher, Ann Riggott, Mark Schibilla, the Elder Board of Autumn Ridge Church, Bob Stanhope, and the staff of Christos Bookcenter. Skilled technical contributions were made by Marge Fynbo (photography), Carol Geselle (transcription), and Davies Printing Company.

Scripture references have been rendered from several translations including the *King James Version*, the *New American Standard Bible*, the *Revised Standard Version*, and the *New International Version*. Quotations from the Scriptures are generally printed in italics. Pronouns referring to God are in lower case to promote understanding and accurately reflect the original biblical languages.

Foreword

He is the son of a British pastor. He is a would-be Royal Air Force pilot. His decision at 16 to commit his life to the service of Jesus Christ led this creative student to theological training at London's finest seminary, and launched an ongoing career of Christian ministry that spans continents and decades. She is the daughter of Lutheran parents who met at St. Olaf college. Educated at UCLA, her career as a successful advertising executive in Southern California was enmeshed with her devotion to Jesus Christ and to a peculiar Englishman whose world travels led to their most unlikely meeting. Married in 1977, neither life would be the same. C. John and Gretchen Steer have been changed by God. They have also changed each other and have changed many lives they have served in 30 years of ongoing Christian ministry in California, Minnesota, and across the world.

Profoundly different in many ways, the Steers nonetheless share distinctives that have made their teaching ministries unique and effective. Fiercely independent, C. John and Gretchen are clever, well-read, well-traveled, thoughtful, sensitive, practical, warm, sharp-witted, stubborn, and determined to honor the One who died for them on a cloudy day long ago outside of Jerusalem. Best of all, these teachers, parents, and shepherds to thousands are also gifted authors. After three decades, each has left a superb collection of ministry writings rich in biblical inspiration, practicality, humor, and honesty. It is this ongoing written legacy that is here celebrated in this collection.

This book samples the first three decades of written teaching by C. John and Gretchen Steer, including sermons, Bible study notes, reminiscences and written contributions to publications and newsletters. The content is as remarkably varied and rich as the intended audiences. The reader will find practical advice, wise guidance, biblical insight, and uncommon freshness of perspective. The collection also reveals with unusual clarity the maturation and seasoning wrought in the lives of two Christian servants surrendered to their God. The authors discuss their grief in the face of astonishing personal calamity and loss, their joys in each other, and their depth of experience in service to family and congregations. Through it all, the reader meets two sojourners anticipating a face-to-face relationship with a timeless God.

The publication of these ministry writings seeks to accomplish three goals. First, to honor Jesus Christ by sharing the biblically-inspired writings of two unique servants; second, to honor the Steers for their 30 years of faithful ministry; third, to raise funds in support of the ministries of Autumn Ridge Church, Rochester Minnesota, as the congregation celebrates 150 years of service.

It has been an honor to develop this collection.

Jim Maher

Brenda Schibilla

David Swanson

Rochester, Minnesota
November 2007

Preface

Re-reading the material in this collection has provided us with a remarkable romp through 30 years of shared ministry. It's our hope that you will find in these pages an accurate reflection of our lives, as well as our desire that others would join us in the joyful, painful, tumultuous, and exhilarating walk that is day-to-day faith in Jesus Christ.

Both of us write as speakers, in the vernacular, rather than as academics or scholars. We both acknowledge the great debt we owe to the commentators and writers we read, and from whom we freely quote in our talks and sermons. In this context, we have chosen not to footnote references in detail. We humbly acknowledge that our work would have been much more prosaic without the contributions of Bible commentators over many centuries. In addition, we're indebted to the suggestions of family and friends. We've begged, borrowed and stolen ideas from preachers, pastors, and theologians, but the greatest sources of inspiration have been our congregations. Their creative comments, questions, and conversations sparked the ideas collected here.

Indeed, these first 30 years have been wonderful, largely because of the two delightful congregations we have been privileged to pastor. Ministers don't often take the opportunity to explicitly state their love for their flocks. We hope this book will help our congregations to know that they have been the objects not only of our ministry but of our love.

Here's to the next 30 (or so!) years of ministry, and to heaven, when all the people with whom we've shared our lives will gather together.

C. John and Gretchen Steer
Rochester, Minnesota
November 2007

Contents

Chapter		**Page**

Chapter 1

But God
John
April 1972

> *In order to be admitted to seminary in England, one has to be sponsored by a local church. Part of this sponsorship involves a demonstration of preaching abilities. "But God" was the first sermon John ever preached in England, at Trinity Baptist Church, where his father was the pastor.*
>
> *Trinity Baptist Church has a balcony, where John's brothers and friends sat during the service. To encourage him in his new calling, they held up numeric scores, as judges do in the Olympics. Fortunately, his admittance to Spurgeon's College was not dependent on the scores: 1.5, 1.0, and so on.*
> *-G.S.*

Today we are going to look at the two biblical words "BUT GOD." These two words illustrate the difference between God and us. They describe who God is and help us to understand what he wants to do in our lives.

BUT GOD chooses the weak. The English Soccer Cup Final will soon be here. The clubs competing for this title will pick the very best players. We understand this is the way of the world. If God were to act in a human fashion we would expect him to pick the best people to be on his team. We would expect him to cream off the most intelligent from our society so that they would be the most able witnesses. But listen to what God says:

> *But God hath chosen the foolish things of the world to confound the wise; and God hath chosen the weak things of the world to confound the things which are mighty. (1 Corinthians 1:27)*

We would choose the strong but God chooses the weak. It is interesting that it was the wise and the intellectuals of their day who put Jesus to death.

BUT GOD reveals. How does God choose the weak? Paul is telling the Corinthian church that Christianity is not a matter of intelligence. We will never convince anyone to become a Christian by clever argument. In Chapter 2 Paul goes on to explain why. He does not want their faith to stand on the wisdom of men but rather in the power of God:

> *Eye hath not seen, nor ear heard, neither have entered into the heart of man, the things which God hath prepared for them that love him. BUT GOD hath revealed them unto us by his Spirit. (1 Corinthians 2:9-10)*

God reveals himself to the weak. This is made by personal revelation. Human wisdom would tell us that God would select an elite. But God chooses the weak and reveals himself to them.

BUT GOD shows his love. We have seen that God chooses the weak but the big question is why? Paul tells us in Romans:

> *But God commendeth his love towards us, in that while we were yet sinners, Christ died for us. (Romans 5:8)*

I like the way the Living Bible translates the previous verse:

> *Even if we were good we really would not expect anyone to die for us although of course that might be barely possible. (Romans 5:7)*

Plenty of people have died for causes. Members of the Irish Republican Army have died in their fight for a united Ireland. No one has forced them but they choose to fight for something they feel very strongly about. This is not surprising. Jesus told his disciples that any person can love their friends. It is easy to love those who love us. What would be amazing is if a member of the Irish Republican Army died protecting a British soldier.

Yet this is what Paul is saying. We would not be surprised if Christ had died for good people, but he died for sinners. This is remarkable because Paul has already told us that God hates sin. The IRA sees the soldier as a representative of the British government. They can't distinguish between the man and the office. But God can. He hates the sin but loves the sinner.

Yet God's love was not passive, it was practical. Christ died for us. As Christians we have God's love in us. Someone once described love as being "down and out." It comes down and goes out. I attended the Festival of Light Rally in London last week. We were reminded that as Christians we can make our point by demonstrating against pornography and other social sins but our main witness as Christians is by the outshining of our love and concern for each other.

BUT GOD gives life. Yet what is the purpose of God's plan? Why does he show his love to us? Paul's letter to the Ephesians tells us. Paul reminds the Ephesian church in Chapter 2 that they were dead in trespasses and sins.

> *But God, who is rich in mercy, for his great love wherewith he loved us. Even when we were dead in sins hath quickened us together with Christ. (Ephesians 2:4)*

So God has given us his life and he has confirmed it by sealing us with his Holy Spirit.

Last summer I traveled to Turkey with my brother. We visited Ephesus. It is an area known for its timber trade. In Paul's day the buyers would come and purchase a consignment of timber. They could not take it home immediately so they would pay for the wood and then put their seal on it. They would come back for it later when they had arranged transportation. Although they had been gone a long time they could identify what was theirs by their seal.

This is what Christ has done for us. He has placed his mark on us. We are not our own for we have been bought with a price and Jesus is coming back to collect us. The difference between us and the logs left at Ephesus is that we are not to wait idly for the Second Coming. We have been purchased for a purpose. We all have a particular task to do. God has placed each one of us in a certain situation. He wants us to witness and live for him in that place.

The other day I was reading a book by Charles Haddon Spurgeon. One sentence caught my eye. It said, "If God has called you to be a clerk, don't stoop to be a king." I had to read that again to grasp the meaning. What Spurgeon is saying is that we can't better God's best. If God has put us in an office and we are fully in his will then that is the best place for us to be. We don't want to stoop to be a king.

BUT GOD supplies our needs. Sometimes as Christians we feel inadequate. We find it difficult to discuss our faith with our friends, let alone with strangers. But God does not want us to push on alone. He doesn't abandon us to get on with the job. Paul tells the Philippians:

> *But my God shall supply all your needs according to his riches in glory by Christ Jesus. (Philippians 4:19)*

We have a big God. He is not frugal. Paul says he will supply all our needs according to his riches in glory. His resources are limitless.

Recently I met a young man of 21 called Mark Sharman. He became a Christian in university last year. He felt God had done so much for him that he wanted to give something in return. He had no money but he wanted to spend a long time alone with God. He decided to walk from London to Jerusalem. It took him five and half months. He met some marvelous people along the way and he raised a great deal of money for Christian Aid. He described how God looked after him and supplied all his needs.

BUT GOD gives strength in temptation. If we believe God is faithful and that he will supply all our needs, we will want to be active for him. The devil does not like this. He will try to prevent us. Under enemy attack we can become very nervous and may consider giving up. Yet Paul tells us:

> *There hath no temptation taken you but such as is common to man; but God is faithful, who will not suffer you to be tempted above that ye are able; but will with the temptation also make a way to escape, that ye may be able to bear it. (1 Corinthians 10:13)*

God has placed a seal upon us so that no one can take us away from him. For that reason God will never allow us to be tempted more than we can cope. He will always supply an escape route. That escape is the person of the Lord Jesus Christ. We are fighting a real battle with a fierce enemy but it is a battle with a difference. We are on the victory side. We fight not to victory but from victory and throughout the warfare we find that God is faithful.

BUT GOD gives the growth. The reason we can be confident that God will use our efforts when they are directed by his Holy Spirit is because he is in charge of the whole operation. Paul writes:

> *I have planted, Apollos watered; but God gave the increase. So then neither is he that planteth anything, neither he that watereth; but God that giveth the increase. (1 Corinthians 3:6-7)*

So we see the whole purpose of God's redemptive activity. God saves the weak by revealing himself to us. He does this because he loves us. God's love is not passive. It is active and dynamic. He wants to use us to be his witnesses. He supplies all our needs. He gives us strength in times of temptation, not simply so that we can just get by, but that he can use us to bring about an increase in his kingdom. This is the God we serve and worship.

4

Three Cheers for the Lord

John
March 1973

> *To this day, Spurgeon's Seminary places a great emphasis on practical preparation for ministry, particularly preaching. One of the more harrowing experiences at Spurgeon's was Sermon Class, where a student preached in chapel before the entire faculty and student body. Afterwards, members of the college community, both fellow students and professors, critiqued the sermon.*
>
> *There was also a great emphasis on oral preparation— speaking sermons out loud in advance in order to prepare adequately for their delivery. "Three Cheers" was the first sermon John preached at Spurgeon's, and he devoted days of preparation by preaching through it in his room. Every time he reached a certain point near the end, his friends (who had rooms along the same corridor) burst into his room, shouting that they had repented. Even then John was well known for the volume of his voice when preaching or singing.*
>
> *-G.S.*

Last month I had the privilege of playing on the Spurgeon's Rugby Team in the London Theological College's Tournament. Our hardest match was against London Bible College and unfortunately we lost. However, at the end of the game I was delighted to hear our captain command, "Three cheers for the London Bible College, hip, hip, hooray." This was our way of thanking our opponents for the game. It is very much a part of our English tradition that we look for a good game rather than just a favorable result.

I wonder what your reaction would be if I said, "Let's have three cheers for God." You might think it is strange. Maybe you would be shocked. Yet I suggest we owe God more thanks than our rugby opponents. However, I won't ask you now to give three cheers for the Lord. Rather I want to bring you three cheers from the Lord that will help us understand why we should be a rejoicing people.

Chapter 2

The first cheer is for sins forgiven.

> *Behold, they brought to Jesus a man sick of the palsy, lying on a bed: and Jesus seeing their faith said unto the sick man, 'Son, be of good cheer; thy sins be forgiven thee.' (Matthew 9:2)*

This poor fellow was so ill he had to be carried to Jesus. He wanted only one thing which was to be made better. Jesus met his need at the same time making him both physically and spiritually well. He called him "son" which was a term of endearment.

Jesus is still doing the same today. He is meeting the needs of people. One of our greatest needs is to have our sins forgiven. We need forgiveness for our shameful pasts. We need a fresh start. The marvelous truth is that when we come to Jesus asking for cleansing he still says, "Be of good cheer, your sins are forgiven."

The second cheer is that Jesus is with us. Mark tells us:

> *For they all saw Jesus and were troubled. And immediately he talked with them and said unto them, 'Be of good cheer: it is I; be not afraid.' (Mark 6:50)*

The disciples were terrified. They were out on the Sea of Galilee in the middle of a dark and stormy night, just the sort of weather conditions for ghost stories. They are having problems with their boat and then they see this figure walking on the water. It was a very natural reaction to feel afraid.

There are times when we too are being tossed around on the storms of life and we are gripped with fear. It might be fear of the unknown or fear of loneliness or fear of failure. At times like this Jesus calls out to us, "It is I, be not afraid."

In his book Strength to Love, Martin Luther King Jr., describes how he was threatened on the phone. He could not sleep. He eventually came in desperation to God. He admitted he had used up all his reserves. The Lord came to him and Dr. King writes, "Then I felt I could go on." He had ceased to be afraid. Jesus was with him.

Moses was a great leader, but he too found himself very afraid. God had just told him that he was going to lead Israel out of Egypt. In panic Moses asked, *Who will go with me?* And God answers, *My presence will go with you.* (Exodus 3:12) We may ask, "Who will go with me into that fearful situation that is confronting me?" and God responds, "I will go with you. Do not be afraid. Be good of cheer."

6

The third cheer is for courage to face the future. In Acts we read:

> *The night following the Lord stood by Paul, and said, 'Be of good cheer, Paul: for as thou has testified of me in Jerusalem, so must thou bear witness also at Rome. (Acts 23:11)*

Paul has written to the church at Rome with some wonderful news. He is going to visit them on his way to Spain. He has wanted to make the trip for a long time but other missionary work has prevented him. Now he has decided to go to Spain and he is going to pop in and visit his friends in Rome on his way.

Paul's journey to Spain is very exciting. It will be the first outreach to that part of the western world. Surely this is going to be for the good of the gospel. Yet things don't always go right even for the Apostle Paul. He is captured in Jerusalem before he starts his journey. He is concerned that now he will not get to Rome or Spain. God gives him this promise that he will get to Rome but there is no mention of Spain.

Now this could have been an enormous disappointment but because Paul believes he is in the divine will of God he accepts it. He is able to write to Timothy and say:

> *I am persuaded that he is able to keep that which I have committed unto him until that day. (2 Timothy 1:12)*

So when Paul's boat is shipwrecked in the Mediterranean, he is able to tell the terrified crew, "We will get to Rome because I believe in God." Paul is willing to sacrifice his own desires to go to Spain. As far as we know he never went.

God is still working his purposes out although we don't always understand them. A gentleman called Peter at Chatsworth Baptist Church illustrated the point well. He became a believer and wanted to express his faith. He was a good wood carver and so he took a beautiful piece of oak and carved the words "Halelujah" on it. He was a great carver but a rotten speller and he spelled halelujah with one l. When this was pointed out Peter was mortified. The task had taken many hours. But then inspiration struck and he added the word "anyway." So it now read, "Halelujah anyway." No matter how you spell it, no matter now complicated the situation, no matter that we don't understand what God is doing, we can still praise him and face the future with courage.

Matthew Poole, the great Puritan theologian, says of this verse in Acts, "The purposes of men are ruled and overruled by the providence of God." Do we have a Spain in our plans? Something which we would like to do but which is not part of God's plan for us? If Christ is to be the Lord of our lives we must trust him, having confidence that he will lead us, and believing that if we are in God's will then we cannot better God's best.

So be of good cheer and face the future with courage. We have three cheers *from* the Lord.

I would like to suggest we can now have three cheers *for* the Lord.

The first cheer is for the past: our sins have been forgiven. The second cheer is for the present: we don't need to be afraid. The third cheer is for the future: we can face it wherever it may lead, for God is with us. Three cheers for the Lord. Hip, hip hooray!

Chapter 3

The Anatomy of Grief

John
1988

One Saturday in May of 1986, Kirstie, our beautiful 16-month-old daughter, slipped through the railings of a bridge near where we live and fell 15 feet onto the concrete channel below. She was unconscious when we got to her. We rushed her to Huntington Memorial Hospital in Pasadena. She died there two days later.

Without a doubt, this was the most grueling experience of our lives. The sense of loss and guilt were overwhelming. It was hard to believe that anything good could come out of such grief. Yet it did. It strengthened our faith and ministry, although the transition back to a feeling of normalcy has been long and painful.

Three factors have proved incredibly helpful. I'd like to share them with you in the hope that they will be of comfort if you are currently in the midst of a loss, or if your congregation needs a model for how to assist its grieving people.

The comfort of God's word. For the first several weeks after Kirstie's death, I found I could not concentrate sufficiently to read my Bible, or even pray. However, I was able to draw on my many years of Bible memorization and began meditating on God's word anyway. The promises of scripture became very precious, and the Psalms, in particular, began to restore my soul. Kind people gave us books, tapes, poems and sermons, but these provided little solace.

The Bible was different. It spoke with authority. It revealed a God who had not abandoned us, who even then was caring for our Kirstie in his heavenly home. It told of a God who was sovereign in both the good and the bad experiences of life. It revealed a Father who also had lost his only child. For this reason, neither Gretchen nor I were ever really angry at God.

The companionship of God's people. At times, when I began to doubt God, I found Him in the midst of His people. From the day of Kirstie's fall until now, the congregation of Eagle Rock Baptist Church has exhibited extraordinary compassion. Within minutes of the accident, several members began to phone through the church directory, inviting people to come to the church to pray. More than 100 gathered that night in the sanctuary. Some remained past midnight. They continued to surround us with prayer for many months, and told us so.

9

At our request, the Board of Deacons came to the hospital to anoint Kirstie with oil and pray for her healing. Members of my staff stayed with us all night and then led Sunday services the next day. The leadership demonstrated a touching sensitivity, offering us a paid leave-of-absence for up to six months. It was only six weeks before I was back in the pulpit, but the offer touched my heart.

Hundreds of people wrote. The most moving letters were from young people expressing their love and sharing amazing insight into our needs. It was a strange reversal of roles, junior high students ministering to their pastor. People were willing to listen and talk. We found it did not matter what they said as long as they said something. They allowed us to grieve, and obviously shared our grief. They invited us to their homes. They brought us meals when we did not feel like cooking.

We discovered the healing power of worship, sitting as members of the congregation. We looked forward to Sundays as the best day of the week. My colleagues displayed pastoral compassion, but refused to treat me with kid gloves. For that, I was grateful. To be frank, for a period of time, I thought I was losing my mind. I confided this to Rick Mandl, my associate pastor, asking him to look out for any peculiar behavior on my part. With an absolutely straight face, he asked, "How will I tell the difference?" Some warned us that in time the church would back off, but that has not been the case. I cannot imagine what more they could have done.

The whole fellowship of the Southwest Baptist Conference was also a great encouragement. We received many visits, calls and letters, the most helpful being from people who had lost children. These folk were a mine of information on what to expect in the different stages of grief. We were amazed at how many pastors had suffered a similar loss. We recognized that the question..."why us?"...was rather ridiculous, and was gradually replaced with the understanding..."why not us?"

The council of good friends.   I was more fortunate than Job. My friends reminded me of some truths I knew, and others I didn't. Here is a sampling of the best of the many beautiful pieces of wisdom they had to offer us:

Guard your marriage.   A horrifyingly high percentage of parents who lose a child end up divorced. We were challenged to work on our relationship to ensure that that did not happen to us.

People grieve differently.   How true. I did not want to talk much about the death, enter Kirstie's room, or look at her photos.   Gretchen had

10

exactly the opposite reaction, even finding solace going back to the scene of the accident. I've learned that it is important to recognize that all expressions of grief are valid.

Change your environment. We did just that, enjoying four weeks in England with my parents. It was a tremendous help and allowed us to spend a lot of time together. Rick and Judy Mandl flew over and joined us for the final week.

Fill up your time. We found it harder to cope when we had nothing to do. So, on our return from England, we both threw ourselves into a frenzy of activity which helped distract us. Gretchen returned to work. I started work on a Doctorate of Ministry. I also plunged into a new hobby of modeling railways. I built a new room to house the layout. I looked forward to receiving packages of models in the mail. It was extravagant, but served as useful therapy.

Plan for the future. There is a tendency in grief to only look back. You are on the road to recovery when you can look forward with hope. We decided to try and have another child immediately. When Gretchen conceived four months later, it was a cause for great joy.

Look for good in grief. We believe that all things do work together for good for those who love God. It is very hard to accept this when you have lost a child, but it helps to try. We offered Kirstie's organs for transplant and were pleased when her liver saved the life of another little girl. We were thrilled to learn that Kirstie's funeral was the means of a neighbor coming to Christ. Since then, he has been baptized, joined our church and is thinking of missionary service. There have been other good consequences, but I must be honest and say I still feel the cost was far too high. All the same, it's good to know her life was not wasted.

Look forward to a heavenly reunion. This is the best truth of all. Heaven is now more real and precious. We have a treasure laid up there. Our little one fell from that bridge, but Jesus caught her in His great, big arms! Kirstie is growing up now in heaven, and what a Father she has! We expressed the Christian hope on her tombstone: "Kirstie, we love you, but Jesus loves you more."

Chapter 4

The Power of Prayer

From a Bible study at Eagle Rock Baptist Church, California
Gretchen
June 1988

Most of us do not need to be convinced of the worth of prayer. In spite of that, most of us still struggle with the way to pray. I once learned two profound lessons about prayer through a difficult personal experience. In February 1988 I took a home pregnancy test, which was positive. Strangely, I didn't feel pregnant, and I had a great deal of pain on the left side.

One week later my doctor ordered an ultrasound scan. It revealed no gestational sac in the uterus and a bulging cyst on the left ovary. I began the first of a series of blood tests to measure the amount of human chorionic gonadotropin (HCG), the pregnancy hormone, in my blood. Before I got the results, John left on a long-planned trip to Africa. The HCG level was 20, which could be construed as indicating that I was just barely pregnant. Worse, it looked as though an ectopic pregnancy was developing.

When you are in need, enlist the help of others. You may be in such a deep hole that you cannot see anything except the darkness around you. That evening I told three people I absolutely trusted, three people mighty in prayer: my friends Becky and Judy and my sister Gail.

The reason I needed their help was that I could not pray rationally for myself. I feared the worst, and knew that a tubal pregnancy could destroy half of my reproductive equipment. I knew that the chance of a second ectopic pregnancy in the remaining fallopian tube was 50 percent.

I knew that I could scarcely bear not ever having a little girl again.

Becky was extremely helpful, allowing me to say all that I needed to say. She reminded me of God's faithfulness in both of our lives. She said, "I'm going to pray that baby gets into the right place and that your blood test results shoot right up." I already believed this baby was lost, but I told her to keep praying.

That night, lying alone in bed, I learned a second lesson. At some point we all stand alone before God. No matter how enmeshed two lives become, we ultimately face God as individuals. Trials of faith often force us to deal solo with God. Despite the fact that my husband was very concerned about my well being and equally concerned for future children, he was in Africa and completely unreachable.

My dear friends and my sister, fully empathetic, could still only lend support. Distraught, I faced God alone that night.

I felt my heart break all over again for Kirstie. I feared that I might never have another little girl, or even bear another child, and I cried. I prayed that inarticulate prayer that has so often helped me: "Lord, comfort me." At times like these the Holy Spirit intercedes and interprets our feeble cries. I did eventually feel comforted that night, but it was the peace that comes from acceptance rather than hope for the future.

The next blood test showed the hormone level at 239, which at least indicated a developing pregnancy. The level is supposed to double or triple every two to three days. Although I was still in pain, I felt immensely encouraged—and ashamed that I had not been able to believe that God would provide a happy ending. It was Becky who had insisted that he could and would.

During these days I was forbidden to travel because of the possibility that I might have a uterine rupture. I longed to visit my dear sister Gail. Instead she came to stay with me. We had the most precious time together that we've ever had. She was a tremendous help to my spirits, and provided further evidence of how God provides in our need. Gail offered not only her prayers but her blood in case I needed a transfusion.

Days went by. The next scan showed no evidence of a baby, but the cyst looked a little smaller.

The following week, one day before John came home, I had a final blood test and scan. When my doctor saw the ultrasound image, his only words were "Praise be to God!" We saw a tiny gestational sac— so small that we couldn't even see an embryo inside, but located where it should be, in the womb.

I am at a loss to explain what happened. My impression is that I conceived, yet nothing developed for a period of weeks. And at the time when my powerhouse of pray-ers started to pray, the baby began developing normally. Later, my doctor said, "I can tell you now how concerned I was. I really thought you had had an ectopic pregnancy, or at the very least that you were going to miscarry." He couldn't explain it either.

Prayer really does work miracles— sometimes inexplicably changing outcomes, as happened this time, and sometimes changing our heart so we're able to cope with an outcome we don't want.

How do we learn a *way* of prayer that shows the *worth* of prayer? We lack time and commitment, and learning to pray means overcoming both. Jesus never had enough time in his days, but still spent time away from the crowds in communion with his father.

You can overcome the lack of time by making prayer a habit. Set aside a specific time each day. I pray when I rock Nicky to sleep at night. Not only does this make me pray, but it allows me to hold and cuddle a little boy who is usually too busy for cuddling during the day.

Pray as the desire or need arises. Seize the moment when you are doing something mindless, such as driving, soothing a child, ironing or cooking.

Pray when a concern crosses your mind—stop then and pray for that one thing before you forget it.

Even finding the time doesn't guarantee a good prayer life unless we also overcome a lack of motivation. You can still pray even though you don't feel like it. Prayer can be developed just like any other habit. Ironing isn't something I ever feel like doing, but the consequences of not ironing my husband's shirts are one of the few areas of conflict in our marriage. I've therefore developed a habit of ironing even when I don't feel like it. Similarly, at times I've not felt like praying. The consequences of not doing so are far worse than my inclination not to pray.

Reflect on God's answers to previous prayers and this can motivate you to pray more. Remember: *What is impossible with men is possible with God. (Luke 18:27)*

Organize your prayer life. I set goals at the beginning of each year. This year I am praying for four people daily. Each week, I additionally pray for one person or situation from Monday to Sunday. It's amazing how often I receive calls on Sunday night or Monday morning from someone asking me to pray, just at the time when I'm trying to decide for whom I ought to be praying.

Pray about people or situations that irritate you. We waste so much energy worrying about things. Prayer is our most effective means of changing situations and people, or at least our own attitude toward them.

Once you get going in the habit of prayer, you will find that duty drops away, leaving you with a burning desire to become closer to God through prayer. Praying becomes its own reward.

Chapter 5

Beginnings

Acceptance letter to First Baptist Church, Rochester, Minnesota
John
February 1989

I know the plans I have for you, says the Lord. They are plans for good and not for evil, to give you a future and a hope. (Jeremiah 29:11)

This promise from God's word has been a great encouragement to us in recent months. We believed that the Lord had a new direction for our lives but were not certain what it was. Now we know, and it is with joy and expectation that we accept your invitation to come to First Baptist Church of Rochester.

Since I was a little boy I have been inspired by the life of my fellow countryman, William Carey, the father of modern missions and the first missionary to India. A few years ago I stood in his pulpit in Calcutta and read again his life's motto on the wall behind.

Expect great things from God; attempt great things for God.

We do expect great things because we so clearly sense the Lord's leading us to you. We know that God's plans are always perfect plans and we believe he has great things in store. We are excited about working and worshipping with you, as together we attempt great things for God in Rochester.

Yet to be honest while we are delighted to come to Rochester, we are depressed at leaving Eagle Rock. It will be very hard to leave our fellowship, our family and our friends. We have grown in Christ together over 13 years and it will be difficult to relinquish the reins of pastoral leadership. Please pray for us as we say our goodbyes and seek to ensure the church is ready for the interim.

We anticipate beginning our ministry with you in early May. We look forward to getting to know you and continuing together on the adventure of faith with its glorious goal of being *complete in Christ*.

We do not know what the future holds, but we know the one who holds the future and it is as bright as the promises of God.

Chapter 6

Redeeming the Time

Departing Eagle Rock Baptist Church
Gretchen
April 1989

Four weeks from today I will be waking up for the first time in a strange house in Rochester, Minnesota. I'll be wondering where's the best place in town to shop for groceries, when our household belongings are going to show up, and how to make new friends. I'll be wondering how I'm ever going to fit into Rochester First Baptist Church like I fit into Eagle Rock Baptist Church.

Although John and I sincerely feel the call of God to Rochester, that doesn't make the actual leaving any easier. Since our decision, I feel the days racing past each other more and more quickly. I see now why God, in his infinite wisdom, does not permit a man to know the day of his death. If I feel this tremendous need to complete everything before I move, how much more difficult it would be if I knew that in four weeks I was to leave this world forever. That thought helps me put it all in perspective. We're not dying—we're simply moving our sphere of ministry. However, neither John nor I anticipated the pain of leaving would be as great as it has been. I recently read a child's poem by Judith Viorst that seemed to sum up exactly how I felt:

Mending

A giant hand inside my chest stretches out and takes,
my heart within its mighty grasp and squeezes till it breaks.
A gentle hand inside my chest with mending tape and glue,
patches up my heart until it's almost good as new.
I ought to know by now that broken hearts will heal again,
but while I wait for glue and tape the pain!
The pain! The pain!

My heart was only broken once before, when Kirstie died. Now it feels as if it's breaking again. I cannot believe how deeply rooted our hearts and lives have become, and that is as it should be, judging by the similar feelings Paul expressed to his churches. Right now I'm waiting for the gentle hand inside my chest to patch up my heart, just as happened after my first great sorrow.

During this painful time of leaving, there is another lesson I am learning. It is the important lesson about what we can do with the time that remains to us— redeeming the time that God has given us.

In Philippians, Paul writes to the church:

> *Not that I have already obtained it, or have already become perfect, but I press on in order that I may lay hold of that for which also I was laid hold of by Christ Jesus. Brethren, I do not regard myself as laying hold of it yet, but one thing I do: forgetting what lies behind and reaching forward to what lies ahead, I press on toward the goal for the prize of the upward call of God in Christ Jesus. (Philippians 3:12-14)*

In order to become what God wants Paul to become, he must to do these things:

Forget what lies behind. Stop sorrowing about wasted time. Our commitment to the Lord may vary tremendously through the years. We must not get bogged down regretting the time we spent as lukewarm, uninvolved Christians, regretting the opportunities for service that we missed, the times when we were more concerned about our home or career than we were about God.

I spent several years very involved in my career, and initially I was far more interested in promotion than I was in growing as a Christian. Consequently, my commitment and my ministry suffered. I have at times tremendously regretted what I now view as wasted years, but I also realize that God is able to use what I learned in that business setting to help me find common ground with women who are going through that same struggle. No experiences of our life are wasted if we turn them over to the Lord for his use. Like Paul, we must "forget the things that lie behind."

Stop longing for the things that are past. Last September I was hugely pregnant with Emily. Somehow each baby seems to do something worse to your abdominal muscles, and I felt and looked as large as a house. Two beautiful young women, friends of ours from England, came to stay with us. They were both single, pretty, working girls with lots of money to spend. They had an exciting vacation planned. As the time wore on, I realized that even though I was only seven years older than my guests, I could have been their grandmother for all the differences that existed between our lifestyles. They knew nothing about the responsibility of looking after a toddler 24 hours a day, nor the time that was required to prepare and serve food for the household. I think the lowest point was when one of them wore a midriff-baring top to dinner and I was confronted by the contrast, not only in our lifestyles, but also our waistlines! Sometimes I feel like I've lived a long life, but I wouldn't trade it for anything. I don't want to wallow in regrets for a stage of life that is past for me, and to which I can never return.

We need to do the same as a church. It will be very hard for John and I to avoid contrasting the people we love here at Eagle Rock Baptist Church with the people we don't even know in Rochester. It may be hard for you, if you've enjoyed these 12 years, to get used to another pastor and pastor's wife. Don't make it any harder on them than it is already. Pray for them, welcome them, and soon you'll find that you love them. The past has been wonderful for us here, but I believe the future will be glorious too.

Press on in the face of changes. Pressing on is one of those great terms that conveys the ability to stick to a task even when it's tough. It's difficult to have the will to press on under changed circumstances. When change occurs, we may need to go through a short grieving period and then try to get on with life. It's probably painfully obvious to all of you that for the first time in my 18 years I have short hair. While some of you, like me, may be thinking that this haircut was long overdue, my hair has been a part of me for a long time. Just like the rings on a tree, I can practically date years of my life in my ponytail. In fact, even when it was cut off I couldn't bring myself to put it away in a dignified fashion: I left it hanging out in the bathroom like a little dead otter for several days trying to get used to the fact that it was no longer attached to my head! Cutting one's hair is pretty trivial, even when it's been 18 years and it's the last symbol of childhood and youth. Other changes are a lot more difficult. We need God's grace to take us through times of change, to know that our anchor is fixed to the one rock that will not change even though all around us the terrain is shifting.

Sometimes I regret the tradeoffs that come with age. Each time I shop at Robinson's, Pasadena, I remember with tremendous amusement the New Year's Day when my brother and I, at ages 15 and 17, climbed up three storeys to the roof to get a better view of the parade. We did it by holding on to the ornamental brickwork that sticks out every 10 inches all the way up. Now that I'm a mother, not only would I resist that temptation, but I would do anything to prevent a child of mine from trying that stupid stunt. When you're 15, you think you're invincible. When you're 30 and have seen death firsthand, you think that everything is a risk. Change can be difficult to handle, but pressing on in the face of change is part of our task as Christians.

Make the most of the present. Every new day we wake up with 24 hours to fill as we please. I find that it helps to pay attention to the tasks at

21

hand, especially when our tasks are repetitive, as child rearing or housekeeping can be.

For example, I'm getting to the stage where I have to carefully think through any disciplinary threats I make to Nicky. I can't just say "I'll spank you if you do that" because I might find myself spanking him all the time in order to follow through. I have to think about which behavior deserves a confrontation and which is merely annoying. He's at the awful stage of always wanting what's on my plate, even if he's got the identical thing on his own. Is it worth creating a tantrum just to be able to eat my own toast for once? Certainly not. Then I can save my "no's" for when he's about to murder Emily. I must at all times pay attention to what I am saying to my young children, so they can hear me saying "no" when it's really important.

I start some days with a desire to accomplish many things, only to later find that I've finished none of them. However, I can always come up with something that I did do, even if it was only that I entertained a toddler and a baby for 14 or 15 hours. Sometimes I find this aspect of motherhood so discouraging that I have to list for myself all my completed tasks. This exercise is far more profitable if I look for spiritual progress each day. You can too. Look for those small areas of victory where, on a given day, you have been able to say "no" to a sin that continually plagues you, or where you have succeeded in reading your Bible despite numerous distractions, where you have held your tongue when you wanted to cut someone to ribbons. Encourage yourself spiritually. Pressing on means that you are making the most of the present.

Reach for the future. Part of the richness of the Christian life is that it is multi-dimensional. Paul has dealt with the past (forgetting what lies behind), the present (pressing on) and now the future (straining toward what is ahead).

The idea of reaching forward to what is ahead implies development of an eternal perspective. It is no problem to look forward to vacations or special events. We all have a natural ability to anticipate those. Instead, we need to turn that faculty toward God and begin to anticipate what his eternal future holds for us.

John and I have recently been reading Elizabeth Elliot's *A Time to Die*, the biography of Amy Carmichael. In her early life, Carmichael attended one of the Keswick conventions, a type of Christian retreat held each year in England. She heard the speaker teach on holiness, and said to herself, "I want to be holy too." To focus on a desire such as holiness is totally different than focusing on a desire for beauty, riches, fame or prestige. It can't be achieved by any measurable path, and those who possess it are usually unaware of it.

Even though holiness is a process, a working out of salvation in our lives, I believe that its origin is the *desire* to be holy. When I read that description of Amy Carmichael, who suddenly realized that holiness was the word for what she had been seeking, I also realized that I want to be holy, and in becoming holy, to understand the very nature of our Holy God.

> *The first man (Adam) was of the dust of the earth, the second man from heaven. As was the earthly man, so are those who are of the earth; and as is the man from heaven, so are those who are of heaven. And just as we have borne the likeness of the earthly man, so shall we bear the likeness of the man from heaven. (I Corinthians 15:47-49)*

I want to bear the likeness of the man from heaven, and in order to do that, I must develop an eternal perspective, keeping the ultimate goal before me at all times. What we experience on earth is not our final destiny, no matter how joyful or painful it is. Simply being aware of that fact puts our experiences into perspective.

Even so, come, Lord Jesus. Lately it seems to me that looking forward to heaven and to a face-to-face relationship with God isn't enough to keep my attention fixed on the future. I am beginning to see how wonderful it would be if our Lord were to return soon—how all the problems created by our leaving would be healed. It is no wonder that men and women who were facing death were often given glimpses of heaven. When Stephen was being threatened in Acts 7 he saw heaven and the glory of God. Moments later he was stoned to death.

Sometimes people reach a point of such weariness and pain that they long for the release that will come with death, and the joy of heaven they will know. John was recently speaking with an older friend who is extremely ill and wants to be home with the Lord. John told her to tell Kirstie that we love her and miss her. Of course we believe we will know and greet fellow believers in heaven, but we don't often have the opportunity to send greetings in advance. How marvelous it would be if there were no partings, if we could perpetually be with those we love, and in the presence of God. That is how heaven will be:

But our citizenship is in heaven. And we eagerly await a Savior from there, the Lord Jesus Christ, who, by the power that enables him to bring everything under his control, will transform our lowly bodies so that they will be like his glorious body. (Philippians 3:20-21)

Now we know that if the earthly tent we live in is destroyed, we have a building from God, an eternal house in heaven, not built by human hands. Meanwhile, we groan, longing to be clothed with our heavenly dwelling, because when we are clothed, we will not be found naked. For while we are in this tent, we groan and are burdened, because we do not wish to be unclothed but to be clothed with our heavenly dwelling, so that what is mortal may be swallowed up by life. (2 Corinthians 5:1-4)

What a great description—having that which is mortal about us swallowed up by life. Develop an eternal perspective in what you are doing in the present—reach forward to what is ahead. Put the past behind you and press on in the present, never losing sight of the future in Christ Jesus.

Chapter 7

Getting Acquainted

Self introduction
John
May 1989

I had the supreme privilege of growing up in a Christian home. My mother and father were both in the British Army and met in Germany toward the end of World War II. After demobilization my father attended Spurgeon's Seminary in London. My mother supported the family by working as a nurse. I ruined that arrangement when I was born! My father pastored two churches in London in his 30 years in the ministry. After they retired, my parents went to Israel where my father was the chaplain of the Garden Tomb in Jerusalem. They now live in the delightful seaside town of Felixstowe in Suffolk, where my father is presently the interim pastor of two churches.

As a boy I was very happy to go to church on Sunday, but my real interest was sport, especially playing cricket, rugby and cross country running. At the age of 16 I attended a young people's house party and a Royal Air Force officer challenged me with Christ's right to rule my life. I began the day knowing about God. I finished it knowing God.

At 18 I left home to go to the University of Newcastle to study for a degree in economics and politics. I was actively involved with InterVarsity Christian Fellowship and began to do some lay preaching in village churches. I enjoyed this but I enjoyed flying even more. Under a special program offered to students, I had joined the Royal Air Force as a pilot and intended to make this my career. However, in my last year at University while attending an InterVarsity retreat in the beautiful Northumbrian countryside, the Lord gave me a clear call to the Christian ministry. In obedience I applied to Spurgeon's Seminary in London. There followed four wonderful years of study, preaching in local churches, and pastoring a small church.

I have always enjoyed travel and one summer decided it would be fun to see the Sahara Desert. Maybe I had just seen Bob Hope's movie "The Road to Morocco"! Well, the desert was a bit of a disappointment, but in one of the oases I met a young American who invited me to California, and who told me about Eagle Rock Baptist Church. My brother had gone to study at the Wharton Business School in Philadelphia the previous year so I was anxious to visit this promised land.

In 1974 I made my first visit to the U.S. and spent three enjoyable months at Eagle Rock. I returned the next year and met Gretchen at a college retreat where I was speaking. On graduation from seminary in 1976 I was invited to join the pastoral staff at Eagle Rock. Gretchen and I were married in 1977.

My two younger brothers also live in the U.S. Andrew is an economist at the World Bank in Washington, D.C. and Simon was ordained last month as Associate Pastor of Basking Ridge Presbyterian Church in New Jersey.

Gretchen's story is quite different. She was born in Hollywood, California, the fourth of five children. Her parents met when they were students at St. Olaf College in Northfield. Her father grew up on a family farm in Waseca, where her uncle farms to this day. Gretchen's sister led her to Christ when she was a teenager. Gretchen was the first person I ever baptized. She graduated from UCLA in 1979 with a degree in history and a teaching credential. Following that, she went to work in the advertising industry and became the first female vice president of her company. When we had children she retired from the corporate fray to look after Nicky, who is now age 21 months and Emily, age four months.

Gretchen has seven relatives who live in southern Minnesota and we are looking forward to getting to know them better.

We both like walking, skiing and reading. I also enjoy gardening and railroad modeling. We look forward to getting to know our new First Baptist Church family in the weeks to come.

Chapter 8

What I Long For

First presentation to First Baptist Church Women's Bible Study
Gretchen
June 1989

I'd like to start by telling you how I came to be sitting here today. I grew up in a Lutheran Church, and one of my clearest childhood memories is meeting our new pastor and his wife at the door of the church. I was about 10, and Mrs. Johnson said to me, "You must be Gretchen." I was so surprised and pleased to be noticed…it made a tremendous impression on me. That's one reason why I tried hard to learn some of your names before we came here.

When I was 13 my sister Gail, who always has been one of the most godly people I know, took me in the bathroom and outlined the plan of salvation. You have to understand that in a small house filled with five kids, the bathroom was the only room of the house where you could have a private conversation. I became a Christian at that time.

By the time I was 17 I was seeking to learn what it really meant to bear the name of Christ. It was then that I met John just before my first year of college, and we married when I was 19. After graduation I accepted a job at a direct response ad agency and soon was entranced with my growing responsibilities and opportunities. At the age of 23 I was flying first class around the country and staying in places like the Waldorf Astoria. This was pretty heady stuff and my energies were directed toward the world rather than toward God.

However, when I had our first child, Kirstie, at 27, I soon realized that her wise little eyes were upon me all the time. Just as I wanted to direct her attention to books and music, I also longed for her to know the Lord. I saw that even by nine months of age she was beginning to imitate me. I therefore rededicated myself to God and asked him to help me rid my life of the things that were entangling me. I began reading my Bible regularly again and praying, and he honored my efforts by drawing closer to me. I am so grateful for those seven months of spiritual preparation, because our beloved child Kirstie died in May of 1986 when she was 16 months old. She fell fifteen feet from a bridge onto concrete, lay in a coma, and was pronounced brain dead after three days.

I have to ask for your forbearance on this subject. I will speak about Kirstie and the lessons I learned from her life and death many, many times, because God used her tremendously in my life and in the lives of many others. I am still grieving.

What I have come to understand is that the wonderful things that came as a result of her death could not have happened in any other way, and for that I thank God.

Since that time I have deepened in my relationship to God and in my reliance on his people. About 18 months ago when the Lord was first speaking to us about moving, I began to pray for guidance. As guidance became more concrete I began to pray that God would give me a ministry at our new church—that he would send us somewhere where both John and I could be used. My former Bible study group at Eagle Rock Baptist Church in Los Angeles has been praying that I would quickly develop friendships and fellowship among the women here. This group has become the answer to both prayers. I was enjoying the fellowship so much, and feeling so forlorn going into a whole summer without a Bible study group, that I was extremely gratified when the opportunity came to lead it. Mind you, that feeling was quickly replaced by terror when I thought of everything I had to do before today!

I've always been a very goal-oriented person. There came a time when I realized that goals could also be made for spiritual things, in order to remain disciplined. Toward that end I'd like to share with you my three goals for this group.

My first goal is that we would draw closer to God; second, that we would draw closer to his word; and third, that we would draw closer to each other. Each of these goals has a sound biblical basis and it is good to know that God delights in honoring our efforts to do these three things.

Drawing closer to God. 1 Timothy 4:15 speaks of being diligent, giving yourself wholly, and making your progress evident. Knowing God is something that becomes easier with practice, just like any other skill. Our familiarity with God is like making a new friend. At first we search for common ground and are a bit guarded in what we say. Gradually the obstacles are removed and with a true friend we can lay bare our souls. Our progress in knowing God is evidenced by our intimacy with him.

The apostle James gives us excellent practical advice in this area. To James there is no mystery about our relationship with God. Draw near to him and he reciprocates by drawing near to us (James 4:8). He honors even our most feeble efforts and he certainly honors our struggles to get up, to get the kids dressed and to rush here to study his word:

> *His divine power has given us everything we need for life and godliness. (2 Peter 1:3).*

How comforting to know that we don't have to manufacture godliness from inside ourselves. He gives us everything we need to pursue it. All we have to do is seek after it, just as we would anything that's important to us.

Last March I cut my hair short for the first time in 18 years. Two weeks before that I got my first set of contact lenses. Now my bathroom cupboards are filled with gel, mousse, hairspray, curlers, curling iron, saline solution, enzyme cleaners, etc. I needed a whole new cupboard for the new me and I often resent the time it takes to get presentable before going out. Life used to be much simpler, but I make time for those things because they are important to me now. How much more important it is to make time for our spiritual pursuit of God.

Drawing closer to his word.

> For the word of God is living and active. Sharper than any double-edged sword, it penetrates even to dividing soul and spirit, joints and marrow; it judges the thoughts and attitudes of the heart. (Hebrews 4:12)

God's word is the only book that has the power to tailor itself to any situation. This is why scripture is so incredibly comforting in a crisis. When I called my friend Judy to come to the hospital after Kirstie's accident, I said "and bring my Bible."

Fourteen and one half months later we were back in the intensive care ward of the same hospital with Nicky. He was seven weeks old and had meningitis. After he'd been moved to a regular room a day later I was attempting to keep up with my daily reading. That particular day I was reading in Leviticus and 2 Chronicles. The Leviticus passage was a section on skin diseases—not much help for an aching soul there. But a verse jumped off the page from 2 Chronicles:

> For the eyes of the Lord range throughout the earth to strengthen those whose hearts are fully committed to him. (2 Chronicles 16:9)

I imagined his eyes roving the earth and settling on me in that hospital room. If ever a person needed strengthening, I did then. I received tremendous comfort from that single verse. God's word always has some new insight for us. No matter how many times you read the Bible, you will always be enriched by his word if you read it with an open heart. I want us to draw close to his word.

Drawing closer to each other. From the first time I visited this group I knew that you had a precious fellowship. I didn't want to force my way into it, but right away I felt you enfolding me. Christian fellowship provides that common bond. We will become friends more quickly than any secular group because our faith in Christ transcends our different backgrounds, tastes and interests.

This time last year we were living in Oxford, England, while John was on sabbatical. He went to the library at Regent's College each morning and reappeared at about 6 each night. I was four months pregnant and Nicky was a year old. I spent my days pushing the stroller around all the Oxford colleges, going to the shops to get dinner items and doing mountains of laundry in the laundromat. Some days I would not speak to another adult from the time John left till the time he returned. I was incredibly lonely and made it so evident to my family that they all feared for my sanity when we said we were moving to Minnesota! This has been a totally different experience. Because we are part of a fellowship here, you have reached out to us and made it easy for us to reach out to you.

My responsibility week by week is to pray for you and to prepare for this study. Already I find your faces and your needs coming to mind during the week as I pray. Your responsibility is to pray for me and for each other, to attend, to consider, and to comment in the discussions that follow.

I am grateful and privileged to be a part of this Bible study. Now you know what I long for—that together we would draw closer to God, to his word, and to each other in the coming years.

Chapter 9

Being Faithful To God

Women's Retreat
Gretchen
April 1990

On October 1, 1987, I was walking around the house holding four-month-old baby Nicky. I had a sheet of notes in my hand; I was going over my speaking plans for the Women's Missionary Society Luncheon that day. We had just returned from England and still had jet lag. Nicky, being on English time, wanted to get up at 5 each morning. As I couldn't sleep, I thought I'd use the time profitably. Just as I hit the page of my notes that spoke about the daily uncertainty of our lives, I heard a noise that sounded like an 18-wheeler semi truck pulling up the street. As it increased in volume, it began to sound more like a freight train about to come through the house at top speed. That noise was joined by the horrible sound of the wood of the house creaking and groaning as the whole structure began to shake violently. As it dawned on me that we were having a major earthquake I ran to the nearest doorway and watched in terror as our two-storey plate glass window bulged inward and outward, and the balcony above me swayed back and forth. The floor was rocking so violently that I could hardly stand. Thankfully it was all over in about 15 seconds—just long enough for me to pray a very fervent prayer for our deliverance. As the noise and shaking subsided there was absolute silence. No birds chirped, no dogs barked, no traffic could be heard, and no sound came from the bedroom above me, where I assumed John had been killed by the fan falling on him. I quavered "John?" and Nicky began to scream for the first time as he heard the note of terror in my voice. Thankfully, John was not dead but had been thrown out of bed onto the floor and had been stymied in the act of trying to put on his trousers, as he couldn't stand up long enough to do so.

The earthquake had been preceded by a week of blistering weather—seven days well over 100 degrees—and the commentators were referring to California as the land of "shake and bake." I certainly did not expect my day to begin that way. My crumpled page of notes will forever remind me of the terror I experienced.

The writer to the Hebrews knew all about the unexpected. The author's world was filled with persecution and uncertainty, yet in Hebrews 13:8 we find: *Jesus Christ is the same yesterday, today and forever.*

In Hebrews 12 the author pens these extraordinary words:

> *His voice then shook the earth; but now he has promised, 'Yet once more I will shake not only the earth but also the heaven.' This phrase, 'Yet once more,' indicates the removal of what is shaken, as of what has been made, in order that what cannot be shaken may remain. Therefore, let us be grateful for receiving a kingdom that cannot be shaken, and thus let us offer to God acceptable worship, with reverence and awe; for our God is a consuming fire. (Hebrews 12:25-29)*

The writer to the Hebrews knew that the readers were living in a faithless world, a world that was full of nasty surprises. In Chapters 10, 11 and 12 they are called to persevere, to be faithful, and to be disciplined. Perseverance, faith and discipline are hardly popular concepts in our disposable world. When all is well it's easy to imagine that life will always be as pleasant and predictable as it is right now. The book of Hebrews helps equip us for those times when life treats us disdainfully and painfully, by showing us the essence of faith.

The first element of faith is *belief*. What does it mean to be faithful to God? Hebrews 11:1 is the only verse in the Bible that attempts to define faith:

> *Now faith is the assurance of things hoped for, the conviction of things not seen.*

The use of the word *hope* in this context is somewhat misleading. It does not mean hope in the sense that we wish these things will happen. Rather, Christian hope means that we KNOW what will happen—that God will see us through this time. In Chapter 11 we read about men and women who were tortured, scourged, imprisoned, stoned, sawn in two. We are told that some refused to accept release from torture *that they might rise again to a better life.* These are not the actions of people who simply hope that there is a better future. These are the actions of men and women who *know* with complete certainty that the future is better, and more reliable than the present. They believe in God's control of the future.

The second element of faith is *worship*. The word literally means *worth-ship,* or *to give worth to.* Worship means a single-minded pursuit of

God that cuts through all the extraneous clutter of our lives. Hebrews 12:2 refers to the example given to us by Jesus:

> *Looking to Jesus, the pioneer and perfecter of our faith, who for the joy that was set before him endured the cross, despising the shame, and is seated at the right hand of the throne of God.*

Think of the experience of childbirth. For the joy that is to come, a woman goes through the indignities of pregnancy and the extremities of labor, despising or ignoring the difficult bits in order to achieve the reward. I had a very difficult pregnancy with our first child, Kirstie. I was sick every day, but didn't have the sense or experience to understand that something was going awry. At seven months I was singing in the Christmas cantata, tightly sandwiched in the choir loft between two other sopranos, when I began to feel faint. Looking around I saw there was no escape. The Christmas tree blocked one exit and the choir blocked the other. I sat down, and promptly threw up all the tuna sandwiches I'd eaten just before the rehearsal. The mess ended up in my lap and long hair. With my face buried in my hands, trying to be as unobtrusive as possible, I thought to myself, *this cannot get any worse.* However, my gaze was caught by a puddle of water on the floor below me and I realized that my water had broken. Then I knew that this child, for whom already I had suffered much, was in jeopardy. My pregnancy was only at week 32. The upshot was that I spent five days in the hospital and three more weeks in bed. On the third of January an ultrasound scan showed that the baby was becoming growth-retarded and there was absolutely no amniotic fluid left. Within hours I was in the hospital having a Caesarean section. My overwhelming reaction through the pain, the humiliation and the suffering, was my joy at receiving a tiny but healthy girl. The joy that was set before me far outweighed the suffering that was necessary to get to that point. Oh, that I would be that single-minded about my pursuit of God, being able to lay aside everything that gets in the way and simply concentrate on drawing near to him. Worship is that pursuit—attributing worth to God through our actions.

The third element of faith is *overcoming*. Overcoming is what we do when we attempt to make progress in ridding ourselves of sin. Sin is like a mint plant that takes over the garden. You may have innocently planted it, wanting a few sprigs, only to discover stubborn mint shoots coming out of the ground long after you tried to destroy the original plant. If you want to get rid of mint you have to dig deeply and keep returning to eradicate the new sprouts that come up. Like mint, sin can start as a good thing that simply gets out of hand.

Sometimes the experiences of life are enough to shock a particular sin right out of us. In England everyone takes an extreme interest in the pastor's life, family and house. Ministry friends of ours in Scotland had the experience of one village busybody telling them, "My, you must have been up late last night. Your bedroom lights didn't go off until 12:30." I love the story of how one gossipy, snoopy lady in the Steer's first congregation was cured forever of her vice.

Chris Steer, John's father, is a late riser. Many times church business kept him out until late and the next morning he would try to recover some rest. One morning the neighbor lady dropped in just before 9, while Chris was in his famously ragged old pajamas, the ones that had no elastic in the waistband. Charlotte's job was to head off the caller, position her in the sitting room near the front door and close that door, leaving Chris free to streak across the entry and up the stairs to dress. All went as planned until the telephone rang. While Charlotte answered the phone the lady made her way down the hall and toward the kitchen. John's father quick-wittedly stepped into the three-foot-wide broom closet.

As nine-year-old John watched in horrified amazement, this woman began opening the kitchen cupboards one by one, working her way around the room. Inevitably, she came to the broom closet. As she opened the door, Chris stepped out with unimpeachable dignity, clutching his pajamas with his left hand and shaking her hand with his right. "Good morning, Mrs. Smith," he said with complete composure and unselfconsciousness. "How lovely to see you." I believe Mrs. Smith made a hasty exit and never again looked in people's cupboards.

I, on the other hand, have so many church people putting things away in my cupboards during events we host that often I can't find things until weeks later. I was particularly amused to discover that someone had stuck two dirty cookie sheets underneath my stovetop, to get them out of the way before the Women's Bible Study Christmas party.

However, not everyone has the luxury of being shocked out of sin. A more reliable means of overcoming is simply to stick with it. Hebrews 12:1 tells us to *lay aside every weight and sin which so closely besets us.*

I think of these "weights" as the inherently good or neutral things that simply get in the way of our pursuit of God. For example, a weight might be busyness created by our acts of service that do not allow us to have time for prayer or for reading the Bible. In and of themselves, the weights are not wrong—but as any runner will tell you, they are not helpful either. The weights must be laid aside if we are to run to our full potential in the Christian life.

But we must also combat *the sin which so closely besets us*. Have you ever walked into a cobweb? Just when you think you've picked off all the sticky pieces you'll notice another strand clinging to your hair or clothes. Worse, you might discover you've also picked up the spider that came with it.

Many of us see ourselves in these verses, because each of us has besetting sins that continue to return regardless of our efforts to eradicate them. Should we be discouraged? No more so than we should be discouraged in our efforts to eradicate dirt in the house, or weeds in our garden. We accept that dirt and weeds will return, and must be confronted year after year. Sin is the same. It must be confronted on a recurring basis, year after year, until finally we are freed from its grasp in heaven.

The final element of faith is *obedience*. We see this in the lives of the saints in Chapter 11— for example, Abraham:

> *By faith Abraham, when he was tested, offered up Isaac, and he who had received the promises was ready to offer up his only son, of whom it was said, 'Through Isaac shall your descendants be reckoned.' (Hebrews 11:17-18)*

These verses show us how improbable God's command must have seemed to Abraham. He was asked to sacrifice his dearest love, the son who was also the living fulfillment of God's promise. Yet we are told that Abraham was ready to offer him up. Genesis recounts that Abraham actually bound Isaac, laid him on the altar, and took up the knife before God stopped him. There was obedience in its purest form— lack of understanding about God's purposes, but willingness to do what God was asking. Abraham understood that God was a loving God who held the future, and therefore, it was safe to be obedient.

These experiences show us the necessity of obedience even when we don't understand. Our son, Nicky, is at the age where he asks "why?" about everything. Quite often, even as he's in the act of obeying, he'll ask why? It's not a defiant question, but one that demands an explanation. The other day he and his little friend were thought to be playing quietly in Nicky's room upstairs. In fact they were opening our bedroom window and sticking their heads out—windows that look onto a three-storey drop. When we made a big fuss about this incident, he wanted to know why. A child cannot possibly see the dangers that adult eyes can see. To God we are like Nicky, unable to anticipate the dangers ahead of us. We demand to know why certain events come into our lives, and yet we are not necessarily able to understand even when we do have the full explanation. Obedience is the answer to this dilemma. When our hearts are breaking and we are despairing, obedience keeps us in contact with the only one who is able to give us assurance for the future. There is a final example of obedience that we must examine if we are to succeed:

> *Therefore, since we are surrounded by so great a cloud of witnesses, let us also lay aside every weight, and sin which clings so closely, and let us run with perseverance the race set before us, looking to Jesus, the pioneer and perfecter of our faith, who for the joy set before him, endured the cross, despising the shame, and is seated at the right hand of the throne of God. (Hebrews 12:1-2)*

It is really only by keeping our eyes fixed upon Jesus that we are able to do any of these things—believe, worship, overcome, or obey. The language translated *looking to Jesus* literally means *looking away from everything else and fixing our gaze on him*. When the verse talks about Jesus as the pioneer and perfecter of our faith, it means that he has physically blazed the trail, or shown the way.

When violinist Jascha Heifetz died in 1988, I asked my sister, a classical musician, why such a fuss was being made. Journalists, commentators, and other musicians described him as the greatest violinist who ever lived. My sister explained that, before Heifetz, no violinist ever attempted to play all the notes exactly as written in the great difficult concertos. Other violinists assumed that certain passages were unplayable as written, and so settled for lesser interpretations. Heifetz assumed that if a composer wrote a note, he intended it to be played, and performed accordingly. Once he made this breakthrough in performance and technique, other violinists followed suit, and a whole new level of musical achievement was reached in this century.

In our pioneer, Jesus, we encounter someone who has gone before us in all things. He has already taken the steps through love, through joy, through sorrow, through pain, through death, that we will follow. How much easier it is to walk in the path of someone else's footsteps—someone who knows the way, and knows how to keep us in that way, until at last our footsteps follow him to heaven.

For the Birds . . .

John
May 1993

Before I came to Minnesota, I hardly knew a thing about birds. I could tell the difference between a pigeon and a penguin, but that was about it. However, since we moved to the land of lakes, my appreciation for our little feathered friends has increased enormously. In Los Angeles I would occasionally hear the birds coughing, but now I awake to a sublime dawn chorus. Our back garden has begun to resemble an aviary. This is mostly due to the small fortune spent on bird feeders that contain a variety of seeds, which the lady in the Wild Bird Store assured me are considered haute cuisine by the local bird population. A number of trees now sport bird boxes, which contain various chirping inhabitants. Our only set-back so far is our martin house, which has failed to attract a single customer. This has been particularly disappointing as the erection of this ornithological version of the Empire State Building almost cost me my life and my marriage. However, while the martins may have turned up their beaks at the accommodations, other residents of the garden have not. We were pleased to see last winter that it became a highrise squirrel condo. With the help of the Audubon Society's Field Guide to North American Birds, I'm now able to recognize some of our guests. In addition to our hummingbirds, cardinals, chickadees and myriad gold finches, we now have three pairs of Baltimore orioles enjoying the oranges nailed to the tree. We've seen a pileated woodpecker, a rose-breasted grosbeak, a summer tanager, an indigo bunting, and a white-breasted nuthatch.

There are still dozens of birds I don't recognize. I believe birdwatchers refer to these as LBJ's (little brown jobs). Yet, even this ignorance can't dispel the joy of watching the aerial antics of these marvelous creatures.

Not only am I seeing birds out of the window, I've started to see them in the scriptures. I've never realized before how often birds are mentioned in the word of God. They're found from Genesis to Revelation. The variety of species reflects the great range of bird habitat in Israel. The mention of birds in the Bible is not merely descriptive—they also have a theological significance. Indeed, they teach us three great truths about our God.

The power of God. The opening chapter of Genesis tells us that when God made the birds on the fifth day of creation he was satisfied with his work. We can understand why.

There are approximately 8,700 living species and more that 1,000 extinct species of birds. The smallest is the bee hummingbird of Cuba, which is 2.5 inches long and weighs one tenth of an ounce. The largest bird is the ostrich, which stands eight feet tall and weights 300 pounds. The wandering albatross has a wingspan of 11.5 feet. Birds are found virtually everywhere on earth, from occasional stragglers over the polar ice caps, to complex communities in tropical forests. Some may believe that this glorious variety emerged from one prehistoric egg. I cannot believe that. My faith is not big enough. Rather, these messengers in the heavens point me to the creative power of our great God.

The providence of God. Birds are the object of God's care. He provides food for the young ravens when they call (Psalm 147:9). Jesus tells us to look at the birds of the air. They do not sow or reap or store food in barns, yet our heavenly Father feeds them (Matthew 6:26). The point is clear. If God cares for the birds, how much more will he care for us?

In addition, God's will governs the life of the birds. Jesus said that a sparrow cannot fall to the ground without the will of our Father (Matthew 10:29). The rooster crowed by divine appointment after Peter's third denial of Christ (Matthew 26:34). At God's command the ravens fed Elijah (1 Kings 17:4). The flocks of quail provided food for Israel (Numbers 11:31). Similarly, God watches over us. Nothing happens to us that is beyond his knowledge. Like the birds, we must learn to trust in his providence. Looking back, we can see how God has carried us on eagle's wings and brought us to himself (Exodus 19:4). The testimony of the birds is, don't worry, God knows all about us and he will provide.

The Passion of God. In one of his most emotional speeches, Jesus said:

> O Jerusalem, Jerusalem...how often have I longed to gather
> your children as a hen gathers her chicks under her wings, but
> you are not willing. (Matthew 24:37)

This is a beautiful metaphor that reveals God's love for us. Most of us have probably seen a hen in a farmyard gathering her brood when danger threatens. So the Psalmist declares:

> He will cover you with his feathers, and under his wings you
> will find refuge. (Psalm 91:4)

God's passion is to draw us to himself. He wants to fill us with his spirit which, interestingly enough, appears as a dove.

Chapter 11

A God of Surprises
John
May 1993

My mother tells me that often she and my father will be sitting in their home in England, having a cup of tea, when my father will say, "Wouldn't it be great if John, Andrew and Simon walked in right now?" He knows it's a rather unrealistic wish as all three of his sons live on the other side of the Atlantic. I live here in Rochester, Andrew lives in Washington, D.C. and Simon lives in Bel Air, Maryland. However, we have decided to grant his wish by showing up for his 75th birthday. He has no idea we're coming, and it's been great fun planning our strategy. One brother favors the three of us standing outside his bedroom window holding a *Happy Birthday* banner, which he will see when he gets up and pulls back the drapes. The obvious drawback to this is that we're not sure when he will wake up and we will feel pretty silly standing in the garden if he chooses, that day, to leave the drapes closed! Another brother suggests dressing as waiters and standing behind the counter at his favorite restaurant when he goes there for lunch. A less imaginative sibling demands the direct approach. He wants us simply to march in and sit down at the breakfast table with my mother and father. The jury is still out on the manner in which we shall announce our arrival. I suspect we will spend much of the flight to London arguing about it. It has been tremendously rewarding planning this venture for a man we love so much. All of us owe our father an enormous debt. As an expression of our affection we have compiled a book that we are dedicating to him. Its title is *Gloria Filiorum Patres* (Latin for *The Fathers are the Glory of the Sons*). I just hope my father does not have a heart attack when he sees his three sons thousands of miles from their homes.

As I have reflected on the pleasure that we have experienced while planning this surprise, I began to think of the pleasure that God must have in surprising us. He begins with the *surprise of new birth*. C. S. Lewis entitled the story of his conversion *Surprised by Joy*. That is an accurate description of what it means to become a Christian. Of course, the very idea that he had to be born again was a surprise to Nicodemus. You can hear the incredulity in his voice when he asks the Master, *How can a man be born again when he is old?* (John 3:4) What a wonderful discovery it is to find that Jesus died for us and rose again for us. How glorious to experience his forgiveness and enjoy the benefits of a new start.

God continues with the surprise of *his presence* in our lives every day. I'm sure my father will be pleased to have the company of his boys for a few days, but the time will come when we must leave. In contrast, God never abandons us once we have committed our lives to him. We have his promise that his Spirit will be with us forever. What a great companion he is. He comforts us in our sorrow, encourages us to be holy, and empowers us for service. I can remember the time when I thought that Christianity was dull. How surprised I was to discover that following Jesus is a daily delight. In John 4:27 we read that the disciples were surprised to find Jesus talking with a Samaritan woman. His behavior broke many of the social conventions of that day. How Jesus loves to break out of our expectations and do a new thing in our lives.

Of course, God's greatest surprise is yet to come when we see the glory of our *heavenly home* that Jesus has prepared for us. The apostle Paul was given a peek into paradise, and what he saw so took his breath away that human words seemed inadequate to describe the scene. He expresses his surprise when he writes:

> *No eye has seen, no ear has heard, no mind has conceived what*
> *God has prepared for those who love Him. (1 Corinthians 2:9)*

The prospect of heaven kept Paul going through the difficult times. It is the destiny of every believer, and when we get there it will be better than anything we have ever known on earth. How glorious to have a God of surprises. I trust you enjoy one today.

Chapter 12

Twentieth Century Apologists
John
May 1993

My tongue is the pen of a skillful writer. (Psalm 45:1)

The church of the '90s faces a new challenge. Today, many seem to regard evangelical Christianity as a threat to democracy, tolerance and even to family life. Some commentators consider Christians to be the enemy. One poll indicated that fundamentalist Christians are feared by many Americans.

How should we respond to these attacks? I believe we can learn from the Christians of the second and third centuries. Their situation was remarkably similar to ours. Back then, there were also great misconceptions about the Christian faith. Believers faced accusations of atheism, cannibalism, incest and idleness. They were also regarded as a threat to the state. These early Christians responded in three ways.

They refused to retreat. The church was gaining attention because it was growing. When there had only been a handful of believers nobody cared what Christians thought or did. It was, therefore, tempting for the emerging church to retreat from the world and become a secret society. Some believers did leave the cities and move to the desert where they could practice their faith undisturbed. Others rightly recognized that Jesus has called them to go into all the world. Christians today have come under attack because, in the last 20 years, we have begun to stand up and be counted. We've become involved in the political process. We've made our voices heard. A solution to our bad press would be to retreat to our churches, raise the drawbridges and keep to ourselves. But that would be irresponsible. The world needs the message of the Gospel now more than ever before.

They began to write. A group of writers called the apologists emerged. An apologist defends the Christian faith. They were men like Justin Martyr, Aristides, Athenagoras, Theophilus and Tertullian. By careful, rational argument they presented the Christian position. They often addressed their apology to the emperor himself. They tried to convince the leaders of the state that Christians had done nothing to deserve the persecutions being inflicted upon them. They demonstrated the advantages of the Christian faith. They sought to eliminate popular misconceptions and create an intelligent understanding of Christianity. Today we need Twentieth Century apologists who will sensitively and graciously contend for the faith.

The letters to the editor page in the *Rochester Post-Bulletin* is an excellent place for this. I'm delighted that so many members of First Baptist are making helpful contributions. I commend you, most warmly, and encourage others to follow your example. Letters can correct anti-Christian bias. They can portray Christian values in a positive light. They can praise activities that are wholesome. For every letter of criticism we write to a TV station or politician, let us make sure we balance it with a letter of commendation for a job well done. The apostle Peter gives good counsel to would-be apologists:

> *Always be prepared to give an answer to everyone who asks you to give the reason for the hope you have. But do this with gentleness and respect. (1 Peter 3:15)*

We must avoid strident and abusive speech. We want to win people—not just arguments.

They lived outstanding lives. The apologists not only wrote about godliness, they lived it. They gained a reputation for caring for the poor and needy. Sadly, many people today do not equate Christianity with Christ-like behavior. But Christians are to be models of gentleness, truthfulness and grace. Again, Peter gives us our cue. Writing to the Christians living under great suspicion he said:

> *Live such good lives among the pagans that, though they accuse you of doing wrong, they may see your good deeds and glorify God on the day he visits us. (1 Peter 2:12)*

Chapter 13

Obedience School

John

November 1994

Recently, Gretchen sent me to obedience school. For company, I took our three-year-old border collie called Lacey. Lacey arrived in our home last June after a phone call to the Paws and Claws humane society. As a boy, I used to watch border collies work the sheep on the Cheviot Hills in the Scottish border country. We don't own any sheep, but we do have three little Steers and I had visions of the dog rounding up the children and bringing them on time to the dinner table.

Lacey's introduction to our home was not an unqualified success. We had lofty ideals that she would stay in the kitchen and keep out of our bedrooms. The first night I tied her up to the kitchen table and went to bed. The howling that followed woke up the entire household. I went down to keep her company. After an unspeakably uncomfortable night on the kitchen floor I opened the door to let the dog out. She immediately ran away. Like most ladies, she headed for the shops and we found her two days later at Fleet Farm.

Lacey was fine when she was with us, but every time we left her, she experienced great separation anxiety. She expressed this by destroying everything in sight. She managed to eat large parts of the lawn mower, our barbecue, a stool and a bicycle. We tied her up with a one inch rope but she chewed through it. We put her in a metal cage and she escaped. We chained her to a tree and she demolished the tree. This devastation was accompanied by barking that could be heard in the town of Byron. Our neighbors were very tolerant, but I knew if it went on much longer that "For Sale" signs would be appearing in the street.

It was clearly time to go to obedience school. I chose a six-week class run by an extraordinary woman named Barbara Mari. She can make a dog do almost anything, and she actually seems to know what dogs are thinking. Lacey is now a transformed canine. She has not eaten anybody or anything for some time. However, she is not the only one to benefit from the class. I have also. Here are three lessons I have learned from obedience school.

Obedience must be learned. Obedience is not natural for a dog or a human. Three of our four children learned to say "no" before they said "yes," and the odd one out soon corrected her mistake

The natural inclination of each heart is to rebel against God. It is not easy to submit our will to God's. We need to be taught. Jesus understood this, which is why in his great commission he told his disciples:

> Go and make disciples of all nations baptizing them...and teaching them to obey everything I have commanded them. (Matthew 28:19)

But how do we learn obedience? I heard the answer every week from the dog trainer: repetition and consistency. It is no use taking Lacey to the class unless I practice obedience with her during the week. So it is for us as Christians. Jesus tells us to *love one another*. We obey that command as we *keep on loving each other as brothers* (Hebrews 13:1). It is not natural for us to love one another so we must practice it each day.

Obedience must have the right motivation. Border collies are considered the most intelligent of all breeds of dogs. Dog intelligence is measured by how long it takes a dog to learn a command. Border collies are faster learners because they have a powerful desire to please their owners. In frustration, we sometimes strike our dogs for bad behavior. That is pointless. Dogs do not equate that form of punishment with their mistake, so they do not learn from it. Fear, too, is a poor motivator. So it is with us. Fear or guilt are poor reasons for obedience. Rather Jesus taught us *if you love me, you will obey what I command*. The righteous man described in Psalm 1 delighted in the law of the Lord. He took pleasure in God so it was not difficult for him to obey God. My dog craves to please me. May I have the same craving to please my Lord.

Obedience has great rewards. We bought a book on dog training. The first chapter began with some firm teaching from the author. It said that training was the only real key to freedom for a dog. With training a dog can accompany its master almost anywhere. With training the dog can be trusted alone in the house. With training the dog can impress family and friends with clever tricks—maybe even bring home a trophy from a competition! A trained dog needn't feel unruly or rejected. The dog can be both clever and self-confident. The author certainly believed that a trained dog is a happier dog.

Indeed, when Lacey was disobedient, we chained her up in a dark garage. Now that she has learned obedience, she gets the run of the house. We no longer even try to keep her out of the bedroom. Obedience has transformed her life.

We sometimes think of obeying God as something dull or negative. Nothing could be further from the truth. Our Lord's commandments are not burdensome. They are given for our health and happiness. Blessing after blessing come to those who obey God.

The rewards of obedience are eternal salvation (Hebrews 5:9) and the joy of knowing God (1 John 2:3). We have the promise:

> *…that if anyone obeys his word, God's love is truly made complete in him. (1 John 2:5)*

The old chorus puts it well, "Trust and obey, there is no other way, to be happy in Jesus, but to trust and obey."

Chapter 14

Where Do We Go From Here?

After completion of First Baptist Church remodeling
John
February 1995

Where do we go from here? We hardly needed to ask that question last year. Church building programs are wonderful because they provide a physical blueprint and direction. They have a clear beginning and end. We can all get involved on some level. But what do we do when the building is completed? That is a harder question to answer. Churches that have successfully built beautiful structures sometimes lose direction once the cement has dried. The people who study church growth have noted an alarming statistic. A high percentage of pastors leave their churches within 18 months of the completion of a new building. Interviewers discovered that once the excitement of a building project had died down, the pastors were not sure what to do next and so, to cover their confusion, they took a new job.

Well, I like it here at First Baptist Church. I have no desire to leave. Thus, I have a vested interest in this question—Where do we go from here now that the building project is behind us?

I knew I needed another blueprint for the next stage of the life of our church. I found it in Solomon's prayer at the dedication of the temple. The building of the temple had dominated the life of Israel for seven and a half years. It is estimated that it cost in excess of $5,000,000,000. It employed 150,000 stone cutters, 550 construction managers, 3,300 assistant site managers. It used 4,000 tons of gold and 29,000 tons of silver. It was finally completed in 960 B.C. Solomon resisted the temptation to sit back and enjoy this magnificent building. Instead he called the people together and outlined for them how the temple was to be used. You can read about it in 2 Chronicles 6-7. As I have read and re-read this prayer, I have come to see that Solomon's plan for the temple is also my desire for this fellowship. Let me explain.

I long for First Baptist Church to be a place where God's presence is felt. As the temple was being dedicated, an incredible thing happened. *The temple of the Lord was filled with a cloud and the priests could not perform their service because of the cloud, for the glory of the Lord filled the temple of God (2 Chronicles 5:13).*

God's presence was so real that it stopped people in their tracks. Wouldn't it be tremendous if God's presence was as real as that to us? Let me tell you what happens when God's presence is felt in this way.

Worship is joyful—I stop asking "Do I like this hymn?" and start asking "Does God like it?"

Service is enthusiastic—It is not a chore or a bore, it is my grateful response to the living God.

Giving is generous—I don't resent giving, I rejoice in the opportunity to give.

When God's presence is felt, time stands still. We don't keep looking at our watches. The dedication of the temple took 21 days and everyone stayed (7:8-9). I plan our services to last an hour and fifteen minutes. I know that can seem an eternity but when God is moving among us, we are not aware of the passing of time.

I long for First Baptist Church to be a place where God's forgiveness is found. Forgiveness is a theme that runs through Solomon's prayer. Here is a typical example:

> *Forgive your people who have sinned against you. (6:39)*

The message of forgiveness is one of the greatest contributions we can make to this community. I am amazed at the number of broken people that God brings through our doors. His forgiveness is the way to their wholeness. The Bible makes it clear that our basic problem is not lack of money, lack of opportunity, or low self-esteem. These significant problems are often only symptoms of a more serious condition known as sin. Forgiveness deals with that root problem. It restores us to a right relationship with God and puts us back in the center of his will.

I long for First Baptist Church to be a place where God's power is experienced. Solomon identifies several ways in which God's power might be seen in the life of Israel. They remind me of certain ministries of our church.

Restoration for the defeated—Solomon prays that when God's people have been captured by the enemy, they may be restored to their land (6:24). Satan has stripped many families in Rochester of their rightful inheritance of joy. One of the main thrusts of our Family Ministries is to restore what the enemy has taken. God wants to rebuild marriages and reunite families.

Provision for the destitute—Solomon prays for rain for those suffering from drought (6:26) and food for those suffering from famine (6:28). There are many serious social problems here in Olmsted County. God's people can be part of the solution. It appears that the government may be withdrawing from the welfare business, which provides the church with a glorious opportunity to express the love of Christ to the needy.

Salvation for the foreigner—Solomon pleaded with God:

> *As for the foreigner, who has come from a distant land…hear from heaven…so that all the peoples of the earth may know your name and fear you. (6:32)*

We have a global God with a global vision. As his people, we must not be parochial. I thank God that First Baptist Church is filled with world Christians striving to see that our "95 by 95" missions project goal is met and surpassed. Let us seek to increase our giving and our going for missions.

Victory over the forces of evil –

> *When your people go to war against their enemies…uphold their cause (6:34).*

Let us be clear that our enemies are not people. Our enemies are spiritual principalities and powers. God's people are called to stand against those philosophies that are contrary to his word. We are to be people of discernment. That is always difficult and often controversial. Our Salt and Light Committee is seeking to help us in this great task.

I long that First Baptist Church will be a place where God's glory is supreme. Notice what happens at the conclusion of Solomon's invocation:

> *When Solomon finished praying, fire came down from heaven and consumed the burnt offering and sacrifices, and the glory of the Lord filled the temple. The priests could not enter the temple of the Lord because the glory of the Lord filled it. When all the Israelites saw the fire coming down and the glory of the Lord above the temple, they knelt on the pavement with their faces to the ground, and they worshipped and gave thanks to the Lord, saying, 'He is good; his love endures forever.' (7:1-3)*

What will it mean for us to desire God's glory to be supreme in 1995? It will mean approaching every issue with this one question: *What will bring the greater glory to our great God?* This is where I believe we should go from here.

Chapter 15

The Face of Suffering

John
May 1995

I recently went on a pilgrimage to the United States Holocaust Memorial Museum in Washington D.C. I was part of a group of 150 clergy from Minnesota. I was invited to participate by Rabbi David Freedman of B'nai Israel Synagogue in Rochester. The visit coincided with the 50th anniversary of the liberation of the concentration camps by Allied troops at the end of the Second World War. Four other pastors from Rochester were also part of the group. We left Rochester at 4:30 a.m. and drove up to the Minneapolis Airport where we boarded a chartered plane. Members of the crew said that they expected a safe flight with so many ministers on board!

On arrival at the museum we were given an orientation by the museum director and the leaders of our group, Rabbi Edelheit of Temple Israel and Father Michael O'Connell of the Basilica of Saint Mary. These two religious leaders of the Twin Cities' Jewish and Catholic communities share a commitment to an ongoing dialogue between Christians and Jews. Rabbi Edelheit said, "I truly believe that if there had been a dialogue between Christians and Jews in the mid 1930's, there would not have been a Holocaust."

The Holocaust museum is located on the Washington Mall. It opened in 1993, and has already attracted 4,000,000 visitors. It contains 10,000 artifacts collected from around the world, including an authentic Treblinka boxcar, an actual barrack from Birkenau, and 2,000 pairs of children's shoes from Auschwitz. Its archives and library of 100,000 volumes makes it the largest Holocaust study center in America.

The museum is a tribute to all the 11,000,000 victims of the Nazis. These include Jews (6,000,000), Poles, Gypsies, homosexuals, Masons, political prisoners, the handicapped, the mentally ill, Soviet P.O.W.'s and Jehovah's Witnesses.

Following our orientation we were given four hours in which to tour the museum. It was easy to become overwhelmed at the hundreds of displays. I found the things that struck me were often the simplest. There were the piles of human hair shaved from victims before they were sent to the gas chamber. There is a three- story tower of photos of the entire Jewish village of Ejszyski in Lithuania where Jews had lived for 900 years. All these people were killed in two days in 1941. There are now no Jews in Ejszyski.

Following the tour we gathered again in the auditorium for a debriefing and closing service of remembrance. On the plane back to Minnesota we had the opportunity to write a note of appreciation to our patron, John Barry, whose generosity made the whole trip possible.

I have been trying to analyze why this visit made such an impact on me. It was not because I was unaware of the evils of the Holocaust. My parents were both officers in the British Army in World War II. They met in Germany during the last year of the war. From my earliest days I remember them telling my brothers and me stories of their experiences in Germany. My mother attended the Nuremburg War Trials. As a college student I began to read about the war. I developed an interest in the Holocaust. I visited the Holocaust memorial in Jerusalem. I went to Anne Frank's house in Amsterdam, and read that little Jewish girl's diary. I walked around the site of the Jewish ghetto in Warsaw and recalled the heroic story of the uprising where Jews armed with little more than stones held off Nazi troops for a month. I talked to the Rabbi of the last remaining synagogue in the old city of Warsaw. In preparation for this pilgrimage I went to the Imperial War Museum in London to see the exhibit of the British liberation of the Belsen concentration camp. Gretchen and I went to the Museum of Tolerance in Los Angeles, which is part of the Simon Wiesenthal Center. I read Schindlers's List and numerous articles, yet none of these experiences touched me like the visit to Washington.

The explanation lies, I believe, in the fact that I was in the company of nineteen rabbis, some of whom had lost loved ones in the Holocaust. They provided the face of suffering. They added a dimension to my understanding that I could not have gained on my own. They helped me take home four lessons:

Mankind is capable of great evil. It is appropriate that the museum is next to the Smithsonian Institute. The Smithsonian represents the accomplishments of civilization. The Holocaust museum speaks of mankind's dark side and the human genius for evil. I was reminded of Jeremiah's words:

> *The heart is deceitful above all things and beyond cure. Who can understand it? (Jeremiah 17:9)*

The power of words. Hitler was not a great military strategist, but he was a brilliant orator. He chose to use his extraordinary gift to destroy. Martin Luther used his gift with words to liberate the church of his day, yet he also made derogatory statements about the Jews that created a climate of anti-Semitism in Germany. We too must be careful of the words we use, for they are powerful weapons. We must beware of making statements like "the Jews killed Jesus." That is neither historically nor theologically true. It is not true historically because the Romans killed Jesus, and it is not true theologically because it was my sins and yours that killed Jesus.

Individuals can make a difference. Even in the face of worldwide apathy to this human slaughter there were individuals (righteous Gentiles, the Jews call them) who made a stand. The Danish people are a good example. The Danish police refused to round up Jews. The Danish people hid them in their homes. In the museum there is a small Danish fishing boat that was used to take Jews from Denmark to neutral Sweden. Recently at church we had a survivor of the Holocaust tell how the Danish people saved him and his family by sending food parcels to him in the concentration camp. Another example of individuals making a difference is the protestant village of Le Chambon-sur-Lignon in southern France. Between 1941 and 1944 the inhabitants helped some 5,000 refugees, including several thousand Jews, to escape Nazi persecution. They were led by their pastor, Andre Trocme, and his wife, Magdu. They hid the refugees in their homes and farms and smuggled them to safety across the Swiss border. Though their actions placed them in danger, the rescuers of Le Chambon-sur-Lignon were resolute. Years later they refused praise for their deeds. One asked, "How can you call us good? We did what had to be done."

God identifies with our suffering. God never promises to deliver us from suffering. He allowed his chosen people to experience terrible tribulation. However, he does promise to be with us in our suffering. We see this illustrated in the Old Testament story of Shadrach, Meshach and Abednego, who were joined in the red hot furnace by one who looked like *a son of the gods. (Daniel 3:25)* We see it demonstrated best of all in Jesus the Jew, who entered our world and shared in our suffering and freely took our judgment and death upon himself. When we look at the cross we see the suffering face of God.

I returned to Rochester reflecting on the evils of our own day. It's easy to blame the Germans of 50 years ago for their failure to speak out against Hitler, but who will speak out today? We still have ethnic cleansing going on in Bosnia, Rwanda and Iraq. What have I done to protest this barbarity? Hitler justified his actions by saying that Jews, Gypsies, Jehovah's Witnesses, etc. were non-persons. They were surplus to the needs of the Third Reich. That justification is eerily close to the argument used to defend the destruction of 30,000,000 babies by abortion since *Roe v. Wade* in 1973. These unborn babies, we're told, are non-people and therefore not protected by the law of the land and are surplus to requirements. The international memorial sculpture at Dachau bears the words, *never again*. For this to be fulfilled we need to believe that there is a set of values worth dying for. Those traditional and biblical values were absent in Germany and are disappearing from our land today. Catholic theologian John Pawlikowski writes in his paper, The Challenge of the Holocaust For Christian Theology:

> *At least indirectly, Western liberal thought was responsible for the Holocaust. By breaking the tight hold the God-concept had on previous generations, it paved the way for greater human freedom and self-sufficiency without realistically assessing the potential of the destructive forces within mankind to pervert this freedom into the cruelty revealed by the Nazi experiment. Thus the Holocaust shattered much of the grandeur of Western liberal thought. In some ways it represents the ultimate achievement of the person totally 'liberated from God.'*

Chapter 16

Immortality
John
March 1996

Do you realize that Adolph Hitler is still alive? I know that he committed suicide 51 years ago but that was just the death of his body. We have no reason to believe that it was the end of him.

The Bible tells us that men and women can never die in the sense that their existence ends. Once we are born we live forever. The curtain is never drawn on our life.

There are hints of our immortality in the Old Testament. Solomon tells us:

> *The dust returns to the ground it came from and the Spirit returns to God who gave it. (Ecclesiastes 12:7)*

However it is from Jesus himself that we have the plainest statements of our inability to escape existence:

> *Do not be amazed at this, for a time is coming when all who are in the graves will hear his voice and come out—those who have done good will rise to life, and those who have done evil will rise to be condemned. (John 5:28-29)*

This is good news for Christians but bad news for others. Some may comfort themselves with the thought of oblivion. Those who have led evil lives are relieved to think that their secrets will die with them and all that they are will be lost in the sea of non-existence.

Some have taken the second death described in Revelation to refer to the annihilation of the wicked but this is not the case. Death in scripture is seen as separation. The first death is the separation of our soul from our body. The second death is the separation of our soul from the presence of God for all eternity. This prospect is so terrible we would never dare to mention it if it did not come from the mouth of Jesus. He tells us that *the unrighteous will go away to eternal punishment but the righteous to eternal life (Matthew 25:24)*. This is the awful consequence of rejecting the son of God.

All this may not fit in with our ideas of God. We are sometimes so eager to embrace the doctrine of the love of God that we forget he is also a holy God who cannot tolerate sin. But even if we were to forget God's hatred toward sin we could hardly believe that a God of love would force his enemies to spend eternity in his presence singing his praises.

Frankly, heaven for a non-believer would be hell. In his mercy God does not consign those who reject him in this life to worship him in the next.

How should we respond to this news that we are immortal beings who will live forever either in the light of God's presence or the darkness of his absence?

We must recognize the seriousness of our situation. We may joke about heaven and hell but God never does. Our eternal destiny is no laughing matter. We may ignore God now (he allows us to do that) but a time is coming when we will stand before him. At that moment he will determine where we will spend eternity. We will stand at that judgment seat knowing that nothing impure can enter God's presence. This rules us out unless we have lived a perfect life. How awful it will be to hear those words:

> *Depart from me, you who are cursed, into the eternal fire prepared for the devil and his angels. (Matthew 25:41)*

We must receive God's remedy for our sin. The remedy is Jesus himself.

> *Believe in the Lord Jesus Christ and you shall be saved. (Acts 16:31)*

There is nothing to hinder us from coming to Christ except our unbelief. If we hold out our hands in faith and our lives as an offering to him, we will be safe for all eternity. Jesus died that we might live. He took our sin on the cross that we might take his righteousness. He came to earth that we might go to heaven.

We must rescue those who are lost. There must be an urgency about our witness to our friends and family who do not know Christ. Their condition is desperate. If they continue to ignore God they face an eternity in hell. We must not be put off by their rejection of us or the gospel. We are on a life saving mission. They cannot see their danger but we can. Love compels us to act. We must pray for them. We must speak with them frankly and honestly about life after death. We must dispel any false ideas they have of either extinction or of an easy passage into heaven based on their good works. We must tell them:

> *He who has the Son of God has life. He who does not have the Son of God does not have life. (1 John 5:12)*

We must invite them to church where they will hear the way of salvation. Time is short. They may die or Christ may come again and the day of opportunity will have passed.

Chapter 17

Reflections on Death
John
July 1996

The phone call I always dreaded finally came at 6:30 this morning. The weeping voice of my mother told me that my father died last night. The next several hours were filled with phone calls trying to make funeral arrangements, flights to England, and ensuring that others will look after my ministry responsibilities in my absence.

I do most of this in a daze. I can't concentrate. I can't taste food. There is a heavy pain in my chest that I remember remained for three months after our daughter died ten years ago. I keep feeling that it's not real, that someone will tell me there's been a mistake, but I know that they won't.

It's now 5 p.m. I've sat down at my desk to sort out my feelings and try and make some sense of it all. Apart from the obvious grief, I can find two other emotions in my bruised soul. The first is thankfulness.

I'm so thankful that our family went to England last month. We almost did not go because of the expense and because of concern about the childrens' readiness for such a long trip. Thank God we did. The children were able to stay in their grandparent's home, spend time with them, and now have the happiest memories of them. It meant that I was able to attend the Spurgeon Seminary Conference with my father. We both love the old place and talked about our student days there. He graduated 45 years ago; I, 20 years ago. On one weekend my two brothers came to my parents' home. We all played cricket on the lawn like we did when we were boys growing up in London. My father acted as the umpire. Just two weeks ago, I spent my last day in England with my dad. We talked about churches and theology and cricket. I see this now as God's gracious gift to me. I'm so thankful, also, for my father's influence in my life.

I am grateful for his example. Hebrews 11 tells us that we are surrounded by a great cloud of witnesses. I was never in doubt of that. I saw the Christian faith lived out in the lives of my father and mother. My dad was a superb example of faithfulness in ministry. He had his own term for it: *stickability*. He stuck with his churches (he only served two in his 30 years of ministry). He stuck with his friends and he stuck with his Lord. He gave his life to Christ when he was eight years old and he followed Christ for the next 70 years.

After he retired, he continued to serve small churches as an interim pastor. He knew that he could possibly extend his life by cutting down the number of his preaching engagements, but his passion was proclaiming the unsearchable riches of Christ. He still found the greatest excitement and satisfaction in seeing people come to Jesus and grow in their faith. The Lord took him home when he was sitting in his favorite chair preparing another sermon. The words of Revelation 2:10 come to my mind, *Be faithful unto death and I will give you the crown of life.*

I am also thankful for his encouragement. His death means that one of the major supports of my life has been removed. All through my life he has encouraged me. When I was a school boy and later a student, he came to watch me run in track meets and cross country races, often driving to different parts of the course so he could cheer me on. Only 16 days ago he accompanied me on a six-hour car drive to watch me and my brother, Simon, play cricket.

He always had advice on how to deal with problems at church. He encouraged me to accept the call to First Baptist Church. He listened to the tapes of the Sunday services I sent him and was always affirming. Sometimes his unfailing support for his son could be embarrassing for my mother as he tended to show the church bulletin, the pictorial directory and First In Touch Newsletter to almost every person he met. It would be easy to dismiss his positive outlook on life as just a by-product of his personality, but in fact it was grounded in his theology. He had a God who was able to *work all things together for good.* He could see no cause for pessimism when God was on the throne. How often I have heard him preach on the themes of joy and contentment from Paul's letter to the Philippians. His life was steeped in scripture. He could quote the King James Version by the yard. He had a verse for every occasion. Driving along at night with a dirty windshield he would observe, *Now we see through a glass darkly.*

The second emotion that comes to the surface during this day is anticipation. I'm looking forward to seeing my father again. His body is lying in a morgue in Felixstowe but his soul is now with the Lord Jesus Christ. He has joined that crowd around the throne of the Lamb. One of his favorite hymns begins:

> *Someday the silver cord will break, and I no more as now shall sing,*
> *But oh the joy when I shall wake within the palace of the King!*

The silver cord of his life (Ecclesiastes 12:6) broke yesterday, July 21, 1996. His faith has now been turned into glorious sight. This is the

Christian hope. This is the ground of my comfort. I used to wonder why young people did not want to go to heaven while many older Christians did. Now I understand. You don't want to go to a place where you don't know anyone. As you get older, you know more and more people who have gone to heaven and you start to look forward to going there too. How wonderful that I shall see my dear earthly father's face again in my heavenly father's home. That's not an abstract doctrine. That's reality. That's my future. Peter puts it well:

> *Now for a little while you may have to suffer grief in all sorts of trials. These have come so that your faith...may be proved genuine and may result in praise, glory and honor when Jesus Christ is revealed (1 Peter 1:6-7).*

Ten years ago, when our daughter died, I caught a glimpse of what it must have been like for God to give up his only son. Now, as a son who has lost his father, I can understand a little more clearly what it was like for the son to give up his face-to-face relationship with his father when he left heaven and came to earth.

Tomorrow I leave for England to be with my mother and brothers. Thanks to the kindness of friends in this church who will care for the children and have helped financially, Gretchen will be able to join me before the funeral on July 29. I am so grateful for the graciousness of the staff in stepping in to cover on short notice. One of the overwhelmingly clear lessons from such a time as this is that God's people do indeed bring God's comfort to life. Thank you for your prayers and your concern. We will need them greatly in the days ahead as I learn to live without my father's presence in my life.

Chapter 18

What Do You Want on Your Tombstone?

John

September 1996

We were driving back from the North Shore when Gretchen turned to me and asked, "What do you want on your tombstone?" I assumed that she wasn't referring to the toppings on my pizza so I replied, "How about 'The Best Husband a Woman Could Ever Have'?"

She laughed so hard that she almost fell out of the van. Somewhat stung by her response, I began to think more seriously about her query.

Each of us would like to be remembered for something worthwhile. Yet few of us will gain a national or international reputation. The Bible tells us that whether or not we are remembered in the pages of the history books is not as important as the legacy we leave through the things we accomplish for the Lord.

A eulogy for King David is recorded in Acts 13:36:

> *For when David had served God's purpose in his own generation, he fell asleep. He was buried with his fathers.*

It is interesting that David is not remembered for slaying a giant or for being a great king but rather for the fact that in his life he accomplished the purpose for which God had created him. We may never be kings or giant killers but we can leave a legacy as great as David's if we fulfill the purpose that God has for us.

The New Testament tells us that God has given all of us gifts to be used for his glory here on earth. This flatly contradicts those of us who say, "I can't do anything." All of us have been called to ministry. The Bible defines ministry as any service visible or invisible that is offered to God. The fact is that any service done for God is eternally significant. The book of Revelation suggests that it is the only thing we can take with us when we die:

> *Blessed are the dead who die in the Lord...they will rest from their labor, for their deeds will follow them (Revelation 14:13).*

Let me suggest a ministry that all of us can have each Sunday morning. As a church we are concerned about communicating to our guests that they are loved by God. One of the best ways to demonstrate this is to show our visitors that they are important to us.

I recently read about a lady who had this wonderful ministry of outreach. She would sit in a different pew each Sunday in order to become acquainted with those who sat in that area. She would greet them, introduce herself, and help them locate a hymn or share a Bible. She would extend hospitality by inviting them to an adult class or a small group. She also practiced the two-minute-rule, knowing guests will generally leave after the service within two minutes if no one has spoken to them, whereas regular attenders are likely to linger longer.

Let me encourage you to make this your ministry also and reserve the two minutes after every worship service as a time for our guests. This may seem insignificant, but it is not. It communicates to our guests that they are important to us and to God.

Every week our services include visitors in great need. Your friendly greeting or word of encouragement may in turn be like a drink of cold water in the desert to them. I encourage you to join me in this ministry of hospitality and welcome. It may not appear on our tombstones, but we can all leave a positive legacy by discovering the gifts that God has given us, and using them like David for God's purposes.

Chapter 19

Salvation
Gretchen
February 1997

Virtually all of us who call ourselves Christians can thank the apostle Saul for our knowledge of Christ. Unless your racial background is Jewish, you probably came to know Christ through the church, or through the Bible, or through another Christian, who came to know Christ in the same way. It was Saul's divinely given mission to bring the gospel to the Gentile, or non-Jewish, world. Because he did, we now have the gospel. If he hadn't been given that task, it's possible that Christianity would have remained a local Jewish sect. One man's obedience led to our belief. We should also put this understanding into personal terms: our obedience may lead to someone else's belief.

There are two dangers in reading the story of Saul's conversion. The first is that, not having had such an astounding experience ourselves, and not knowing anyone else who has, we tend to disbelieve that it could ever happen again. The second danger comes when we compare our conversion experience to Saul's and realize that nothing so dramatic happened to us. That comparison can make us doubt the validity of our own conversion.

At the very least, the account makes us wonder whether there might not be two models for the way God calls men and women: Saul's way, and the mundane way the rest of us come to faith.

Lest you think that no one today gets called by God, my oldest sister described her conversion at the age of 42 as a "Damascus Road experience." She said it was so sudden, such a breathtaking reversal, and so compelling, that she had no choice but to follow Christ once he'd revealed himself. My husband has described how he heard an audible voice just once in his life at a critical moment of decision, directing him to abandon his vocational plans and go into the ministry.

If you are one who came to know Christ in a dramatic moment as did Saul, rejoice and remember that moment when the going is tough. If you are more like the disciples, who lived with Christ for three years and yet didn't really understand who he was until the resurrection, cling to the knowledge that what you came to understand slowly and deliberately is of just as much value. Being human we can often feel shortchanged if we don't have a dramatic testimony, but the capitulation of the wicked human heart is just as dramatic in the sight of God whether it is a heart that appears to be good or whether it is a murderer's soul like Saul's.

I went through a fairly dreadful experience of doubt several years back. It was the first time I had ever really experienced doubt in what I believed. I remember sitting in church during this stretch, hearing words that had caused me to rejoice all my life, and thinking, "But how can anyone really believe these things?" It was awful. It was impossible to worship in any meaningful sense. I didn't feel like there was any point in praying, because it was hard to believe that anyone was there to pray to. I kept on with my Bible reading, but it was like reading Grimm's Fairy tales—it didn't seem to have much basis in reality.

This experience for me came on quickly and left quickly, almost as if someone suddenly pulled a dark curtain off my head and left me blinking in the sunlight of a normal world. A few days later I could scarcely remember why I ever found it difficult to believe. The convictions that had driven my life for the past many years were completely back in place.

On reflection, I found that this stretch, while awful to experience, was a valuable learning experience. It was like having one's toes on the abyss and swaying over the edge. It was truly frightening to catch a glimpse of what life without Christ is like, chilling enough to make me determined to safeguard my spiritual life and yet revealing how extremely difficult it must be for someone to come to Christ for the first time. When in that state of unbelief, all the words a believer can say about Christ's love are just that...words. It taught me that faith is a marvelous gift from God, one to be valued, cherished and protected by the way we live. As a wise friend told me during that time, God desired intimacy with me. Seeking that intimacy over a period of time seemed to be the thing that turned the tide.

If you grew up in a Christian home with loving parents and gave your heart to Jesus when you were a little kid in Sunday school, be grateful today that you didn't have to go through the bitterness of soul that confronted poor Saul on the road to Damascus when he realized that he had been trying to harm the risen Christ. Be grateful that, unlike him, you do not have on your conscience the murder of innocent people. Be grateful that God spares many of us the consequences of a life deliberately and fully screwed up by sin. Belief is truly a sovereign gift from God. If you have it, value it as much as did Saul. This I have learned only because I nearly lost belief.

God puts us, like the apostle Paul, through times of testing. There are times when we feel like we're being told, "I will show you how much you will suffer for my sake." I don't like to suffer, but on the rare occasions when I've faced suffering, it has each time been a learning experience. What's more, suffering validates to me the value of the faith I hold in Jesus Christ. The key of conversion merely opens the door to our real lives—lives meant to be filled with both suffering and joy for the Lord's sake.

Chapter 20

Visit to a Monastery

Gretchen
March 1997

There are some lessons that I just cannot seem to learn in my spiritual life, and so God patiently teaches them to me year after year. Probably the biggest one concerns God's sovereignty and his right to run my life. It becomes very, very difficult to listen for the still, small voice of God whispering when all around me life is shouting "Do this!"—"Do that!"

One way that God reinforces our attention to him is by the surprising events of life. Several years back my mother and I went walking through her neighborhood and journeyed into the nearby graveyard. I hadn't been there in years, since I stood there with a crowd of friends from our old church and watched as John conducted a graveside service for a friend of ours. Six weeks after our daughter died in 1986, a young father and husband in our church died of a brain tumor. I remembered the location of his grave and uncovered the stone, which was covered with leaves and dust. "Bruce J. Bibelheimer, 1953-1986: Beloved husband and father." In that year when we were still reeling from our daughter's death, our friend Becky lost her husband of six years. She had a daughter just Kirstie's age, and she was also five months pregnant at the time of his death. It was a year when the sovereign power of God to shape our lives through circumstance was brought home again and again. Do any of us know what our future holds?

When we always put first ourselves, our own aims, our busy little pursuits, we are in danger of missing God's desire for us, which is that we know him more.

Several years back my sister gave me a gift of one night as a guest in a monastery for a spiritual retreat. The monastery is the New Camoldoli Hermitage near Lucia, California, and two miles above the coast on a deserted stretch of Highway 1 just below Big Sur. All sorts of stresses conspired to keep me from going. At the worst end of the scale was the discomfort I was causing to my relatives by traveling across the country from Minnesota to see them, and then going away alone for 24 hours.

I arrived at the monastery late Sunday afternoon. The monk who showed me to my guestroom was cheerful and friendly. We had a conversation lasting two or three minutes, and from that time on, silence reigned. The rooms are built along a cliff, simple and bare, with just a bed, a desk and a toilet. The back of the room consisted of a huge window and a door into a walled garden.

Within that little garden, about 10 feet by 12 feet, it was completely private. At the back of the garden was no wall, but rather just a railing, as the cliff fell away below it. The view out the back of my garden was of the whole Pacific Ocean with the sun setting beyond it. No other person was visible. No sound could be heard but the natural sound of birds and small animals rustling in the brush.

What happened to me during my night and morning there is largely a private matter between me and God. However, it seemed clear to me that I was there for a specific purpose and I used every moment of that time to refresh my soul and listen for God's voice through reading, prayer and meditation. I attended vespers the first night, and was grateful that the service consisted only of sung scripture. A cantor sang the first line of a psalm, and the monks and few guests responded with the next line. There was no speaking, no explanation, no bulletin, just the musical setting of five or six lengthy passages of scripture concluding with 1 Peter 1. The singing finished with half an hour of silent prayer in the chapel—again, no explanation, no leading, just silence, completed by the tolling of the monastery bell atop the chapel. Yes, it was strange to be visiting in a community of 20 or so silent monks and five or six other silent strangers. Yet somehow that extraordinary beauty of the setting and the purposefulness of my visit there made the hours fly by until, all too soon, it was time to pack my few things and go. I was able to continue my silently happy thoughts for another three hours until I was home again among my very non-silent family.

I recognize that this opportunity was probably a once-in-a-lifetime thing. However, what it showed me was the deep craving I have not only for silence but for occasional separation from all the responsibilities and relationships that press in on me, demanding my time, drawing out my best efforts, and in the process, quietly driving a wedge between me and the God who desires intimacy with me. Neither intimacy nor love flourishes among strangers. They are by-products of spending time together. I know that I need to preserve and guard the relationship that I have with God more zealously. The subtle danger of pride can creep into our spiritual lives as we begin to believe that we are self-reliant and self-directed.

When I look back at some of the deeply affecting things that I thought about while I was there, I have concluded one thing very powerfully. This experience came about not only by the grace of God, who welcomed me graciously into his presence, but also by the grace of my family who were inconvenienced by my absence. More than that, it came about by the grace of friends who remembered to pray for me. I rely on the prayers of others for my ongoing preparation and ability to teach and minister within this church. I do not want to make the mistake of being self-reliant, not only because that would be putting myself in the place of God, but also because it would diminish the role of others who are helping me to become the woman that God wants me to be.

Chapter 21

How Can We Be Sure We're Going to Heaven?

John
April 1997

I wonder if you ever think of heaven. You should, for it is going to be your residence for a lot longer than this earth is going to be your home. I know it is hard to imagine what it is going to be like because:

> No eye has seen, no ear has heard, no mind has conceived what
> God has prepared for those who love him. (1 Corinthians. 2:9)

Nevertheless, Scripture does tell us to fix our mind on heavenly things and to seek those things that are above. From time to time it is good to reflect on our heavenly home.

An old joke tells about a tourist who was driving through Iowa. He stopped an old farmer to ask him how to get to Chicago. The farmer scratched his head and after a moment's thought said, "Well you can't get there from here." That's not true of heaven. You *can* get to heaven from here. You can be certain of your eternal destination. You can be sure you are going to heaven. You can have a spring in your step and a song in your heart because you know that whenever the Lord comes for you, you're ready to go. The message is simple but also effective and a good one to review any time you are tempted to doubt God's love for you.

We can be can sure we are going to heaven because of the promise Jesus made. John 14 is one of the loveliest chapters of the Bible, describing Jesus' last night with his disciples before his death. They have sensed that something is very wrong and that Jesus will soon be leaving them. They have a pretty good idea that he is going to die and, like us, they hate the thought of loosing a loved one—of being left behind without him and never seeing him again on earth.

So Jesus addresses their anxiety. He tells them, *Do not let your hearts be troubled.* He urges them to put their trust in God and also in him. Then he makes them this marvelous promise:

> In my Father's house are many rooms; if it were not so, I
> would have told you. I am going there to prepare a place for
> you. (John 14:2)

This is one of the clearest promises that Jesus ever made—and the good news is we can trust Jesus' promises.

This was a solemn time for Jesus. He was not in a frivolous mood. He selected every word carefully. The message he chose to convey to his disciples in that last meeting in the upper room was that they were going to spend eternity with him in heaven. They were not going to be separated from him. They were not going to lose him forever. They had his word on it that he was going to his home to prepare a place for them.

Second, we can be sure because of the prayer Jesus prayed. John 17 is one of the most sacred scenes in all of scripture. Jesus is waiting to be arrested and he uses the time for a few moments of final communion with his Father. In this chapter we are privileged to hear the Son pouring out his heart to his Father. As we read through the gospels we know that Jesus often spoke to his Heavenly Father, but seldom do we learn the content of those prayers. Yet here we see right into the heart of our Lord. There is mystery and there is wonder.

Jesus first prays for himself. He then prays for his disciples. Then looking down the centuries, he prays for you and me. In verse 24 he makes an impassioned appeal:

> *Father, I want those you have given me to be with me where I am, and to see my glory.*

Here we have Jesus' last request before he goes to his execution. The extraordinary thing is that he is not thinking of himself but of us. He beseeches his Father that we might be with him in heaven, that we might behold his glory. This is a prayer that the Father would be delighted to answer because it summarized the purpose for which Jesus came. Jesus laid aside his glory when he left heaven to come to earth in order that he might clothe us with his glory and take us back with him to heaven. This is Christ's greatest longing for us. His ultimate desire is not that we should necessarily be healthy or wealthy or even comfortable or happy. His desire is that we will be with him in heaven and that we might see his glory.

Third we can be sure we are going to heaven because of the price Jesus paid. Peter tells us in his first letter:

> *It was not with perishable things such as silver and gold that you were redeemed from the empty way of life handed down to you from your forefathers, but with the precious blood of Christ. (1 Peter 1:18-19)*

Paul tells us:

> *You are not your own; you were bought with a price. (1 Corinthians 6:20)*

The price was the precious blood of Jesus. With these words we discover that Jesus has paid the entrance price for us to get into heaven.

Ice hockey is very popular in Minnesota where we live. Several years ago the owner of the Rochester Mustangs called me up and invited me to come to a game and to bring the family. He graciously added, "Just stop by the ticket booth on your way in and mention my name."

So my family, who I am ashamed to say know almost nothing about ice hockey, went along to the Recreation Center. There was a long line outside the ticket booth and I must confess I felt rather awkward as we waited there. The thought went through my mind, "What happens if I get up to the window and nobody knows anything about these tickets?" My worst fears were realized when my turn came and I said, "I am John Steer and I have some tickets waiting for me." The lady looked at me utterly blankly and said, "I'm sorry, we know nothing about you."

I became rather flustered. There was a large crowd behind me and I could imagine they were all thinking, "Who is this guy trying to get free tickets when all the rest of us are paying?" In desperation I mentioned the name of the owner. A smile now came over the ticket lady's face. She said, "Oh, that's alright then, how many tickets do you need?"

I said, "Five" but I think I could have asked for 55 and it would have been alright. You see I knew the owner; he had paid the price for my admission so that I didn't have to. It will be the same when we get to heaven. There will be no use in me saying, "I am John Steer and I have been the pastor of First Baptist Church—an above average church—and I did this and I did that for the Kingdom of God." I will get a very blank stare indeed from the reception committee. But when I say, "I know Jesus and he has paid the price on the cross for my sins," well then I am going to get a very warm welcome indeed.

It is important for us to understand the nature of the price Jesus paid. Peter tells us that we were redeemed with the "precious blood of Christ" and that is something that people do not admire today. They find it distasteful. Some churches regard it as rather old fashioned, so they are removing the hymns about the blood of Jesus from their songbooks. But it is because of the blood of Jesus that we can be certain of heaven. That blood must be applied to our lives. We need to acknowledge that Jesus went to the cross for us and recognize that we are sinners who need a Savior. We need to surrender our lives to him so that we can leave here absolutely sure of our standing with Christ and our eternal home.

Gretchen and I had the awesome experience of being in the Supreme Court when it was in session. We sat before the nine black-robed justices and heard the attorneys present their oral arguments. It was a very solemn scene. There was great tension in the air and no one made a sound. One was almost afraid to breathe. As I sat there in that stately room, looking at the imposing figures of the Justices, I thought of the day of judgment when each of us will stand before God. We will be on trial for our lives. How we lived and in what we placed our faith will be revealed for all to see.

That is a prospect to make any person nervous. If we have rejected Christ, if we have seen no purpose in his sacrifice, no value in his blood, then we have every reason to fear that scene. On the other hand, if we have acknowledged Jesus Christ as our Savior and Lord we can face that day with assurance. For the Bible tells us:

> *There is no condemnation to those who are in Christ Jesus. (Romans 8:1)*

We can be confident that the judge will hold out his arm and beckon us to his side.

Perhaps you have heard the gospel before but you have never made a commitment to Jesus. Perhaps you are a Christian but there is some uncertainty in your mind about whether you will go to heaven and you would just like to make sure. In the silence of your heart you can pray to invite the Savior to come into your life and cleanse you of your sin and empower you to live a life that honors him. That prayer will make you a new person, a new husband, a new wife, employee, or citizen.

You can be absolutely certain that you are right with God and you are going to heaven. You can know that you are going to heaven because of the promise Jesus made, the prayer Jesus prayed, and the price Jesus paid for your salvation.

Chapter 22

The One Thing You Need
John
May 1997

We all like to get free advice. My cousin is a doctor in Hong Kong. When he is at parties, people are always coming up to him wanting a free consultation. He has a good way of dealing with this. He tells them to undress so he can examine them.

Architects, interior designers, painters, plumbers, and electricians also find people asking them questions. So do clergymen. I find that when someone discovers I'm a pastor their conversation changes. They tend to clean it up. They avoid doubtful stories that might offend the tender ears of a minister. They also ask me questions about matters of faith. They ask if I believe there is a heaven or what hell is like. I welcome this, and I've had some good conversations with people who are interested in the things of God.

The same thing happened to Jesus. He was known as the up-and-coming religious leader so people came to him with their questions. On one occasion a young businessman came to see him. Matthew and Luke tell us he was a wealthy man—a ruler. His question was so important to him that when he heard Jesus was in town, he ran all the way and knelt down before him. That must have been a strange sight—a young aristocrat kneeling before a penniless preacher. He turned to Jesus and asked, *How can I get to heaven? What must I do to inherit eternal life?*

That is a very good question and one that we all need to ask. We don't know when we are going to die and it is wise to plan for the future. It is good to plan for our school, our career, our family, our retirement and to plan for our death. This young man wanted to know what he should do to get ready for that day. And in response Jesus looked at him and loved him.

Isn't that marvelous? Jesus is just about to leave on an important trip. This young man is delaying him, but instead of getting irritated, Jesus loved him. Jesus was not always so patient. He got angry at some of the questions of the Pharisees and religious people. What was so appealing about this young man?

The man wanted life; he wanted real life, eternal life. He was willing to admit openly that his life was lacking. He recognized that if he was going to get life, someone had to give it to him.

The man was prepared to do something to get it and he believed the answer lay with Jesus. He felt there had to be something more so he came to Jesus.

This young man had tried to keep the Ten Commandments. Not claiming to be perfect he said, *I've tried that, I've tried being good, I've tried keeping the commandments and being decent but it doesn't bring life.* And Jesus loved him for his honesty and sincerity. So Jesus informed him, *There is one thing you lack.* Many commentators say that one thing is poverty. But that is not what Jesus means. He says there is one thing you lack, not one thing you've got that is causing all the trouble.

It was not anything to do with money. Rather Jesus says the one thing you need if you want eternal life, is me. You need to follow me. But the trouble is that something is going to get in the way, and that is your money.

You see we cannot have Jesus and everything else. When we come to Christ there will be one thing, at least, that Jesus will tell us to release. He'll say, *Go and deal with that and then follow me.* It may be a possession, it may be a person, or it may be a principle.

For the disciples it was their nets. They had to leave their nets before they could follow him. For us it may not be money, as it was in this young man's case. But still Jesus says, *Give it up or you will not be able to follow me. You can't serve two masters.* The one thing this young man lacked was Jesus. It was not poverty, because there had been plenty of rich people who had found Christ.

This young man's face dropped when he heard what he had to do. *Go sell everything you have and give to the poor.*

There is ironic humor in his response. *He went away sad because he had great wealth.* Would you be sad if you had a large bank account? But it was that wealth that kept him from Jesus. He turned around and left and in so doing, turned his back on heaven. He must have been an utterly miserable man, because there is nothing worse than to come so close to eternal life and then miss it because you won't pay the price.

So here is the story of the poor, rich man. It is a story that tells us the way to heaven. It shows us that respectability is not enough, although many people think it is. Respectability consists in not doing things. The commandments are mostly negative. Christianity consists in doing things, putting Christ first, helping others out of our abundance.

This man had never stolen anything, but neither had he given anything. It may be respectable never to take anything from anyone but it is Christian to give everything to someone. Christianity is Christ and he gave himself for us. In reality, Jesus was confronting this ruler with a basic question: *How much do you really want to be a Christian? Do you want me enough to give your possessions away?* In effect the man answered, *I want you, but I don't want you that much.*

Jesus watched the man go. There was sadness in the heart of Jesus that day, for God desires that none should perish but that all should come to repentance and live. It was the sadness of seeing a man deliberately choosing to fail to be what he might have been, and could have been.

Jesus looks at you with the same appeal of love. He challenges you to embark on the adventure of following him. God grant that he may never have to look at any of us with sorrow because we refuse to be what we might and could have been.

Chapter 23

The Importance of Values

John

June 1997

When I was a boy growing up in London, I liked to visit the graves of famous people. Two memorials stand out in my mind. The first is the grave of Karl Marx in Highgate Cemetery. The second is the memorial to William Wilberforce in Westminster Abbey. These were both men who made an incredible impact on the world of their day.

One wrote *Das Kapital* in the British Museum Library. The philosophy of this book resulted in the slavery of millions to communism.

The other man, a member of the British Parliament, campaigned for 46 years against slavery. His work resulted in the freedom of millions when slavery was finally abolished throughout the British Empire.

Growing up, I wondered why one man could do so much good and the other man so much harm. Was it simply an accident of history? Would it have been possible to have reversed the roles so that Karl Marx became the liberator of slaves and William Wilberforce the inventor of communism? When I looked into their lives, I found that their actions were not arbitrary, but rather were the outcome of their values. In their formative years, their parents, their families and their communities gave them values that stayed with them throughout their lives. The way that Karl Marx and William Wilberforce looked at life determined what they did in lives. Their world views determined their contributions to the world.

It was a Jewish King called Solomon who said 3,000 years ago, *As a man thinks in his heart, so is he*. Christians recognize that Solomon's observation still holds true today. As a person thinks, so will they act. That is why we are interested in values.

All of us have values. Each family has values. Each institution, whether a private company, a non-profit organization, or a government department has values. We need to examine these values. We must ask: are these values helpful? Will these values contribute to the strength of our community? Will these values unite families or divide them? As Christians, we make at least two assumptions as those interested in values.

We do not believe all values are equal. Despite what some may say, no one really believes that all values are the same. In the movie Schindler's List it is apparent to any thinking person that the values of the German industrialist who tried to save the lives of Jews are not morally equivalent to those of the Nazis who wanted to eliminate the Jewish race.

It is clear that there are higher values and lower values. There are values that elevate the human condition and values that drag us down. For a family, a church, a community to be strong, we need to embrace those higher values.

We believe it is possible to distinguish between good and poor values. We believe that there is such a thing as absolute truth. The framers of our constitution affirm the same idea. They said, "We believe these truths to be self evident." They accepted the notion that there are certain truths whose relative merits need not be debated. As a nation, we still believe that certain truths are self evident. The Chinese government may accuse us of cultural imperialism when we criticize their human rights record. They tell us we are just imposing our Western values on them and we do not understand their situation. We rightly dismiss their complaints because we intuitively believe that there is a better way than theirs. We do not believe that imprisonment and torture of those who disagree with the party line are the moral equivalent of freedom of expression for all citizens.

Now where do we get our idea of "a better way" or a "higher standard?" We get it from a higher being. It is God who has revealed these truths to us.

In 1993, Pope John Paul II published an encyclical that all thinking people should applaud. It is called Veritas Splendor—The Splendor of Truth. John Paul notes that the modern world has a lot to say about freedom, but freedom must be grounded in truth. Freedom is not enough, for freedom standing by itself inevitably degenerates into license, and license quickly becomes the enemy of freedom. John Paul contends that power and freedom can and must be made accountable to truth.

"Authentic freedom," he says repeatedly, "is related to truth." Not my truth, your truth or her truth. Not the truth of a class or a nation but truth as in absolute truth.

The central text of the Pope's argument are the words of a Galilean carpenter recorded for us in John's gospel where Jesus says:

> *You will know the truth and the truth will set you free. (John 8:32)*

Some will object that we live in a pluralistic society in which there is no agreement as to what truths we hold. We respond that it is precisely because we live in a pluralistic world that we urgently engage one another in civil arguments about the truth that undergirds our laws. Our mission is to bring the voice of biblical values, based on absolute truth, into the marketplace of ideas.

In 1984, theologian and social critic Richard John Neuhaus gave us the phrase "naked public square" to describe the difficulty of civic discourse without the benefit of moral insight. As a church, our task is to bring moral insight into public discourse in Rochester's "naked public square." We desire to clothe debate with the garments of truth.

Every community has values. The question is, which values will influence our community life? Will they be values that encourage responsibility for our actions, respect for others, and reverence for God? Or will they be values that emphasize personal satisfaction regardless of the cost to others? Values that ridicule honesty and purity? Values that undermine the freedom that has been our heritage? There is a price to pay for dismissing values. If we fail to lay a strong foundation of values in Rochester, we will pay for it in more police, more judges, more jails, more vandalism, and more serious crime.

The alternative is to go God's way and to follow the path that leads to peace. The Apostle Paul tells us which way to go:

> *Whatever is true, whatever is noble, whatever is right, whatever is pure, whatever is lovely, whatever is admirable, if anything is excellent or praiseworthy, think about such things...put it into practice and the God of peace will be with you. (Philippians 4:8-9)*

Chapter 24

Roughing It

A Steer Vacation Saga
John
August 1997

> *Roughing It was the title Mark Twain gave to the journal*
> *of his travels through the American West in 1860.*

We leave on a high note for our annual vacation. The Lakeside Baptism has just concluded. Fourteen people professed their faith in Christ in the waters of Lake Interlachen. It was a glorious evening with some amazing testimonies and the high point of the year for me, thus far. We resolve to leave at 4 a.m. after a few hours' sleep. At 4:30 a.m. we wake up, having both slept through the alarm. We're on the road by 6 a.m.—a record for the Steer family, to leave only two hours after our estimated time of departure!

We set off heading east toward Chicago until it dawns on us we should be going west. I show great restraint in not rebuking the navigator. We travel through Iowa and into Nebraska, paralleling the Mormon and Oregon Trails. I marvel at those early pioneers and try to imagine what it must have been like to make this journey in an ox-drawn wagon. Traveling with three young children also has its challenges. I must remember to send a memo to the makers of the Dodge Caravan, encouraging them to offer the option of a soundproof glass window that could be raised immediately behind the driver's seat, thus cutting out all sound from the rear of the van. It would be a big seller with parents.

Driving on the interstate I offer a quiet word of thanks to those magnificent men and women who labored to raise the speed limit to 75 mph. It's not that the traffic is going any quicker but at least we are traveling legally. We stop at a rest area and the children discover a colony of prairie dogs. Emily, the great animal lover, persuades the prairie dogs to come out of their burrow with the offer of bread. They scurry up to her and she's able to stroke them. The children are delighted with their new-found pets until a man comes and informs them that the animals are carrying the plague. We tell the children to wash their hands and proceed with our journey.

We had planned to camp that night, but true to Steer vacation form, the heavens open and we are treated to a spectacular display of lightning.

We press on and instead spend the night in a motel in Cheyenne, having managed 850 miles for the first day's travel. This is only the second time the children had ever been in a hotel. The novelty and the long journey causes them to treat the bed like a trampoline while we are outside unloading the car. Within five minutes of our arrival the management calls to ask us to keep the noise down as the neighbors are complaining.

In the morning we tour the modest State Capitol building with its glittering golden dome. We admire the statue of Esther Morris. This lady was instrumental in women being granted equal rights in Wyoming in 1869, the first government in the world to do so. We make our way to Laramie, named after the trapper, Jacques Laramie. We take the scenic route through the Medicine Bow Forest, over the Snowy Peak Pass. All the guide books told us that the scenery is spectacular. Unfortunately we can't see it because it is pouring rain. One of the purposes of this trip is to show the children some of the outstanding sights of our country. For the most part they remain remarkably unimpressed. However, they do enjoy one aspect of our day's travel—Gretchen's family had a tradition of stopping for an ice cream once a day on a long journey. The children anticipate this moment and savor it far more than any sunset or historic monument.

We drive through Salt Lake City and on into Nevada. I spot two large birds sitting in the road in front of me. Despite honks from my horn, they refuse to leave the road kill they are enjoying. I pull up beside them. To my amazement, they are two golden eagles. They stare at us for some time, unwilling to leave their dinner, then stretch their enormous wings and take off into the wild blue yonder.

In the afternoon we arrive at Great Basin National Park. At last the sun is shining! We set up our tent at 7,500 feet in a campsite offering only pit toilets and a faucet for water. Due to the absence of any towns nearby, the sky here is jet black at night. We see more stars than we've ever seen before. The verse from the Psalms comes to mind, *When I consider the heavens, the work of your fingers, the moon and stars that you have set in place, what is man that you are mindful of him?* I remember reading somewhere that there are billions of galaxies, most of them undiscovered by man but each one known by God.

We begin the day with a tour around Lehmann Cave. These caves were discovered in the last century when Mr. Lehmann's horse suddenly started sinking into the ground. The guide explains that the caves were formed when the area was a vast inland sea. We wonder if this was Noah's flood. We hike with the children up to 10,500 feet. The air is thin

84

but the view of 13,000 foot Wheeler Peak is spectacular. Setting off again we travel down Route 50, the old Pony Express route. It is described as the loneliest road in America. It goes through historic mining towns like Ely, Eureka and Austin.

One of the advantages of these long road trips is that it provides opportunity for unhurried conversation. Today we discussed the doctrine of sin. Gretchen asked me if I thought of myself as a sinner. Suspecting that I'd been found out in some transgression, I decided to play it safe and changed the subject.

I don't approve of gambling but I do approve of the discount rates that casinos offer for food and accommodations. We spend the night in a casino in Fallon. I take the children on a tour of the casino and give them the assignment of noticing the expressions on the faces of the gamblers. At the conclusion I am very pleased when Nicholas says, "They all look so sad." The atmosphere of despair that hangs over these places is oppressive. It exposes the fallacy of those who would claim that gambling is just entertainment.

It is a perfect day of Nevada sunshine with the temperature at a dry 95 degrees. We stopped to enjoy the refreshing blue water of Lake Tahoe. I remember learning to water ski in these clear, frigid waters 24 years ago. The backdrop is spectacular with the Sierra Nevadas rising to 12,000 feet, still snow-capped. Emily is reading Patty Reed's Doll, a true story of a little girl's doll that was taken along with the Donner party. We have almost exactly paralleled their route on this trip.

Gretchen's four siblings and their families have gathered in San Luis Obispo, California, to celebrate their mother's 70th birthday. Following a wonderful dinner we enjoy an evening of music, poetry and tributes to this extraordinary lady who raised five children. It is unfortunate that in our society we tend to regard people of 70 as past their prime. In countries like Korea they are honored for their wisdom and experience. In Biblical days people like Abraham, Moses and the Apostle John did their best work after 70. The New Testament makes it clear that the role of elders is all-important in teaching the younger members of the church how to live. True to form there is plenty of hilarity and, I notice with a sinking heart, 300 or more old slides to show.

We worship at Grace Church, San Luis Obispo. One of the members of the fellowship has recently had an accident and been paralyzed. The pastor speaks on how good can come out of suffering. It is an excellent exposition, clearly addressing the fears and concerns of many members of the congregation. In this university town Grace Church has a thriving ministry to hundreds of college students. The service is much like ours at First Baptist. The pastor introduced a new element this Sunday. Apparently, like many of us, he loses track of time and often preaches for an hour. He asked the organist to begin to play softly after he'd been going for 45 minutes in order to warn him it was time to wrap up. This she did and to his credit he concluded two minutes later.

In the evening we watch with amazement as thousands of pelicans congregate on the rocks and small islands of Shell Beach. They are responding to the Creator's mandate to go forth and multiply. These birds, which look so ungainly and foolish on land, are graceful and majestic in flight.

We arrive at Summerdale, a glorious campground just outside Yosemite, run by the National Forest Service. Gretchen and I have spent many happy summers here in the past, but this is the first time the children have seen it. A mountain stream meanders through the campground. I take my rod down to one of the deeper pools and within 30 minutes have caught three 12-inch rainbow trout. Of course, it helps that the D.N.R. stocked this stream in the past 24 hours! The scenery of this alpine meadow is glorious and I can hear my father's voice quoting one of his favorite Old Testament verses: *The lines are fallen unto us in pleasant places.*

We visit the Mariposa Grove in Yosemite. It is incredible to look up at the giant sequoias. These towering trees are both the largest and some of the oldest of all living things. It's amazing to think that some of these trees were growing when King David was ruling Jerusalem in 1,000 BC.

We drive into Yosemite, sometimes called "The Incomparable Valley"— the world's best known example of a glacier-carved canyon. In few places is the sense of scale so dramatic. The towering splendor of El Capitan and Half Dome never fails to thrill me. We park in Curry Village and walk up to Vernal Falls, a four mile hike rising over a thousand feet. I am pleased that all three children make the summit. The view from the top of the waterfall is spectacular, although we feel the need to keep a firm grip on all small hands because of the huge cliff. We return to camp and visit the local swimming hole fed by a small waterfall. We haven't had a shower in three days. It is time to practice full immersion as good Baptists. We plunge into the icy waters and discover we can swim behind the waterfall. It's a mystical experience to watch the curtain of water fall just a foot in front of our faces as we sit with our backs to the rock. Coming out through the waterfall our bodies are massaged by the cascading waters. We are camping with Gretchen's sister, brother-in-law and two of our nieces. As we sit around the campfire in the evening I am asked to read some of James Herriot's dog stories.

When Baptist minister Frederick Gates went on his vacation 100 years ago, he read William Osler's Principles and Practices of Medicine. It changed the course of medical history, for on his return he persuaded John D. Rockefeller to invest in medical education and research. Holiday reading does not always have such dramatic consequences but it can be both enjoyable and stimulating. Along with the usual theological journals, I have brought some books including: Carl Sagan's *Contact* and Os Guiness' *Dining With the Devil,* a disappointingly-written tirade against the mega-church movement. Os clearly has the gift of admonition. I can't recall him writing anything positive about modern culture.

We journey from Yosemite to Las Vegas today, traveling over the Tehachapi Pass into the Mojave Desert. Tehachapi bills itself as the world leader in wind power. It's an extraordinary sight to see hundreds upon hundreds of windmills on the top of the ridge. These are not the sort of picturesque wooden windmills seen in Holland, but instead have a sleek, futuristic look with three propeller blades on a tall pylon. It's an otherworldly sight to see them all turning at slightly different speeds. Other windmills are in the shape of an ellipse about 30 feet high. They look like giant egg beaters on the top of the mountain. With all the wind we have in Rochester, this seems like an excellent way of producing cheap electric power. The valley floor is dotted with Joshua trees, so named by early pioneers because they looked like Joshua with his arms outstretched in prayer before the Lord. The Mojave, where the space shuttle often touches down, is a hot and barren desert. The only thing growing is sage brush, which survives because its tap root can reach down 22 feet to find water in the otherwise parched environment. The air is so dry that the airlines store their unneeded airplanes out on the desert floor. These can be kept here for years without any rust developing. Should they be needed for service again they can simply be maintenanced and flown out.

We worship in a tiny Baptist church in Mesquite, Nevada. There were about 35 in attendance meeting in a converted storefront. A visiting preacher gives an excellent message on Psalm 100, focusing on contentment. It's wonderful to know that God's Word is being faithfully proclaimed in this stronghold of Mormonism. We drive on to Zion National Park in Utah, named by Mormon pioneers. It brings back happy memories as Gretchen and I camped here on our honeymoon 20 years ago.

Methodist minister Frederick Vining Fisher thought that the massive, multi-colored vertical cliffs and deep canyons were a foretaste of heaven and drew on his biblical knowledge in naming the Great White Throne, Angels Landing, and the Court of the Patriarchs. Like the other places we've stayed, this campground doesn't have any showers but it does have two sinks and flush toilets—sheer luxury!

Throughout the trip, the children have been searching for license plates from every state. It becomes a running joke to claim that someone has spotted Hawaii or Alaska, and for that reason no one believes Nicholas when he actually does encounter an RV with an Alaska plate. Because the car radio is broken and we haven't bought any newspapers, we haven't heard any news for over two weeks now. There is something wonderfully liberating about being totally ignorant about national and local crises. Surrounded by mountains that have been here for millions of years, helps me to focus on eternal verities. Being with my family for 24 hours a day enables me to learn the news of their personal and spiritual development. In the midst of this rugged beauty, the latest fluctuations of the Dow Jones seem gloriously irrelevant.

After spending most of the day playing in the Virgin River, we hike up to Emerald Pools. The National Park Service should be sued for misleading advertising. These are not so much emerald pools as muddy puddles. On the way back we meet a large tarantula spider walking along the path. This little creature seems quite unconcerned by the crowd of humans standing a respectful distance from it. However, one of our little creatures refuses to go to bed that night until the entire tent and all sleeping bags are thoroughly searched and declared to be tarantula-free.

We drive to the North Rim of the Grand Canyon and eat our picnic lunch on the veranda overlooking the valley. The drive to Grand Canyon takes us along the Kaibab Plateau North Rim Parkway, which has been described as the most beautiful 44 miles in the United States. It begins at Jacob Lake and winds through dense forest and alpine meadows. This is the first time I have seen the Grand Canyon from the north. It truly is one of the world's most outstanding spectacles. In form, glowing color and geological significance it is unsurpassed. The canyon is 277 miles long and averages 10 miles in width from rim to rim. It is 5,700 feet deep at the North Rim. Nicholas is intrigued to see Bright Angel point after reading Brighty of the Grand Canyon, a true story about a burro who helped create the trail from the North Rim to the bottom of the canyon.

There is even a statue of Brighty, named after Bright Angel Creek, in the lodge. We take a short journey down the South Kaibab Trail. Several mule trains carrying less energetic folk pass us on the way up. Gretchen and I promise ourselves we will return someday and walk down to the Colorado River, a 28 mile round trip.

We travel to Arches National Park. Temperatures are in the 100's but the scenery is incredible. There are more than 2,000 arches ranging in size from a three-foot opening, the minimum considered an arch, to the longest one, Landscape Arch, which measures 306 feet from base to base. We hike the two miles to stand beneath it, a little nervously, as in 1991 a slab of rock about 60 feet long fell from its underside. This is in an area called The Devil's Garden. It's interesting that while the National Park Service attribute the creation of the parks to evolution, those who name our national treasures clearly had a different world view as their supernatural nomenclature acknowledges the spiritual world.

Spend the evening in Denver with Doug and Fiona Bowman. Doug and I reminisce over our student days together at Spurgeon's Seminary. Doug has just been called to be the new pastor at The Vineyard Church in Santa Barbara, California. He will do a splendid job in this new denomination founded by John Wimber in the past 20 years.

We return to Rochester, driving 888 miles in 15 hours. While Minnesota may not have the weather of California, it has the cheapest gas we found anywhere in the whole United States. We begin this day like many others by praying that God would watch over us and bless us. At the end of 5,200 miles it's been evident that he has honored our prayers and granted us an experience we will never forget.

Chapter 25

For Those Far from God

John
October 1997

Luke provides a detail about the crucifixion scene that no other gospel writer gives us. He tells us that all those who knew Jesus stood at a distance from the cross watching what was happening.

> *All those who knew him, including the women who had followed him from Galilee, stood at a distance, watching these things. (Luke 23:49)*

The Greek word for distance is *makron*. It is variously translated as *a long way off* or *far off*. In Acts we receive the good news about the implications of the cross of Christ. Here we find that the promise of God's forgiveness is explicitly offered to us. Peter tells us:

> *The promise is for you and your children and all who are far off. (Acts 2:39)*

The *you and your children* refers to the Jews and their families that were present on the day of Pentecost, but the *far off* applies to us. We are *far off* in time because we are reading this 2,000 years later. We are *far off* in race because we are not Jews. We are *far off* in every respect from God, yet it is for people just like us that Jesus came and gave his life. In fact Peter tells us it is: *For all whom the Lord our God will call.* And God is calling us today to come to his table and to remember the death of his son and receive his gift of forgiveness.

The *Boston Globe* ran a news report in June 1990, describing a most unusual wedding banquet. Accompanied by her fiancé a woman went to the Hyatt Hotel in downtown Boston to order the meal for her wedding reception. The two of them pored over the menu, made selections of china and silver, and pointed to pictures of the flower arrangement they liked. They both had expensive taste and the bill came to $13,000. After leaving a check for half that amount as a down payment, the couple went home to flip through books of wedding announcements. The day the announcements were suppose to hit the mailbox the potential groom got cold feet. "I am just not sure" he said. "It is a big commitment, let's think about this a little longer."

When his angry fiancée returned to the Hyatt to cancel the banquet the events manager could not have been more understanding. "The same thing happened to me, honey" she said and told the story of her broken engagement. But about the refund she had bad news. "The contract is binding. You are only entitled to $1,300 back. You have two options. You can forfeit the rest of the down payment or go ahead with the banquet. I am sorry, really I am."

It seemed crazy but the more the jilted bride thought about it, the more she liked the idea of going ahead with the party. Not a wedding banquet, mind you, but a big blowout. Ten years before this same woman had been living in a homeless shelter. She had gotten back on her feet, found a good job, and set aside a sizable nest egg. Now she had the wild notion of using her savings to treat the down-and-outs of Boston to a night on the town.

And so it was in June of 1990 that the Hyatt Hotel in downtown Boston hosted a party such as it had never seen before. The hostess changed the menu to boneless chicken "In honor of the groom" she said, and sent invitations to Rescue Missions and homeless shelters.

That warm summer night people who were used to eating half-gnawed pizza out of dumpsters, dined instead on chicken cordon bleu. Hyatt waiters in tuxedos served hors d'oeuvres to senior citizens leaning on aluminum walkers. Bag ladies, vagrants and addicts took a night off from the hard life on the sidewalks and instead sipped champagne, ate chocolate wedding cake, and danced to big band melodies late into the night.

That is a picture of what God has done for us. As a consequence of the cross he invites those who are *far off* from him to come and sit down at his banquet table. The communion table is a foretaste of that day. When we come and take bread and wine we are pointed back to the cost of our salvation and we are pointed forward to that day when Jesus himself will sit down with us at the wedding supper of the Lamb.

One day Charles Haddon Spurgeon, the great preacher of the last century, was out for a walk when he met a boy who had a sparrow in a cage. Spurgeon asked the boy what he was going to do with the bird and the boy replied, "Play with it for awhile, then torture it and kill it."

Spurgeon asked how much the boy wanted for the bird as he would like to buy it. The boy remarked, "It is a worthless bird. You don't want it." But Spurgeon persisted and the boy eventually sold it for 5 English pounds, a fabulous sum in those days. When the money changed hands and the cage was handed to him, Spurgeon opened the cage and set the bird free.

The next Sunday Spurgeon took the empty cage and placed it on his pulpit. He told his congregation how just as he had done with the boy, Jesus went to the devil and engaged in a similar discourse, "You don't want those people the devil mocked. They are worthless." The devil said he planned to play with them and then torture them. But Jesus wanted to purchase the people in the devil's cage, so the devil finally relented. He would sell them—but it would cost Jesus his blood.

That is what Jesus did when on the cross he bought our freedom and our life with his own blood. The problem is that some people are still trapped in the devil's cage because they don't know they can get out. The communion table reminds us that the door is open and we can leave the prison of our sin and discover the freedom that is in Jesus Christ.

Charles Wesley was one of the founders of the Methodist Church. He was a priest in the Church of England. He was a member of the Holy Club at Oxford University. He spent his life doing good deeds and trying to get right with God, but no matter how hard he tried he found no peace.

But then one day he realized that the cage was already opened. He saw that Jesus had died on the cross for one such as him—one who was "far off." One wonderful day as an ordained minister of the church he became a believer in Jesus. He described it in one of his great hymns:

> *Long my imprisoned spirit lay, fast bound in sin and nature's night.*
>
> *Mine eyes defused a quickening ray, I woke the dungeon flamed with light.*
>
> *My chains fell off, my heart was free, I rose, went forth and followed thee.*

The cross is for those at a distance from God. We who have been brought near by the blood of Christ must never forget it.

Chapter 26

Good News for Strangers
John
December 1997

Growing up in a minister's home, I was accustomed to having all sorts of visiting preachers and missionaries staying with us. Each Sunday afternoon we had various church folk over for afternoon tea and this was acceptable because we got better cakes than had it just been the family.

However, one thing I didn't think was acceptable was my mother inviting all sorts of strangers to join us for Christmas Day. It seemed to me that Christmas was sacrosanct. It was a time for the family to be together. I didn't want all sorts of outsiders hanging around the house on this most important day of the year.

Yet, my mother took very seriously Jesus' parable that we should go out into the highways and byways and compel people to come in. So each Christmas Day we had a motley crew join us for the turkey, Christmas pudding, and Christmas crackers.

As I say, I was initially hostile to this idea. But over the years I came to appreciate it, and the reason was the eccentric personalities of two particular elderly ladies who joined us each Christmas.

One was called Miss Castle and the other was called Miss Smith. As far as I know they had no other living relatives and had it not been for my mother they would have spent Christmas on their own.

Miss Castle had been in service as a maid when she was a younger woman. She was clearly from "below stairs" as they used to say. Miss Smith didn't have a penny with which to bless herself but she imagined that she came from the upper classes and spoke in an exaggerated upper crust accent. These two would engage in low-intensity class warfare throughout the day and it was hilarious to watch.

At one point in the afternoon everyone was expected to take a turn providing some light-hearted entertainment. Miss Smith invariably recited Rudyard Kipling's poem, "If" with all the melodrama of a music hall actress. Miss Castle, not to be outdone, would sing, "Bless this House." At least I think that is what she was singing. As her notes bore no relationship with the original, it was hard to tell.

My brothers and I found these talent displays incredibly funny. I remember stuffing my handkerchief in my mouth to stop from guffawing in the wrong places. These remain some of my happiest memories of Christmas from my childhood.

Christmas is a time for gathering the family, of course, but it is not just for our family. Christmas, rightly understood, is a time to embrace the stranger and to minister to the marginalized. That is why we send cards to our shut-ins and gifts to the families of prisoners. It is why people will serve Christmas dinner to the homeless at rescue missions across the country and put money in Salvation Army kettles where it will be used to help the needy. We understand instinctively that Jesus came for people like this.

Unwittingly, my mother taught me a very important lesson about Christmas: Christmas is for strangers. It is not just a time for family, for in fact at Christmas God broke up his family when he sent his Son for all the strangers in the world.

Chapter 27

Jesus, the Defeater of Death
Gretchen
February 1998

In the eleventh chapter of John we read the miraculous account of Jesus raising Lazarus from the dead. From this story we can learn why Jesus sometimes delays answers to our prayers.

Jesus' first comment upon receiving word about Lazarus' death was:

> *This sickness will not end in death. It is for God's glory so that God's Son may be glorified through it (John 11:4).*

Even though this passage goes on to say that Jesus loved Martha, her sister and Lazarus, when Jesus heard that Lazarus was sick, he stayed away for two more days. One of the most striking things we learn about Jesus from this passage is that his delays are the delays of love, not indifference. He doesn't delay because he doesn't care, or because he's too busy or to preoccupied to notice that someone's hurting.

Sometimes Jesus deliberately delays answering to reshape our wills. We know that God's timetable is unknowable. All we know is that sometimes God doesn't seem to want to answer right away. We talk a lot about praying in Jesus' name, or praying within the will of God, but there are times when that will is not clear to us. A delay in answering can take us through a searching process that helps us recognize, gradually, that our original prayer may not have been within his will for us.

I think these sorts of delays are most apparent when we are praying for something in our lives that we believe to be good (or at least not immoral) but may not be within his plan for everyone. How many of us have prayed for a marriage relationship when we were single, or for a baby when we were married? We know these good things are not morally opposed to the will of God. However, it is also clear that God doesn't have the same life in mind for everyone. A delay in answering can help us understand God's will for *us*, not just his general will for everyone.

Sometimes Christ delays answering our prayers to strengthen our faith. When we begin praying about something it can be difficult to know at the outset what God may desire for us. A delay in answering can bring us to our wits' end. When God does answer, we are then at a point of extremity that causes us to recognize his help when we really needed it… at our lowest point, or our point of greatest need.

97

Sometimes Christ delays answering our prayers to bring glory to God. There are times when God doesn't answer us until it is so late we *know* the answer came from him. This way it is impossible to mistake it for anything but God's provision at exactly the time when it was needed.

When Jesus delayed coming to Bethany, his goal was the same as for all his other miracles—that God might be glorified. By waiting two extra days it was clear to everyone that Lazarus was really, really dead and gone, not just sleeping. There was no mistaking God's hand in the outcome of this situation. It was to bring glory to God that Christ waited to come to his friends.

Jesus reassures Mary and Martha with these words:

> *I am the resurrection and the life. He who believes in me will live, even though he dies, and whoever lives and believes in me will never die (John 11:25).*

This one verse explains why Christian funerals are often really joyful occasions. Two and a half years ago my father-in-law, Christopher Steer, died in England. The memorial service we had for him was one of the most uplifting church services I have ever attended. It was a joyful occasion to commend to God a man who had lived fully for Jesus his entire life. We just knew he was now delightfully happy, face to face with God.

Chris Steer accepted Christ when he was seven years old. To my knowledge he never wavered once in his belief and went on to live a life poured out for God. The church was filled with the people who had been affected by his 30 years of ministry in England...men and women he had led to Christ, baptized, married, helped. It was really hard to let him go in the normal human sense, because we all miss him greatly. Yet, it was so clear that Chris himself would be doing exactly what he'd done his whole life...praising and worshiping God...that we could hardly begrudge him the chance to go home to heaven and be with his heavenly father. When a believer dies, it is a literal home going. The person is going to a place that *is* more their home than is earth. That is why death should have no terror for us. I know that all of us will face the fear of disease or being disabled or even the uncertainty of what happens when we physically die, but there is not the terror of death that comes from uncertainty about where we are going.

The reason for our belief is Jesus' words: *I am the resurrection and the life.* He knew that he was going to conquer death, forever. Lazarus was just a little demonstration that death was going to loosen its hold over mankind.

Jesus looks to his heavenly father, acknowledges that God always hears him, and knows that God has the power over death. He then calls out in a loud voice *Lazarus, come out!* Some commentators have remarked that Jesus is angry at death, that his shout is his notification to Satan that death is about to be finished and done with forevermore. I think of this scene more as a parent going to reclaim a child from the place they've been playing. At our house, the children often play in the woods in the summer and to recall them from their forts and tree houses I need to really yell so they will hear me. Eventually I hear a little voice piping in the distance, "Coming!" and they reappear. I have reclaimed them from where they have gone. It is the sound of my voice and their obedience to it, that brings them back. Jesus shouted to Lazarus to reclaim him from the land of shadows where Lazarus had gone. His voice, and Lazarus' obedience to it, brought him literally back from the dead.

Jesus, in one sense has recalled us from the dead. Unlike Lazarus we haven't physically died, but he has already recalled us from the natural inclination toward the world that we have. Yet the world without Jesus is dying, and so is everyone in it. The sound of Jesus' voice speaking to us recalls us away from what we are doing here and toward him. The sound of his voice calling us will be the last thing that we as Christians hear when we close our eyes in death.

Our daughter died after three days in a coma (see The Anatomy of Grief, page 9). From the moment I could get to her after she fell I lay down on the ground and began speaking to her. I spoke to her continuously through those three days in the Intensive Care Unit. They told me that people in comas can sometimes hear. I had no indication that she could, but I wanted her to know that I was there with her. And so I spoke and talked about all the familiar things of her little life and told her I loved her.

But a stronger, more compelling voice than mine was calling her to heaven. The one who died to defeat death forever was calling her home, and reclaiming his child. His claim was greater than mine, and so she heeded his voice and disobeyed mine for perhaps the first time in her 16 months of life. It was very hard to let her go to the one who had prior claim, but I did, knowing that someday, he'll call me too. When he does, I know where I am going. I pray that you do too.

Chapter 28

Traveling Hopefully

A Steer Vacation Saga
John
August 1998

"To travel hopefully is better than to arrive."

— Robert Louis Stevenson

We set off on our yearly exercise to test the stability of our family—
normal people call this a vacation. Once again we head west in our
continuing quest to see as many of the national parks as possible. The
children are given $5 in quarters as we begin. They are told that each
day they behave they will be given an additional 25 cents. However,
every act of misbehavior will cost them a quarter. I sometimes wonder if
this is teaching them godliness or greed. However, it seems to cut down
the rioting and sedition in the van. As a pragmatist I can ask for no
more. Crossing the bleak landscape of South Dakota we stop at the only
tourist attraction for miles, the Corn Palace in Mitchell. This is a
building decorated with colored ears of corn that create various murals.
The guidebook recommends at least an hour here. We allot 10 minutes
and discover it is five too many.

Stopping at an interstate rest area I talk with a sad-looking lady
employed by the South Dakota State Tourism Department. After she
answers several of my questions I thank her for her helpfulness and
playfully tell her I would recommend to the governor that she be given a
big raise. She immediately brightens up and thanks me profusely. She
introduces me to her colleague and both of them proceed to give me
enough literature to wallpaper our house. They ask if I would mind
filling out a customer satisfaction form—to which I gladly agreed. We
part as if we had been friends for years. No wonder the New Testament
tells us to encourage one another. We all need it. It is a ministry that
costs so little and gives so much. We stay in a very inexpensive motel.
As far as the children are concerned it could be the New York Plaza
because it has a pool.

We arrive in Grand Tetons National Park. All the literature we are given
by the rangers warns us of the bear danger. If we go for a hike we are
supposed to sing in order to alert the bears of our presence. I suggest a
round of the old hymn "Gladly My Cross I'd Bear" as particularly
appropriate if the animal is suffering from strabismus. If we are
approached by a bear we are to talk in a monotone. I mentally rehearse
my sermon in case it is needed:

101

"Mr. Grizzly, I would like to remind you of St. Paul's words to the Galatians, *Bear one another's burdens.*" The children encourage me by saying, "Don't worry, Dad—if the bears are like the congregation they will fall asleep before you are finished."

Entering Yellowstone National Park, we await the eruption of Old Faithful geyser. I recall the last time I was here in 1975. I was visiting Los Angeles one summer and my brother Andrew was in graduate school in Philadelphia. We decided to meet in the middle of the country and Yellowstone seemed a reasonable spot. The only landmark known to both of us was Old Faithful. We arranged to rendezvous at 4 o'clock on a certain day. I hitchhiked out from Los Angeles and arrived with an hour to spare. Andrew was traveling in a rickety old van and got there the next morning.

The beautiful state of Montana does not have any daytime speed limit, but our aged van can't take advantage of this luxury and we chug along at 70 mph. After 350 miles we find an isolated National Forest Campground, just outside Glacier National Park. We spot a bear on the other side of the deep and swiftly flowing Flathead River and trust that he is Episcopalian and doesn't believe in full immersion.

As we are many miles from the nearest town we decide to have our own church service. All the children take part. Preaching on the subject of Zacchaeus, my sermon is interrupted when one of Emily's teeth falls out. We all have to stop and admire it before I can continue. Gretchen points out that despite the small congregation and meager offering, I still spoke for half an hour.

I get up at the crack of 9 a.m. Gretchen is already out cycling. The children emerge in the next half hour. Gretchen returns and cooks a wonderful breakfast of fried eggs, bacon, sausage and toast—"Heart attack on a plate" as the English would call it. It tastes like the nectar of the gods in this setting.

It is the practice in Montana to mark road fatalities with a white cross at the side of the highway. Sometimes there are several crosses together. On one occasion we saw nine. I wonder about the lives these crosses represent and reflect on the fact that even in our increasingly post-Christian society, the cross is still a universally recognized symbol of both tragedy and hope.

We take the Going-to-the-Sun Road. We stop at Logan Pass on the Continental Divide and make the four mile hike to Hidden Lake. It is an area filled with lush meadows and wild flowers and surrounded by jagged peaks. We experience the thrill of coming across a herd of wild mountain goats and strain to see five longhorn sheep almost invisible against the mountains. We drive to Many Glacier where we take the three mile hike around Swiftcurrent Lake. The trail takes us through a huge patch of huckleberries that thrive in this climate and are a favorite food of bears. A spectacular thunderstorm descends and we take refuge in the Swiss style—Many Glacier Hotel with its huge tree trunk pillars and comfortable sitting rooms.

The local paper, *The Missoulian*, makes interesting reading. A woman is advertising for a husband: "Mountain warrior seeking combat-trained male survivalist, 43-55, wanting wife to live off land in mountain wilderness. Believes God is holy." There is a great opportunity for some lucky fellow!

We arrive back at Yellowstone Park and walk to Inspiration Point. We have a superb view of the Grand Canyon of the Yellowstone. This is the very spot upon which, 50 years ago, Gretchen's parents had their picture taken during their honeymoon. We hike around Mammoth Hot Springs and Norris Geyser Basin. The highlight of the day is when we spot a black bear on the side of the road. Like us, all the other drivers stop and leap from their cars in order to get a better view. We get within 15 feet of the bear and eagerly snapped photos. It is an interesting insight into the process of education. We have been told again and again not to approach the bears because they are highly dangerous. Intellectually we knew what to do, but emotionally we still think of this animal as simply a larger version of the teddy bears we have known as children.

Returning to our cabin I find a message from home. We discover that one of our church families has suffered a tragic bereavement. I reflect that death does not take a vacation, but how good it is to know that the Gospel offers hope, the Holy Spirit provides comfort, and the Lord Jesus has won eternal life for those who love him.

We drive to Theodore Roosevelt Park in North Dakota, the only National Park named after a president. Roosevelt first came to the Badlands to hunt buffalo in 1883. We walk through the cabin that was his home. Roosevelt later said, "I would not have been president had it not been for my experience in North Dakota." He was a man who knew much sadness. Both his wife and mother died on Valentine's Day, 1884. His journal that day reads: "The light of my life has gone out. My life is over." However, his stay in the Badlands gave him new hope and purpose and he returned to New York to stand as a candidate for mayor.

We find ourselves in the middle of a herd of about 40 buffalo crossing the road. They are magnificent beasts. It is extraordinary to think that the great plains were once filled with 60 million of them.

We arrive home in Rochester, grateful for traveling hopefully over 4,000 miles.

Chapter 29

Helping Jesus Build His Church

John
September 1998

One of the most encouraging things that Jesus ever said is found in Matthew 16:18 where Jesus declares:

> *On this rock I will build my church and the gates of Hades will not overcome it.*

Jesus had just concluded a discussion with his disciples at Caesarea Philippi. This was a city on the northern coast of Israel. Jesus had now been with his disciples for about two years. He posed them a question:

> *Who do people say that the Son of Man is?*

They gave him the gossip that was going around Galilee. Folk had been observing the miracles of Jesus. They had been listening to his unusual style of teaching. They realized that he was different. Some thought he was John the Baptist come back from the dead. Others argued for one of the great Old Testament prophets like Elijah or Jeremiah.

Jesus then made the question personal. He asked:

> *But what about you…Who do you say I am?*

It is Simon Peter, aided by divine insight, who provides a staggeringly, accurate answer:

> *You are the Christ, the Son of the Living God.*

In that statement Peter acknowledges that Jesus is the Messiah, that Jesus is divine, and that Jesus is God's anointed one.

It is in response to Peter's declaration that Jesus announces, *On this rock I will build my church.* Jesus is making a pun here. In the Greek, Peter's name is *Petros*. The word for rock in Greek is *Petra* from where the Christian rock band gets it name. Jesus is informing us that on the firm foundation of Peter's confession of faith he will build his church. For the past 2,000 years as men and women, boys and girls have acknowledged that Jesus is the Christ, the son of the living God, they have been added to the church and the promise of Jesus has been fulfilled.

I find this promise tremendously encouraging for three reasons. First, because it is a statement of hope. It is an antidote to the pessimism that can sometimes pervade the church. We look around and Christians appear to be in a minority. Self-proclaimed prophets pronounce the demise of the Christian faith.

Sometimes we can feel like Elijah, that only we are left. Jesus tells us not to be so naive He is going to build his church. We have his word on it. The church will never die because it is the body of the living head. Christians have fewer reasons to be pessimistic than any other group in the whole world.

Second, I find the promise encouraging because it is an assurance of growth. Jesus is going to enlarge his church. The church will not get smaller and smaller, but bigger and bigger until ultimately every knee shall bow before king Jesus and every tongue in every language will confess him Lord of all.

Sometimes people say to me they don't want to join our church because it is too big. I don't know what they are going to think about heaven. There will be billions of people there. More people than the US census bureau could ever count. Jesus is building his church.

Third, the promise is a declaration of victory. Jesus goes on to add that *the gates of Hades will not overcome it.* This is a statement of Jesus' ultimate triumph over Satan. Some scare mongers would have us to believe that Satan is all-powerful. . . that he is having his way in the world, and that nothing can stop him. But Jesus stopped him on the cross.

Sometimes we get the impression that the church is a little fortress being bombarded by the attacks of demons and it seems we can't hold out much longer. Here Jesus provides a different picture. Hades is facing a withering attack from the forces of General Jesus. The Son of God is battering on the doors of Hades and they can't withstand the onslaught. The doors cave in and the army of God sweeps in to take over.

Gates are used for defense, not attack. This is not so much a picture of Satan attacking God as God attacking Satan. Nothing can prevent God's victory. I want you to be encouraged. Jesus Christ is building his church —all over the world.

Back in 1994 the US Center for World Missions did some research. They said that 37,442 born-again believers are added to the church every day. That means 13,666,330 are added every year. In total there are 304,000,000 evangelical Christians worldwide. The church of Jesus Christ is not some small struggling band.

We have evidence of that growth in our own fellowship. Today, many individuals have made a profession of their faith to the Board of Elders who are recommending them for membership in our congregation. This church is growing just as Jesus said it would. Tonight I want to speak directly to our new members. We are delighted that you are joining us. We are grateful that God has brought you to us. We look forward to serving God together with you. I want to tell you how you can help Jesus build his church. I want to tell you how you can be part of his great plan for extending his influence here in this community.

There are three things I want to ask you to do.

Be proud of your church. You can be proud of your church because Jesus is proud of his church. You can be proud of your church because the church of Jesus Christ is the greatest force for good in the world. You can be proud of your church because the church of Jesus Christ is the only organization in this world that is going to last forever, and it is the only institution in this world that is offering lasting answers to the eternal questions of humanity.

Let me suggest three practical ways that you can demonstrate your pride in your church.

First, you can attend it. Make sure that you are here regularly. The way we spend our time demonstrates what's important to us. We may say that our faith is important but if we are seldom in church then these are only words. The book of Hebrews tells us:

> *Let us not give up meeting together as some are in the habit of doing, but let's encourage one another and all the more as you see the day approaching. (Hebrews 10:25)*

This verse tells us that one of the main reasons to attend church is encouragement. We receive encouragement when we come, and we are a source of encouragement when we come. We encourage others as we speak to them. We also encourage people by our presence. If a visitor comes in and sees a half-empty building, they are not likely to be impressed. But if they come in and see a church full of people with their Bibles open, singing enthusiastically and praying fervently then it announces that something is happening here. God is at work. They will want to find out more.

Second, you can defend it. There is a lot of criticism leveled at the church of Jesus Christ. Sometimes it is justified, such as when television evangelists make ridiculous claims and embezzle the money of their followers. More often the criticism is not justified and we need to address it.

For example, you might hear someone say "the church is full of hypocrites." That gives you the opportunity to stand up and say, "Well not in my church. I don't find hypocrites, I hear people freely acknowledging their imperfections."

You can go on to say: "I meet people that want to make a difference in their community. I observe people helping Habitat for Humanity and providing gifts for prisoners through the Angel Tree program. I see people volunteering their time to work with children and young people and going off on mission trips to help villages in Africa and Alaska and the Dominican Republic." We don't need to be pushy about this. We can simply declare the facts. We are defending our church.

At other times people will say things like, "Well of course the Bible is just a bunch of fables." Again, we can defend our faith.

Perhaps we can turn to the individual who made the statement and ask, "Would you be interested in reading this book? It is by a scientist who examined all the facts. It is called *Surprised by Faith* (by Don Bierle). Why don't you look at it and we'll talk about it next week after work or during the lunch hour." Many of the criticisms leveled against the church are based on ignorance of the facts. They provide us with an opportunity to present the truth.

A third way we can show our pride in our church is to commend it. If you know people who are looking for a church, invite them to your church. If your friends don't have a church, bring them along to a suitable event. Introduce them to others. Help them feel at home.

So be proud of your church. Love your church. Jesus does! Paul tells us:

> *Christ loved the church and gave himself up for her.*
> *(Ephesians 5:25)*

Paul goes on to tell us that Christ cares for the church. As his followers we can do no less.

Promote your church. Peter, to whom Jesus' commendation is given, tells us in his first letter that we are to:

> *Declare the praises of him who has called us out of darkness*
> *into his wonderful light. (1 Peter 2:9).*

The word "declare" means to "advertise" to "promote." In promoting our church we are acting in partnership with the Lord Jesus who wants to build his church. There are two ways we can promote our church.

First, we can support it. We can support our church by our giving. Contributing to the financial need of our church is the best investment we can make. Some of us thought we had done rather well in the stock market until the summer of this year, when all our gains were suddenly wiped out. The stock market plummeted.

There is "no sure" thing in earthly financial markets, but there is a sure thing in heavenly markets for investing with God brings eternal rewards. In Revelation we read:

> *Blessed are the dead who die in the Lord . . . they will rest from their labor for their deeds will follow them. (Revelation 14:13)*

It is often said that you never see a hearse pulling a U-Haul trailer, but the child of God is able to lay up treasure in heaven—our deeds follow us. We can know that there will be people in glory who will welcome us because our giving made it possible for them to hear the gospel.

Second, we can also promote our church through our service.   God has given each of us gifts to use for his glory. This church requires hundreds of people in order to make it work. Sometimes people come into this fellowship and they see it working smoothly so they think they are not needed. That is simply not true. Everyone is needed in this church. Our annual Christmas outreach events take between 200 and 300 people to produce.

One hundred volunteers are needed every month to staff the nursery and 96 teachers and leaders are needed every week to provide Sunday School and the other children's programs. There are ministries not yet underway because no one has yet come forward to start them. Perhaps you are that person.

Church was never intended to be a spectator sport. Some people choose that level of involvement, but it is very unfulfilling. What tends to happen is that we become critical because we have too much time on our hands and we get irritated at those who are doing the work. We become spiritually obese by taking in spiritual food and never working it off. God's plan is that we should keep spiritually fit by first taking in, and then giving out. Paul puts it this way:

> *Work out your salvation with fear and trembling.*
> *(Philippians 2:12)*

We grow spiritually as we put ourselves in positions where God has to step in to help. If we never do that we never give him a chance. You will know joy and fulfillment and satisfaction and you will see God answer your prayers and work in your life when you get involved in an area of ministry— especially one that taxes you to the limit.

A third way to promote your church is to speak well of it. Let me just say a word to parents here. Our children are always listening to what we say. They form judgments based on what they hear in the home. Let me tell you why I love the church and why I have given my life to serving the church and why I feel so positive about the church.

It is because I grew up in a home where my parents spoke well of the church. Now we didn't belong to a perfect church, and there were problems in that church, but my mother and father didn't air those problems in front of us. . . certainly not when we were young. I grew up with the impression that church was a good place.

I have a friend who was at school with me and played on the same cricket team. His parents also went to church, but every single week my friend heard from his father how bad their church was and how poor the pastor was and how weak the leaders were. He heard nothing but criticism of the church. My friend decided quite rightly that he wanted nothing to do with a church like that, and so he abandoned the church and his faith along with it.

There is no perfect church—least of all this one. There are problems and we need to address them. We need to do that in the right place and in the right way. Our staff and our Elders are always open to meet with people. We welcome this. Let us be sure to keep things in perspective and not give the devil an opportunity. He would love to divide this church; to split us, to set us against one another.

Thankfully that has not happened, at least not in my years of involvement here. I thank God for the wonderful spirit of unity on our staff and leadership. Let us not take it for granted. Let us speak well of our church. It is hard to criticize your church and then compliment your Savior.

Finally, pray for your church. This is what Jesus does. In John 17 he offers one of the greatest prayers that has ever been given for the church of Jesus Christ. Let me select a few of his petitions:

> *My prayer is not that you take them out of the world but that you protect them from the evil one. Sanctify them by the truth. I pray also for those who believe in me. . . that all of them may be one, Father, just as you are in me and I in you.*

Do you know what Jesus' ministry to his church is right now? He is praying for us. He is interceding as our High Priest, sitting on the right hand of his Father. He is praying for his church.

The Apostle Paul, the great church planter of the First Century, was constantly praying for the church. As he writes to the churches at Rome, Corinth, Galatia, Ephesians, Philippi, Colossae and Thessalonica, he tells them that he is praying for them. O how I hope you will pray for your church; to petition the blessings of God to descend upon us; to pray for our pastoral staff.

Please pray for me. As you see me walk into the pulpit on Sunday mornings will you pray for me? As you see the Elders serve communion, will you pray for them? Pray for your child's Sunday school teacher. Pray for the teacher of your Adult Discovery class. We have prayer guides available to help you pray for our missionaries.

They don't have to be long prayers. Most of the prayers in the New Testament are very brief. But do pray that God will build his church here at First Baptist Church—that he will add people to his family. Pray for yourself that you will be an integral part of what God wants to do here and in this community.

If you don't know where you should be serving, pray that God will show you an open door of opportunity. Pray that God will use you every day and bring people across your path who need God's help. Pray that he will give you wisdom to know what to say. God loves to answer prayer, especially prayers for the glory of his Son and success of his church.

So welcome to First Baptist Church! We are glad you are here. Together, let's help Jesus build his church.

Chapter 30

Facing a Mid-Life Crisis

John
November 1998

Before the dawn of the Twentieth Century no preacher would have thought it necessary to preach on mid-life crisis. In 1901, life expectancy for Americans was only 50 years. This is much higher than it was in the Middle Ages when the average age of death was 37. It is substantially more than during the days of the Roman Empire when life expectancy was only 18. Today, however, the average life span for men is 73 years, for women it's 77 years.

Somewhere around the mid-way point we go through a myriad of changes that psychologists have labeled a mid-life crisis. This event doesn't affect everyone the same way, and because of this there's no one cure for the condition.

Some people suggest that the most effective way to deal with mid-life crisis is to laugh about it. In fact there are many funny things about this time of life. One woman described it as being "too young for Medicare but too old for me to care." A cartoon showed a man telling his friends about his weekend. He says, "I went to my high school reunion and everyone there had become so old and fat they didn't even recognize me."

Studies by Meyers-Briggs psychologists reveal that adults who experience mid-life crisis often display some or all of these characteristics: a newly developed discontentment with life; boredom with things and/or people who were previously considered fascinating; risk-orientated thrills gained by doing things never done before; the questioning of values that have shaped past behavior; confusion about identity and direction.

The national average age for mid-life crisis is 42 1/2 but it can start as early as 30 or as late as 60. Mid-life crisis may be a new term but it's not a new condition. You can find mid-life crisis described in the pages of scripture.

For example, we find many of the characteristics of a mid-life crisis in the book of Ecclesiastes, which was written by Solomon. The interesting thing about Ecclesiastes is that it was probably written when Solomon was an old man and yet he expresses concerns that are most often felt by people much earlier in life. This tells us that if we don't deal with these problems, they're going to remain with us for the remainder of our days.

This is Solomon's response to years of looking for fulfillment in different things:

> *When I surveyed all that my hands had done and what I had toiled to achieve, everything was meaningless, a chasing after the wind; nothing was gained under the sun.* (Ecclesiastes 2:11)

I think Solomon points out a basic cause of mid-life crisis. When our eyes are on the wrong goal for the first half of life and we discover from harsh, personal experience that the dreams we're chasing and the ambitions we're pursuing do not provide fulfillment. The fact is that the answer is not found "under the sun" (which refers to the things of this world). It is found beyond the sun.

Most of us work for about 40 years. I think for many men, in particular, those 40 years are divided into two 20-year periods. The first half of our working life is concerned with success. We want to "climb the corporate ladder," we want to "make it to the top." By our mid-forties many of us have achieved our goals and frankly we're not as thrilled as we thought we would be. There's emptiness in our souls and we find ourselves asking "is this all there is?"

The second 20-year period is concerned with significance. This search for fulfillment is seen in the increased average age of those entering seminary. When I went to Spurgeon's Seminary in the early 1970's the average age of the incoming students was 22. It is now 35. When I talked with the principal of the seminary, he told me that men and women in their 40's and even 50's are coming into seminary after a career in medicine, engineering, government, and other fields, because they hope this second career is going to provide for them the significance not provided by their first.

Another trend is emerging across our own country. Women who've achieved success in the business world are giving it all up and becoming stay-at-home moms. They found that success didn't satisfy them, and they're hoping that spending time with their children is going to give them the significance that they desire.

I believe that one of the main reasons mid-life is such a crisis for some people is that they fear they will spend the rest of their lives with this feeling of discontentment. This fear of discontentment is so real that they do all sorts of things to overcome and escape it.

It explains why men who have been models of propriety will suddenly throw themselves into an affair. It explains why women who have always been wonderful mothers will suddenly abandon their children in search of a new life.

So how can we escape this fear of discontentment? The answer is surely to discover the secret of contentment. Here the apostle Paul is our model. We find him as a middle-aged man sitting in a prison in Rome. He has every reason to be miserable yet surprisingly we find him saying this:

> *I have learned to be content whatever the circumstances. I*
> *know what it is to be in need, and I know what it is to have*
> *plenty. I have learned the secret of being content.*
> *(Philippians 4:11)*

We will never find contentment in middle age or any other age outside of a relationship with Jesus Christ. Augustine put it well when he said, "Our souls are restless until they find their rest in you." In Philippians 1:21 Paul says, *For me to live is Christ.* Paul doesn't say *for me to live is myself,* or *for me to live is my job,* or even *for me to live is my family.* Those things lead to discontentment because they cannot ultimately satisfy us. Rather he says, *for me to live is Christ.* Contentment is living for Jesus

A mid-life crisis requires a mid-life correction. It requires putting the focus of my life onto Jesus. It is interesting that the people, who do this early on, do not experience mid-life crisis, because Jesus Christ does not disappoint. Other goals do. It may take us 20 years to realize it but sooner or later they let us down.

It can be very helpful to make changes in our lives. We can learn from the example of Chuck Swindoll, who seemed to have it all. He was the pastor of a huge church in California with a daily radio audience that numbered in the millions. His best-selling books made him a fully fledged Christian celebrity. Then a few years ago he decided to make some major changes in his life. He resigned his pastorate, traded wearing a suit every day for casual clothes, and took a job as president of Dallas Theological Seminary.

He then did something he always dreamed of doing. He bought a hog—not a pig—but a Harley-Davidson. He also bought a leather jacket. You should see him and his wife, Cynthia, on the back of their bike. He rides all over the country and they are having more fun than ever before. Someone asked him if he was worried about what people think? He said, "No. When I am on the road with my Harley I introduce myself to people as Dr. James Dobson."

Chuck Swindoll reminds us that it is okay to make changes in our lives. Just be sure they are changes we can ask God to bless. We must make sure the changes bring about the best in our marriages, our relationships with our kids and our friends. Above all I must make sure any changes validate my relationship to Jesus Christ.

Paul's second secret of contentment was that his life was Christ-controlled. Paul is not down in the dumps although he is sitting in a prison cell, because he believes that the circumstances of his life are being directed by a sovereign God.

> *Now I want you to know, brothers, that what has happened to me has really served to advance the gospel. As a result, it has become clear throughout the whole palace guard and to everyone else that I am in chains for Christ. (Philippians. 1:12)*

He is not in chains for Rome—he is in chains for Christ. God has allowed him to go through this experience. Paul understands that suffering is part of his calling.

If I believe that my life is Christ-controlled, I don't need to be despondent over all the imagined lost opportunities that have passed me by. I may not have won Wimbledon. I may not have made my first million by age 30. I may not have the perfect spouse, children, home or job, but God is in control. He is working through me to glorify his name. He has a purpose and plan for my life. So I am not the victim of circumstances. I am the object of his electing love; the apple of his eye. My life is hidden with Christ in God and therefore it has purpose and meaning.

The third secret of Paul's contentment is that his life was Christ-connected. In Chapter 4, verse 13 he says, *I can do everything through him who gives me strength.* Paul has learned the secret of being content in every situation, whether well fed or hungry, whether living in plenty or in want. We live in a world that is desperately looking for contentment. There are many things that can provide that contentment in the short term. But in the long term only Christ provides it. When my life is Christ-centered, Christ-controlled and Christ-connected I then can be content in the most difficult of circumstances.

In 1918 a Christian friend gave songwriter Helen Lemmel a tract. A particular sentence in that pamphlet inspired her and through her it has since helped thousands of Christians to refocus their lives on the source of true lasting contentment.

From a single haunting phrase Helen penned a song that instantly became a favorite around the world. It says everything Paul wants to say to us who pursue contentment.

> *Turn your eyes upon Jesus.*
> *Look full in his wonderful face,*
> *and the things of earth will grow strangely dim*
> *in the light of his glory and grace.*

We don't need to fear a life of discontentment if our eyes are turned to the Lord Jesus Christ.

Chapter 31

I Love You
John
February 1999

Those three little words pack dynamite. Many people have trouble saying them to their romantic interest. Once they are uttered there is an implied commitment that moves the relationship to a new level.

Have you ever realized how hard it is to say those three little words to God? We speak of people who love the Lord, meaning they are true believers, but how many times have we heard people say in public prayers, "I love you, Lord?"

I guess we hesitate because of the same implied commitment. Jesus put it this way:

> *If you love me keep my commandments. (John 14:15)*

If we say the three little words to God we can't go out and live in a way that displeases him. Therefore we avoid saying them.

The Old Testament law includes the powerful command:

> *Love the Lord your God with all your heart and with all your soul and with all your strength. (Deuteronomy 6:5)*

Nothing is more basic to the faith of Israel and yet I am aware of only one instance in the whole Old Testament where these three little words are spoken by a believer to God. They occur in Psalm 18:1 where David says, *I love you, O Lord, my strength.* There are many others passages where we are exhorted to love God, but only this one where a believer says, "I love you" to God.

Jesus elevated this Old Testament teaching about loving God with all one's heart, soul and strength by calling it *the first and greatest commandment.* (Matthew 22:38). Throughout his ministry Jesus emphasized the importance of loving God, yet in the entire New Testament there is only one instance where the three little words are actually spoken to the Son of God. It is Peter's deeply felt statement to Jesus after the resurrection, *Lord you know that I love you.* He actually repeats it three times. (John 21:15-17).

If loving God is so important, why are there so few references to individual believers actually saying, "I love you" to him? The answer might be found in a closer look at those two instances. What the statements have in common is that they are not words spoken by new Christians in the first flush of their "puppy love" for God.

These "I love yous" were spoken by mature believers who had gone through life's troubles and trials and experienced God's sustaining presence.

The author of Psalm 18 had struggled with distress, powerful enemies, the cords of death, and the torrents of destruction. Through it all God was his deliverer who never failed him. Based on his own life experience, David could say, *The Lord lives.* That is why he opened his beautiful Psalm with the words *I love you, O Lord.*

The disciple Peter had walked with Jesus for three years, experiencing all the ups and downs. He thought he loved Jesus, but when the moment of truth arrived, he bolted and ran. While Jesus was being tried and beaten, Peter was denying that he ever knew him. If he had said, "I love you" before, it would have seemed hollow and phony as he shrank before the angry crowd and the menacing soldiers.

But after the cross and the resurrection, Jesus approached Peter with forgiveness and affirmation. In fact the Son of God said he wanted to use this denying disciple as a leader to build his church. Peter's repeated *I love you*s were based on a rich experience of God's grace through wrenching defeats. This *I love you* was sincere and heartfelt.

The Psalmist and the disciple both earned the right to say, *I love you* to God. After many negative experiences each was finally able to love his Lord with his whole heart, soul and strength. God longs to hear these three little words, *I love you*, from his seasoned saints.

Chapter 32

Farewell to a Mother

John
April 1999

The phone call came at 8 on Thursday morning. It was my brother Simon in England informing me that my mother had suffered a stroke and had been taken unconscious to the hospital. She was not expected to recover. As the implications of the news sunk in, I realized the place I most wanted to be in all the world at that moment was beside her. My colleagues were wonderfully understanding. They quickly picked up my responsibilities. Brenda Olson was providentially off work and was able to move into our home and look after the children. We managed to get the last two seats on the non-stop flight from Minneapolis to London.

Ten hours later Gretchen and I were on the plane making our way across the Atlantic. A wonderful peace descended over us as Gretchen realized that the Elder Board was praying for us at their monthly meeting. I asked God to preserve my mother for at least another 24 hours so that I might see her alive for one last time. I fell into a deep sleep and woke up refreshed.

May 2001—John: My mother, Charlotte Steer, was born in the Scottish border town of Kelso. Her father was a fly fisherman who worked for the Duke of Roxburgh. He took the Duke and his aristocratic friends fishing for salmon in the River Tweed that ran by the bottom of their garden.

My mother trained to be a nurse in Edinburgh. She then did her midwifery training in Glasgow, delivering dozens of babies in the Gorbels, one of the worst slums in the nation, where the homes had dirt floors. This experience made her a lifelong socialist with a tremendous passion for the underdog.

As soon as Britain declared war on Germany in 1939 my mother joined the Army. She nursed wounded Allied soldiers along with captured German prisoners of war. She followed the troops over to France on D-day and was a nursing sister in a MASH hospital on the front lines.

My father was also in the British Army and they met in Germany in the closing years of the war. She was not a Christian. He shared the gospel with her, led her to Christ and when they were demobilized back to England after the war, he asked to marry her.

Faithfulness

While my father was attending Spurgeon Seminary in London my mother provided for the family by working in a London hospital, where I was later born.

Upon arriving in London we drove to Ipswich, the country town of Suffolk, and made our way to the local hospital. Ma (as I always called her) was in the geriatric wing of the hospital. I went up to her bed. She seemed so small and frail but it appeared that she was simply having a wonderful deep sleep. There is little reason to think that people in comas can hear conversation but there is also little reason to think that they can't (as it is rather hard to do research on the subject). We spoke to her as if she was fully conscious, prayed with her and told her all that she meant to us. I was so grateful she hung on until we arrived.

She was in a small ward with five other beds all occupied by elderly ladies. Over the next week we got to know them well and learned their life stories. They took a tremendous interest in us and in the welfare of our mother.

The British health system is socialized medicine, which means among other things that there will be no bill for her treatment, nor for the ambulance that brought her to the hospital. It also means that no unnecessary tests are done if they are unlikely to change the outcome. She has no attached monitors, for which I am grateful. She only has an intravenous drip. Being an English hospital the tea lady comes four times a day to provide cups of tea, the cure for every possible problem. There is open visitation and even pets are welcome. It is a warm homey atmosphere and the buzz of conversation echoes through the room, especially when the other patients are receiving visitors.

We decided that we would not keep a 24-hour vigil, so after a few hours we returned to my mother's house in Felixstowe. The absence of her vivacious personality made me terribly sad. I felt almost like an intruder as we had to get our room ready and prepare a meal.

I went down the street to thank the observant neighbor who noticed that my mother's curtains had not been drawn at 9:30 in the morning. Having a key to the house, he went in to investigate and discovered her unconscious in bed. How grateful I am that she did not lie there for several days before anybody found her.

The next to arrive would be my brother Andrew, who is coming from Hanoi, Vietnam. He won't get here for two more days and, like us, would love to see his mother alive. In the meantime we visit the hospital on a regular basis. I read scripture to my mother and reminisce with her.

My last precious conversation with her had been on Easter Day. She was so interested to know about our Easter service at John Marshall High School, and was pleased that it had provided a solution to our overflowing facilities. We talked then about the great doctrine of the resurrection. How wonderfully comforting it is at a time like this; her own body is wasting away but her inner being is being renewed as she prepares for that greatest journey of all, to that city whose builder and maker is God.

And yet how I hate death and what it is doing to my mother, this fine, striking woman who through osteoporosis has lost almost a foot of height and who has lost all her hair because of a thyroid problem. What an appalling enemy is death. It steals our loved ones and reduces them to dust. Gretchen reads the words from 1 Corinthians 15:

> *Where, O death, is your victory? Where, O death, is your sting? But thanks be to God who gives us the victory in our Lord Jesus Christ.*

We are all doing a lot of crying. We grieve because God has made us emotional creatures in his image. We mourn the fact that we will not converse with our mother again on earth and that the family home will have to be broken up and sold.

> *May 2000—John: One of my most vivid memories is of a Good Friday when I was eight years old. I had no idea what Good Friday was about and I asked my mother to explain it. She described Jesus' suffering on the cross with such clarity and conviction that I began to weep. I was so touched by her narrative I felt I was witnessing the scene. Seldom in my life have I had such a clear understanding of the atonement.*

> *Years later when I was a seminary student I went through a period of great despair. I wondered how I would manage to prepare a morning and evening sermon and a Wednesday night Bible study for the congregation of my small student pastorate in the village of Binfield in England. My mother calmly explained to me that those the Lord calls he also equips. She said, "God called you into the ministry and he will provide the necessary resources to do the job." She was right and I cheered up.*

> *At age 26 when I left England to take a church in Los Angeles I think she knew I would not be returning but she was content*

in the knowledge that I was where God wanted me to be. That was enough for her.

On Sunday we go to the local parish church. As an Anglican church they follow the church calendar and the theme is still on resurrection. It is so comforting to be worshipping with God's people. We go forward to the altar rail to receive the Eucharist and hear the familiar words, "the body of Christ broken for you, the blood of Christ shed for you."

Andrew arrives and brings with him his new fiancée. At age 46 he feels it's time to settle down. It is the first time we have met her. She is a lovely young lady from Belgium who teaches at the London School of Economics. Her actual name is Liesbet but I immediately christen her Hercule Poirot in honor of Agatha Christie's famous Belgian detective.

We meet with the doctor who tells us that he does not expect our mother to live more than 48 hours. He asks us our wishes. She has often told us that she wanted no heroic measures such as being put on a ventilator. We have already decided that a feeding tube would be both uncomfortable and unproductive. The hospital had planned to do a CAT scan of her head but we decline as it will involve moving her and in no way will it affect the outcome or the treatment that she is receiving. The stroke, which we believe was caused by a hemorrhage, has affected both sides of her brain and she is totally unresponsive.

The next day the nurse calls to inform us her breathing is now irregular and that this may be the end. Once again we travel the 12 miles to the hospital and sit around her bed. I go to the hospital chapel and find some hymnals. We sing some of her favorite hymns including *And Can It Be?* and *Glorious Things of Thee Are Spoken*. We read scripture, pray and say good-bye. She surprises us and survives the night and the next day.

We reflect that some cultures set aside one or two weeks to grieve. That seems excessive in our action-packed, fast moving society. Yet we are now being forced to do a similar thing and it is very good for us. The rest of our lives have completely stopped. We are not thinking of home or work. We are simply giving a week of our lives as three brothers, to honor the woman who gave us life. Sitting beside her the time passes very quickly as we weep, pray, reflect, read scripture and talk to the other patients in the room.

We receive calls from Pastor Doug Weincouff and Max Gernand informing us that the Elders would like to put our three children on a plane so they can join us. We are overwhelmed with this generosity and thoughtfulness. It is a lovely gesture that encourages us enormously. On reflection we feel that it will be best if the children remain at home and Gretchen returns as planned on Wednesday. The response of our church family has been incredible and we are so grateful to be part of such a caring community.

Mother's heart is turning out to be much stronger than anybody imagined. She is still holding her own. Every time we leave we say farewell. It is becoming like a Minnesota good-bye and it is taking an emotional toll. Now that Andrew has arrived my prayers have changed. I just want the Lord to take her to be with himself.

> *May 2001—John: Mother was a totally contented woman. She always believed that every stage of her life was the very best stage to be in. She loved being single for 32 years. She loved being a nurse. She loved caring for wounded soldiers in the war. She loved married life and she loved having young children.*
>
> *When my father took his first church in London she threw herself into the work of ministry though she knew nothing about Baptist church life until that time. For over 20 years she ran a young wives group in her home. She served these young women coffee and dessert and then taught them about being a wife and mother and instructed them in the Christian faith. She lived out Paul's instructions that the older women should instruct the younger.*
>
> *She was a very popular preacher and went all over England taking services in evangelical churches of various denominations. We often joked that she was in more demand than my father. This was remarkable because it was during a time when women preachers were relatively rare.*
>
> *She loved retirement and as she got older she talked with great affection about heaven. As she was dying we discovered that she had given away almost everything she had. There were only two sets of clothes hanging in her closet. She was content to die.*

She's contracted pneumonia and her breathing is labored. I reflect on how very difficult it must be for families who have a loved one in a coma, not just for days, but for months or even years. About the worst thing that could happen now is if she were to wake up and make some form of partial recovery. She always told us that her greatest dread was being put in a nursing home, where she would be washed, changed and fed by others. Thankfully she has been spared that indignity and managed to stay in her own home right until the end.

With no change in sight, I take Gretchen to the airport to return to Rochester and look after the children. She would love to stay for the funeral but my mother was always a great one for emphasizing the living over the dead.

> *April 1996—Gretchen: My mother-in-law, Charlotte Steer, is someone who has lived a life of servanthood towards other people. As a pastor's wife for 50 years and the mother of three boys, the oldest of whom is my husband, John, she has modeled for me what servanthood is all about. When Charlotte first qualified as a nurse, in Scotland in the 1930's, she went out to work for her first job. She took her very first pay check, one month's wages, and bought her own mother a string of pearls. At that time they cost her about 25 English pounds. Today they are worth $500 or $600. She wanted to show her mother how much she loved her, and she went without things that she desperately needed as a newly independent woman in order to give her mother this gift. Her mother wore them until her death in 1961. Charlotte took back the pearls at that time. She later had them restrung and, a few Christmases ago, gave them to my oldest daughter, Emily. As I received the pearls from Charlotte's hand in keeping for Emily, I was reminded of the relationship they symbolize, and I hope that I am as close to my children as Charlotte was to her own mother.*

Returning to Ipswich I pass a signpost to the village of Kelvedon. It rings a bell—I pull off the road and inquire about the location of a certain house. The owner of the grocery store gives me directions and I walk 100 yards up the road and stand in front of the place where Charles Haddon Spurgeon was born in 1834. I give a silent prayer of thanks for the impact he had on the Baptist denomination around the world and on my life in particular.

Today we found mother's instruction for her funeral. They were typical of her, self-effacing, humorous and concise. She begins:

> *Suggestions when Charlotte Steer bids you a temporary farewell. Please, no viewing of the body—ghoulish practice! That is not me, just a dried up husk. Remember my Scottishness, so no gush. I remember a little old lady who lived unobtrusively in an Alms house but listening to her*

> *funeral oration, one would have thought she had been a mixture of Joan of Arc, Boadicea and Saint Therese of Lisieux, with Juliana of Norwich and Mrs. Thatcher thrown in. If the old soul was listening she didn't know who they were talking about. The Scots are not like that and the nearer I get to my New Beginning the more I feel my Scottishness.*

She requested that the theme of her service would be "continuity." As a young girl she used to love hiking in Scotland from one youth hostel to another with her sister. She describes her death as:

> *Like the last night in a youth hostel. After a glorious holiday, you have regrets about leaving the lovely surroundings and lovely people but a glorious realization that you are going home to an even more loving parent, a good bath and clean clothes.*

She instructed that I was to lead the service. She had chosen the hymns and scripture readings. She asked that prayers be made for missionary endeavor and particularly for Indonesia and Israel where she had lived. Gretchen was to read 1 Peter 1 and Simon was to read John Donne's poem *Death Be Not Proud.* There was no place for a eulogy. She concluded:

> *After the service have a lovely meal in a nice hotel, taking the cost out of my estate, and try to remember me laughing.*

It has been nine days since her stroke. We meet with the doctor who tells us he is surprised that Ma has lasted this long. She has overcome pneumonia without antibiotics and could conceivably live several more weeks. We have all been here long enough and have said all that we need to say. The needs of the living now take preeminence. Andrew returns to Vietnam and I decide to fly back to Rochester the next day.

Before I leave her hospital bed I read Revelation 21 and 22 to my mother. It is a beautiful description of heaven. I thank God for her life and her influence upon me. I praise him for the example she has been of a godly wife, mother and grandmother. I tell her that I love her and that I will see her again on the resurrection morning. Knowing that this is the last time I will see mother alive in this world I bid her farewell and kiss her on the cheek. The doctor is right—there is a sense in which she died 10 days ago when she had the stroke. I wonder where the soul of an unconscious person resides. Perhaps she is already with the Lord.

Nineteen days after her stroke Charlotte Steer went to be with Jesus.

May 1999—John: I am convinced that one of the greatest things a mother can do for her children is to pray for them, fervently, frequently and faithfully. On the very first Mother's Day without my mother, just two weeks after she died, I realize just how I terribly miss her. However I am grateful for the extraordinary impact she had on my life and particularly for her prayers for me.

When I was back in England with my two brothers for her funeral we found her prayer diary. There was nothing fancy about it. It was an unused 1992 Day Timer. As a good Scot my mother believed in the adage: "waste not, want not." She was recycling things long before it was popular. Although her prayer diary is not very posh, it is very precious.

On the opening page scribbled over February 12th is J.A.S., which stands for John, Andrew and Simon—her three sons. It is clear she prayed for four passages of scripture to become real in our lives. The first is Ephesians 1:17-19:

I keep asking that the God of our Lord Jesus Christ, the glorious Father, may give you the Spirit of wisdom and revelation, so that you may know him better. I pray also that the eyes of your heart may be enlightened in order that you may know the hope to which he has called you, the riches of his glorious inheritance in the saints, and his incomparably great power for us who believe. That power is like the working of his mighty strength.

She then goes on to ask God for: *Their individual needs and work, help, wisdom (like their father) and love.* This is the greatest legacy my mother left me. Far greater than any possessions or property are her prayers, which have eternal significance.

Chapter 33

The Inner Core of Holiness

Gretchen
August 1999

I'm going to begin by acknowledging that for the past 22 years I have felt strongly called to teach. . . to teach women, that is. I actually have done very little teaching of coed groups, primarily because the opportunities haven't arisen. In pondering what to teach the men of the Joint Heirs Adult Sunday School class, one of my first reactions was the pleasure of realizing that I'd have 40 minutes to harangue a captive audience of guys! However, on reflection I thought better of that and so I'd like to begin with a little gender-destroying anecdote from my home life.

For the first 20 or so years of my married life, John and I had unusually clear divisions of labor. These fell along very traditional lines. I cooked, he did the yard work. I did diapers, he played with the baby, and so on. One of these divisions of labor concerned ironing. For twenty years I faithfully *ironed* clothes and he faithfully *wore* them.

A curious trend occurred a few years ago when I began working part-time. I was often so far behind in the ironing that John, with a great sigh, would pull out the board and iron his own shirt each morning. Before long it was clear that I had managed to divest myself of the ironing job for good. We had a really crummy old iron, which didn't steam, and often wouldn't heat up at all unless the cord was in a certain position.

For Father's Day this year I went to great trouble to buy John the very best iron I could find… an iron, in fact, that cost as much as a really good power drill.

I'm not normally much of a gift giver on Father's Day. I was a bit concerned that John might think he was getting a really cool gift in that big box and then be disappointed. Believe me, I was well aware of the comic potential of this gift, so along with the traditionally mushy card I taped a note to the side of the box saying "I know it's really crass to give your spouse a household appliance, but at least you can get a sermon illustration out of it." (Little did I know that I'd be the one using the sermon illustration.) I'm happy to report that John was absolutely delighted with his new iron and has been happily ironing ever since.

I love this story for a number of reasons. First of all, it shows that every good marriage breaks the rules. Men, what have you been told in marriage seminars? Never, *ever* give your wife an iron for her birthday or Mother's Day. Yet this was John's favorite Father's Day gift… ever.

Second, it shows the remarkable truth that old dogs can indeed learn new tricks. Who would have thought that after 22 years of marriage he'd be doing the ironing and I would be taking the van to the mechanic?

But, third, it shows something far more profound... that on the level where love operates, you throw away gender and use a different yardstick: *To what does the other person really respond?*

In the most crucial arenas of our lives, like showing love, we deal with each other as individuals, not as stereotypical men or women. That brings me full circle to my point:

> *In Christ there is neither Jew nor Greek, slave nor free, male nor female, for you are all one in Christ Jesus. (Galatians 3:28)*

Christ, because he loves us, deals with us as individuals regardless of our gender. Once I understood that principle I was more at ease with teaching men. We need to remember that these words are equally applicable to all of us, men and women, because they concern our relationship to Christ as individuals first, not as men or women.

Ephesians 4:17-24 talks about what it means to live as Children of Light... not *men* of light nor *women* of light, but jointly *children* of light. This passage contrasts the consequences of separation from Christ with the consequences of joining with Christ.

This passage contrasts the life of one who knows Christ with the life of one who does not know. It also acknowledges that it is possible for those of us who know Christ to live as though we don't. I have to be strictly honest and admit that of the six commentaries I read on this passage, no one applies it to the sinning believer. However, in my observation of the Christian life over the years, I have perceived that even Christians can become so entrenched in sin that they start, for a time, to display these same characteristics shown by unbelievers. The difference is that no believer can go on in this state indefinitely without coming under either judgment or conviction.

In verses 17-19 Paul talks about the characteristics of those who do not know Christ... but as I've just mentioned, they can also be the characteristics of one who knows Christ but is not living accordingly.

I see around me people whose lives fall everywhere along the spectrum. We expect bad, rude selfish behavior from those who have never known Christ's influence in their lives. But within the church we see lots of people who are living nominally Christian lives. Scratch the surface, or deal out some suffering, and we see these same characteristics… bad, rude, selfish and sinful behavior. The difference is that they're not happy about it. A cognitive dissonance occurs in the soul of the person who has yielded himself to Christ, but who is living as though it makes no difference.

John MacArthur had a rather poetic way of putting this struggle between the new nature in Christ and the old nature. He said it's like a smelly old coat encasing new, beautiful flesh. We have to ruthlessly tear off that dirty old coat to reveal the newness within. Sadly, that's easier said than done.

To put it really bluntly, all around us are people who are really messed up: unhappy marriages, addictions and lusts, boredom, depression. In fact, if we're honest, most of us can point to stretches in our own lives where we fully caved in to sinful impulses, where we struggled in our Christian lives, and where we didn't see a lot of difference between our supposed new lives in Christ and those around us.

In this passage, Paul insists that there must be a difference between the life in Christ and the life outside of Christ. If there isn't, then something is far wrong. The incredible truth is that there's a way out of the downward spiral—through Christ.

The first consequence of separation from Christ is ignorance. Paul is speaking to Gentiles, or those who do not know God. However, these same consequences happen when we willfully separate ourselves from fellowship with Christ. We are still believers, because Christ will never let us go, but we are willfully sinning believers, and so we suffer many of the same consequences of separation as those who never knew Christ.

We are stuck wearing the smelly old coat. If we continue to separate ourselves from Christ through sin, we become ignorant. We become ignorant of the things of God, the standards of God, the delights of God and the fellowship of God.

This ignorance works itself out in practical ways. First, we become disinclined to read the Bible, listen to sermons, be with other Christians. There is an ignorance of God that comes from a lack of interest and a lack of effort.

But there is another kind of ignorance, and it originates from willful sin in the Christian's life. When we deliberately sin, we separate ourselves from Christ. In that condition, even trying to draw near to God won't succeed, because it doesn't address the root problem.

Let me give you an example. It's human nature to compartmentalize, and so we falsely believe that if we are going to church, praying, and so on, it's simultaneously possible to ignore a glaring issue of sin. This tendency to think we're OK as long as we act like Christians on the outside is a form of ignorance, or self-deception.

That is why it's possible to have well-known Christian leaders and pastors carrying on affairs while running a successful church. That's why it's possible to have Christians embezzling from their companies, or beating their wives, or visiting prostitutes. They've fallen into the trap of thinking that if they're striving after God in most areas, the one sinful corner somehow doesn't matter.

I've given some extreme examples, but I think the same principle operates with any area of willful self-deception in our lives. This is the difference between saying "OK, God, take all of my life," and saying, "OK, God, take all of my life except that one little corner I don't want to give up."

Ignorance is therefore one of the first consequences of separation from Christ. We become ignorant because we are not growing in our faith, and we become willfully and increasingly ignorant of the things of God when we go on in deliberate sin.

The second consequence of separation from Christ is a hardened heart. This is what happens when prolonged and willful sin is allowed to flourish.

A hardened heart is a more serious problem than simple ignorance. It's the difference between a blister and a callus. A blister hurts a lot more because it feels like an injury. It demands attention. But repeated use of an area of skin produces a callus, not a blister. The skin thickens and becomes coarse in order to protect the tender part underneath. A callus is good, in the sense that it cushions pain, but it does so by deadening sensitivity.

A hardened heart is cynical about the words and motives of other Christians. A hardened heart sits in church and critiques the worship team, musicians, and pastors. A hardened heart has learned to always put itself and its own needs first, even when others need attention.

So, it's a useful exercise to ask ourselves as believers: Is there any area where we willfully and always put ourselves at odds with Christ's standards? What is so important to us that it takes precedence over service, over family, over God?

Let me throw out one possible candidate, and that is the role of work in our lives. Rochester is filled with bright, intense, successful and driven people. It's culturally unusual in that most people seem to love their jobs. But any time we are engaged in something that fully occupies us, it vies for our allegiance alongside God, our family, our spouses and everyone else.

Perhaps this is even more true in the medical and helping professions. During the past year, I had two extraordinary conversations with friends who are surgeons. The first mentioned that, as a surgeon, it was very difficult to avoid the feeling at the end of a successful operation that "I've saved a life! I've cheated death!" and conversely, to feel at the end of an unfortunate operation where the patient dies, "I've failed!" I reminded this man of God's sovereignty in numbering our days (Psalm 139:16) before we are ever born. He talked about the seductive lure of the power of curing or healing people. Yes, he has the skills. But even the best surgeon cannot save where God's sovereign will has determined death. Work becomes a snare when it makes us feel equal with God.

The second surgeon mentioned another area of struggle, the idea that the healing professions excuse one from work in the local church. In other words, if everyone knows you're a doctor and you're really busy putting in long hours saving lives, then somehow you are exempt from all the requirements given to every other Christian... the need to worship together (Hebrews 10); the necessity of service; the carrying out of the Great Commission (Matthew 28); even, perhaps, your responsibility to family. He said that it's very easy to hide behind the schedule and the essential nobility of the work to, in effect, shirk one's duties as a Christian in a socially acceptable way.

How many of us are engaged in work that we think should take precedence over God's work? If we just finish that bit of research that will save the next generation of lives... if we untangle the scientific secrets of the universe... if we can help our company generate such profits that we raise everyone's standard of living... why can't we let these noble goals take precedence over the simple requirements of following Christ?

I'm not saying that we aren't accomplishing great things with our hard work and our commitment to excellence. Believe me, I struggle with this issue on a daily basis. It is impossible for me to do a job partway. I just want to caution all of us against letting our work seduce us away from the responsibilities that God has given each of us in Christ—to raise our children, love our spouses, and guard our hearts from becoming hardened.

Please notice that what I'm saying does NOT necessarily translate to "I'll shorten my working hours to spend more time with my family" or, "I'll shorten my working hours so I can have a more comfy life."

On the contrary, what I am advocating here translates to: "I'll shorten my working hours so I can follow Christ." It's not enough to give money instead of service. Neither money nor time is what God wants, unless they are propelled by a passionate love for Christ.

What God desires from us is our hearts, not burnt offerings and sacrifices. What he might be calling you to do is serve him in the church, reach out to your unchurched neighbor, go to the mission field with your vocational skills, or, perhaps, spend time with your family. In our culture, family can become just as much of an idol as work, and as great an excuse to avoid service. When we truly follow Christ all the parts of our life will fall into balance.

I'm also not suggesting that all of us high-achieving, driven types are living this way because we have hardened hearts. I simply want to raise the issue that anything, even something inherently good, like meaningful work or devotion to home life, can take the place of God in our lives if we let it. When we let anything take the place of God, we run the risk of becoming first, ignorant and second, hardened to his voice.

The third consequence of separation from Christ is loss of sensitivity (Ephesians 4:19). This can lead to full indulgence in sensual pleasures.

I'm speaking to both men and women here. This verse is not referring to sexuality alone, but about all the pleasures that play to our bodies... eating, obsession with appearance, sexual immorality (both in the body and in the mind), emotional affairs, and substance abuse.

After all these years in the ministry, I don't think I could be surprised by anything that befalls people. After all, when we fully indulge ourselves, this verse tells us that what satisfied us initially will not satisfy for long. There is a continual upping of the ante. People who give in to sin with abandon will become more and more perverse.

Let's say you have a romantic streak and get caught up in soap operas, sleazy movies and novels. Constant immersion in that way of thinking will dispose you toward extramarital affairs, whether or not you give in. No day-to-day marriage can live up to romantic fantasy.

Let's say you start flirting with pornography on the internet. It's safe, no one knows, it's late at night, what's the harm? But the sites that initially satisfied you won't for long. Pornography can become an obsession once it's indulged.

We are able to go deeper and deeper in sin because continual, repeated sinning lets us lose our sensitivity to God's voice and God's standards. It's a downward spiral. Once we've become ignorant of God's standards and hardened our hearts, there is nowhere to go but down.

Sin is extremely seductive, so strong—especially sexual sin—that there is really no antidote. No antidote, that is, except Jesus Christ. There is no logical, rational deterrent that will stop us if we are determined to go ahead with sin... not the fear of consequences, not the fear of losing our marriage or job or position in the community. That's a pretty bleak picture, but I believe it is realistic. The only true preventative for sin is an inner core of holiness that says, "By the grace and the power of God I WILL walk away from this temptation."

In a new building I toured recently, there is a firewall. In the kitchen is a large metal slatted door that drops down from the ceiling when the smoke alarms go off. Its purpose is to keep conflagration from spreading throughout the rest of the facility. Of course, if the fire is hot and strong enough, this firewall will only delay, not contain, a fire that could potentially burn down the building.

We can build firewalls into our own lives in the form of accountability groups, restricted internet access, avoidance of situations where alcohol is served, and so on. These firewalls make good sense, and they should be part of our defense. But they must not be mistaken for prevention. The only way we are going to be kept from sin is to throw ourselves on God's mercy every single day, asking for help to walk in Christ's footsteps. It is a daily yielding to the Spirit that keeps us from becoming ignorant, then hardened, then completely insensitive to God.

What we need to develop is the inner core of holiness that operates even when we are all alone and no one is looking. When we are in a hotel room and lonely and tired and the "adult" channel beckons, or the streets, or the bar, or the co-worker. When we are resentful at home and exhausted from raising small children, we don't think we love our husbands any more, and we've started flirting. What we need is an inner core of holiness that grows very, very slowly over a long period of obedience.

When we planted pine trees at the edge of our front yard nine years ago, they were so small that John brought ten of them home in the back seat of his VW Rabbit. Now each is 16 feet tall! These trees looked like little shrubs for about the first five years of their lives on our lawn, then they began to shoot up. There is no stopping them. I understood that pine trees slowly put down roots for the first few years and only then, when the roots are deep enough, can they grow to their full potential.

The inner core of holiness grows very slowly and puts down roots over a long period of time. Yes, obedience does become easier when practiced over the long haul. After many years we may find the same leap of progress and growth that the pine trees experience. Initially, the inner core of holiness is enlarged one act of obedience at a time.

It would sound impossible and discouraging if it weren't for the following verses:

> You were taught, with regard to your former way of life, to put off your old self, which is being corrupted by its deceitful desires; to be made new in the attitude of your minds; and to put on the new self, created to be like God in true righteousness and holiness. (Ephesians 4:22-24)

These verses tell us that we are not alone. The first consequence of joining with Christ is that we put off the old self. When we come to Christ, we are made new creatures, but we are only made into *infant* new creatures. Just as a newborn baby is alive, but needs help in order to grow and mature, so do we in Christ. That maturing process starts with the putting off of the old self. The old self is the smelly old coat of sin that needs to be forcibly shed. The old self is the one that is ignorant, has a hardened heart, and has lost all sensitivity. Putting it off makes us ready for the next step, which is being made new in the attitude of our minds.

Here's an illustration from the kitchen. If you want to make a smooth, creamy soup, you have two choices. You can puree the soup in the food processor until it is really smooth. After it's smooth you add cream and seasoning and transform it into something entirely new.

However, this method can have its drawbacks if you're cooking, for example, asparagus soup. Asparagus contains stringy tissue that sometimes can tangle in the processor, without ever being cut. If you want to make really smooth asparagus soup, you have to use the older cooking technique of pressing the whole mess through a sieve before pureeing it. That's the only way to make sure that the stringy part of the asparagus has been removed.

Our new nature involves being put through the sieve rather than just being pureed. We are actually shedding off the old bits before we are thoroughly smoothed out and the final ingredients are added. Our new nature is different. We suddenly can achieve discipline in a measure that we've never known before, because it comes from outside ourselves.

If your experience of the Christian life has involved one defeat after another, it's possible that you've never understood fully the capabilities that we have in Christ. Of course we can't get rid of entrenched sin, or habits, or bad relationships, if we're trying to do this on our own. But in Christ, with our new nature and attitude, we can.

Here's what's at stake: we can go along our whole lives in a sort of insipid and uninspired parody of what the Christian life is meant to be. Our church will take on that same protective coloration, because the church is, of course, made up of us. At the end of our lives we will have nominally served Christ, grown a little bit, and probably refrained from public sin, but not necessarily. Many of us will have stumbled publicly and disgracefully.

When we're old, if we've lived the kind of life that hasn't touched our inward being, we will enter our elder years increasingly embittered by our inability to exercise our sinful passions. We'll be the kind of old people that my friend, a nurse at St. Marys, describes as "guys who throw their bedpans and swear."

What entering my forties has taught me is this: I'm trying to live as though I'm already out of time. I'm becoming more comfortable with aging. Sure, it's hard to give up some of the dubious pleasures of youth as our bodies start breaking down. How much more important it is to give up the dubious pleasures of sin, which are dragging us into the downward spiral of ignorance, hardened heart and loss of sensitivity, and instead to put on the new nature and learn to really like it.

So I've decided that my goal in life is to try to follow as closely as I can in the footsteps of Christ, and in the decades ahead, to strive to become one of these nice old ladies who have a surprisingly tart sense of humor, and an enormous reservoir of prayer power.

Oh, and I've also decided that I'm going to get John a new ironing board for his birthday.

Chapter 34

For Better or Worse

John
August 1999

My brother, Andrew is finally getting married. After 47 years of enjoying the single life he has decided it is time to settle down. His fiancée is Liesbet, a 29-year-old economist from Belgium. They agreed to get married in April but couldn't quite decide where. Should it be in Belgium where her parents live, or England, where Liesbet now works, or Vietnam where Andrew makes his home? They eventually decided on Washington, DC, where neither of them live and where Liesbet does not know a soul. Grateful that they had pinned down the place, I pressed them to choose a date. This they finally did last week informing me that it would be Friday, August 7th, and by the way, would I perform the ceremony?

Now it is not every day that you get to marry your brother and I need to think of what to say to him at the wedding. It is a serious thing to stand before God and your family and friends and promise to love your spouse, "for better for worse, for richer for poorer, in sickness and in health."

The odds are against a good marriage. The average marriage today lasts 7.2 years. Even marriages that last aren't always happy. So how can we ensure that the reality of married life lives up to our expectations? When I am preparing couples for marriage I ask them to do some research. I invite them to discover three or four couples who have excellent marriages and ask them about what they believe is the secret of their success.

Neil Clark Warren has gone one better. He interviewed 100 happily married couples and discovered ten practical secrets for a great marriage. He published these in his book *The Triumphant Marriage.* Here they are:

- Dream a dream! Construct a vision of everything you believe your marriage can be.

- Get tough! A triumphant marriage requires two strong skillful, thoroughly committed partners.

- Maximize the trust factor! The spouses in a solid relationship have complete faith in each other.

- Get healthy! A triumphant marriage requires two emotionally healthy people.

- Work on chemistry! Maximize passion and romance.

- Learn to talk! Become masters of good communication.

- Work it through! Conflict is inevitable so learn to handle it productively. A happy marriage is the happy union of two good forgivers.

- Negotiate a mutually satisfying sexual relationship! A great sex life builds intimacy in marriage.

- Get connected! Recognize the role of children and friends in making your marriage triumphant.

- Pursue spirituality! Partners in great marriages find significance in their spiritual lives.

These are principles that are not only helpful to a couple like Andrew and Liesbet, who are just starting out, but also to Gretchen and I, who have just celebrated our 22nd wedding anniversary.

Above all else I want to tell my brother that marriage was God's idea and when Jesus Christ is invited into our heart and is the center of our home, the honeymoon does not need to end. Solomon tells us that a three-stranded rope is not easily broken. I think this is a wonderful picture of marriage when the three strands represent the husband, wife and the Lord Jesus Christ.

Paul tells us that the marriage relationship between husband and wife is to be a living illustration to the world of the love of Jesus for his church. I also want my brother to know that another of the similarities between the Christian faith and marriage is that they both get better as the years go by.

Now if only I can persuade Andrew to send out his invitations before the wedding!

Chapter 35

Living Well Through Sharing

Gretchen
September 1999

My husband keeps bees, and during this time of year there are many "bee things" to be done. I personally stay as far away as possible from the hives, but I know that they bring John a lot of happiness. One of the peculiarities of this hobby is that he has to dress up in some strange clothes, a hat, veil, gloves and so on, to protect from stings. Of course, it's hot and sweaty in this getup. The bees get more and more aggressive as he messes with their hives and so, by the end of each bee excursion, they are quite riled up.

One day this summer John lost his glasses somewhere in the woods when he flung off his bee hat. Because he was moving quickly to get away from the bees, he had no idea where his glasses went. Now, because I *care*, I decided to look along the path. As I went deeper in the woods, engrossed in looking at the ground, several bees got in my hair. I know, you're supposed to be calm, but instead I began sprinting along the path, squealing and making frantic air washing motions with my hands. I say sprinting, but because I was wearing flip flops I was really only very quickly mincing along trying to keep my sandals on my feet so I didn't *step* on any bees.

Now here's the bad part. As I emerged from the woods onto the lawn, I discovered that my husband was leaning out the upper storey window, laughing and saying, "Good show! Good Show! Very impressive!" Well! I guess he can look for his own glasses next time. Is that what you get for caring? All too often we care and risk, and the result is not at all what we think. People misinterpret our motives. They laugh at us, or become our enemies. But even when the outcome is not what we expect, it doesn't absolve us of the responsibility to care for each other.

In the fourth chapter of Philippians Paul says:

> *Yet it was good of you to share in my troubles. (Philippians 4:14)*

The caring that steps in when things aren't going well is very important to our well being. A time of trouble is the perfect time to show our tenderheartedness toward others. Paul goes on to mention four groups of people sending or receiving greetings. One group is the "saints in Caesar's household." These were civil servants who had come to hear the Gospel.

That one phrase illustrates the fact that the Gospel message had penetrated to the highest reaches of Roman society. Think about the cost of following Christ if you were in the service of Rome. Roman citizens were to worship the emperor as a god. How difficult it must have been, and how dangerous, to profess Christ. Yet they sent greetings to other Christians. They were interconnected. They *cared:*

> *Not that I am looking for a gift, but I am looking for what may be credited to your account. I have received full payment and even more; I am amply supplied, now that I have received from Epaphroditus the gifts you sent. They are a fragrant offering, an acceptable sacrifice, pleasing to God. (Philippians 4:17-18)*

One of the best principles that we can teach our children early on is to share. We start by teaching them to share toys, or perhaps a room, or a special treat. But very soon we should give children the opportunity to share by giving.

This fact was brought home to me by two experiences. One was in my own childhood, where our church had a stewardship drive. When I was in fourth grade I pledged to give 25 cents a week to the offering. I filled out a card and promptly forgot about it. You have to realize that, at this time in my life, my weekly allowance was a dime, and half the time my parents forgot to give it. The end of the fiscal year rolled around and my parents received one of those nice little cards from the church showing that I had given 50 cents toward what should have been about $15 for the year. We had a long talk about responsibility and the upshot was that they paid my "debt" to the church...but they also insisted that I didn't fill out another stewardship card unless they had a chance to see it first.

My children also sporadically receive an allowance. I tend to forget, too, when it's time to deliver. However, because they never spend money, all of them have amassed little piles of dollars in their piggy banks. At different times each of them has come home from something at church and said, "I want to give my money to the missionaries," and several times they have given $20 or $25 to a mission appeal. I haven't stopped them. I think the best way to teach children that money is to be given is to give them chances to give. I hope they never forget the great feeling that comes from placing everything you have in the offering plate and asking God to use it.

Teaching our children to share with others in need is an important part of the legacy we give them.

Knowledge is also meant to be shared. I've been delighted with one of the books that I inherited from my mother-in-law, a book called *Mrs. Beeton's Book of Household Management.* This book was written in 1861. The book was a complete how-to manual of the English middle class during the Victorian era and beyond. I was familiar with Mrs. Beeton's as a famous cookbook, but I didn't realize what else it contained. Literally, you could ask this book anything and Mrs. Beeton would have an answer. Want to know the housemaid's daily duties? See page 1,039. How about what to do when a person has been struck by lightning? Page 1,121. How to cook snipes? See page 538.

If Mrs. Beeton found time to run her own household, perfect these principles, and write a 1,139 page book in the days before word processing, she was clearly Superwoman. She admits in her preface that if she had known beforehand what labor the book would cost her, she never would have been courageous enough to attempt it. But most great things in life *are* accomplished by people who were too blind, too naïve, or too brave to notice the obstacles. What she did was to share an incredible wealth of knowledge. One of the most potent kinds of sharing is the sharing of help and information. Again, this is a biblical principle: the older women are to instruct the younger. And now I can at least tell myself that I'm getting more and more biblical because I'm getting older and older! If we don't have the material resources to share with each other, each of us has experience and time that we can share with one who needs us.

But the Philippians are commended by Paul because they shared their material possessions with him. The Philippians are notable because for a long time they were the *only* church who supported Paul. Can you believe that of all the places in which Paul ministered, only *one* church felt called to support him? I'm sure that was part of the reason they were so dear to him.

But Paul points out an interesting fact: their giving benefits them as much or more than it does him. The giving provided Paul with food, comfort, perhaps warm clothing, but for them it provided an eternal entry on God's balance sheet showing that they cared enough to share what they had.

God is pleased to see us giving our money, time and goods to honor and worship him. Yes, the recipient is helped, but the giver is helped far more.

I am going to give you a set of guidelines that I hope will enlarge your attitude toward giving and possessions. They come partly from biblical principles, partly from common sense, and partly from personal experience. The first is:

Don't cling too hard to possessions. If possessions are merely here to help us on our way, then it makes sense not to give them too high a place in our lives.

I have been pondering this concept a lot recently. When we moved here from LA it took three packers working four days straight to empty the contents of our large home into a moving van. When we unpacked those contents, it appeared there was plenty of room in our large home here. Now, ten years later, the house is stuffed to the gills with things…clothes, serving pieces, ten years of Bible study and work files, books, all that relate to the life we live. We didn't set out to acquire more possessions than a small country. We just did.

So about four months ago I began trying to empty the house. I sent twelve garbage bags out from the basement. I took a full load of stuff to a garage sale, including over a hundred books. I gave away 16 bags of clothes. I threw away countless papers, files, useless objects and junk. Now there is a little extra room, but I have scarcely made a dent. It is a project for the rest of my life. I don't need all the stuff I've acquired. I'm going to spend the next few decades un-acquiring it.

But what hardened my resolve to have fewer possessions was the experience of emptying my Mother-in-Law's home in England. I went through her dresser. Everything was tidy, and I was astounded at how few personal possessions she had kept. Almost everything she had was identifiable as a gift given by one of us. All her clothing would fit in a two-foot closet rail. If I dropped dead suddenly, I wince to think of all the junk through which some poor soul would have to wade. In the end, we each took a few things that particularly reminded us of Chris and Charlotte. In my case, I took the seven or eight pieces of china that remained from her wedding set. They are faded and chipped, but they represent the countless meals she served us over 22 years. They speak of hospitality to me.

I think Charlotte had the right idea. She had gradually divested herself of a lot that formerly tied her to this world. In the end, it was the few photos, the prayer journals, and the four or five letters from her own mother that meant the most to her survivors. Don't cling to possessions. To a large extent they weigh us down on our journey to heaven.

Practice the discipline of simplicity. There is a cost attached to every possession we own. First, there is the cost of purchasing it. Next, there is the cost, in either time or money or insurance, of maintaining it. Do you want a beautiful lawn? Then you have to spend time mowing, fertilizing and watering. Do you want a great new car? You have to work to make car payments. There is a cost attached to every possession. The fewer possessions we have, the greater freedom we have.

Have funds ready to respond to someone in need. It's a good discipline to keep some cash or liquid asset handy in order to help someone who needs help. If we are so chronically strapped for cash that we cannot pay our own bills, how can we possibly respond to need in the life of another? There is a tremendous joy in giving gifts to others.

Need may not always be obvious. If the Philippians hadn't been concerned about Paul, they never would have thought to set aside money for his ministry. Yet that gift of money not only helped his need, but tremendously lifted his spirits. What's more, it was pleasing to God.

Tithe everything. The Bible teaches that giving a tithe, often ten percent of one's income, is a good starting place for us to recognize that God is the giver of everything we have. Ten percent may sound staggering to you, especially if you are not in the habit of giving. Why not start with something a bit smaller and work up to it. I think the important principle is that part of your income is set aside for God's work and it goes there automatically, despite whatever else is going on in your life. Tithing is giving for the long term. It teaches us to budget our income so that we are not chronically short of money. It teaches us to give back to God in recognition that God has given everything to us. The money given provides the means for churches and Christian organizations and missionaries to do God's work in the world. It also teaches us to hold money lightly.

God also knows how many hours we have in a day. Consider tithing your time as well. Most of the work in churches and other Christian organizations is done by volunteers. However, those who have to recruit workers are discovering that people would rather give money than time, or not give at all. This fact is increasingly impacting church life. God sees our priorities in the way that we use our time. If none of our time goes to his work in the world, except for the one hour a week that we sit in church taking in, then we are not witnessing well about the importance of our faith. Tithing is a good discipline, whether it is time or money.

Distinguish between needs and wants. We all want things. I want a new piano, but I have a perfectly good one. I don't *need* a new piano, I just *want* one. If I never get a new one, I still will have the pleasure of playing on the one I have, and that is a lot more than having no piano at all.

There are things we *need* in order to work efficiently. There is no glamour in struggling along doing God's work with ill-fitting tools if the proper means are right in front of us. We just have to be certain that what we need is not just what we *think* we need...or what we *want*. Keep this principle in mind when you are evaluating purchases, especially big-ticket items.

At one stage of your life you might need help—financial or otherwise. You may or may not be able to return kindnesses to the people who help you. The important principle is that you return them to *someone*.

The movie *Elizabeth* is about Elizabeth I, the Sixteenth Century queen of England. The movie contains a scene when the young Elizabeth is thrown into the Tower of London by her half-sister, Mary Tudor. One of the noblemen accompanying her gives Elizabeth his coat as she is sent into the dank tower cell. She says to him, "I will not forget this kindness, sir." Within the decade she herself is queen of England, and in dealing with a plot against her life, she encounters this man as one of the treasonous plotters. Reminding him of his former kindness, she spares his life while the others are put to death. The world's point of view sees such an action as honorable and noble, which it was; yet how much more noble would it have been if she had spared the lives of the other traitors? Christianity deals in grace. As we fail to repay our enemies with evil, and as we offer grace and help to strangers who have never helped us, we are showing the world what Christ has done for us. He offered us grace when we didn't deserve it.

Remember your partnership with God. By this I mean that in your giving, be daring. Dare to remember that God provided everything for you, and he will supply what you need again and again.

If we are to take the following verse literally, then we have to dare:

> *And my God will meet all your needs according to his glorious riches in Christ Jesus. (Philippians 4:19)*

When we take this verse literally we are free from fear. We understand that God will not leave us helpless and hopeless, no matter what circumstance comes into our life. When we take this verse literally we understand that God will give to us in proportion to his riches. He gives and gives, in proportion to what he has, and yet it is never exhausted. When we take this verse literally, we understand that God will give us what we *need.* What we need may not necessarily be material blessing. God may intend for us to learn to trust him through hardship and deprivation. He may put us through bankruptcy and unemployment. He may put us through widowhood and a tiny pension. He does so in order to bring us what we need.

Paul prayed three times that God would remove a "thorn in his flesh." Whether that thorn was loneliness, or depression, or chronic illness, or pain, we don't know. But we do know that God supplied all of Paul's needs, and he evidently didn't think Paul needed to be rid of his thorn. Ultimately, its presence drove Paul to his knees and brought him to a deeper understanding of God.

You might not be giving thanks for a thorn in your flesh right now, either. But remember that the God who supplies all your needs will have a purpose for any affliction in your life.

One final point: Paul says, *My God will supply all your needs…* If Paul's God is not your God, then none of these promises are for you. They depend upon a personal, living relationship with Jesus Christ as your savior. If you do not know Jesus Christ in this intimate and personal way, I long for you to know him. But if you can think of God as *your God,* then all the resources of God's mighty and infinite power are yours. May we learn to use them to their full extent.

Chapter 36

God's Plan for Your Family

John

January 2000

God created your family to reflect his glory. Dietrich Bonhoeffer, a Lutheran pastor sitting in a Nazi prison cell, wrote in a wedding sermon to his niece who was about to be married:

> *Marriage is more than your love for each other. It has a higher dignity and power, for it is God's holy ordinance through which he wills to perpetuate the human race to the end of time. In your love you see only your two selves in the world, but in marriage you are a link in a chain of the generations, which God causes to come and pass away for his glory. In your love you see only the heaven of your happiness, but in marriage you're placed at a post of responsibility toward the world and mankind. Your love is your own private possession but your marriage is more than something personal. It is a status, an office.*

Bonhoeffer was making the point that the Christian family does not exist for our benefit. Rather, God has created it to bring honor and glory to himself. The goal of family life is not our happiness. Our happiness is a by-product of realizing that God created the family to reflect his glory.

In Genesis we read of the creation of the first family.

> *God created man in his own image, in the image of God he created him; male and female he created them. (Genesis 1:27)*

Here we learn that God created us in his likeness. This is not referring to physical features because God does not have any. He is spirit, not matter. When God is described, it is in terms of his glory. We are made to reflect that glory.

Here is the first family. There are no children at this point, just a man and a woman, and yet they are a family and God says, *it was very good.* God concluded the first five days of creation, by saying, *it was good*, but on the sixth day he said, *it was very good.* The crowning act of God's creative work is the making of men and women in his own image. This is why the family will always survive in spite of the attacks from the world and the devil, because it is God's idea.

First and foremost then, it's essential to understand that God created our family to be a reflection of his glory. We're like those reflectors at the side of the highway. We don't notice them in the daytime, but when our headlights hit them at night they light up to give out a message. Our families are to be like that.

We don't have any glory of our own. We're to reflect God's glory and send out the message of his love. Jonathan Edwards wrote, "Every family ought to be a little church connected to Christ and wholly influenced and governed by his principles."

Some, in their concern to protect the family, speak as if the family itself is the ultimate reality. To hear some folks talk you get the impression they want to re-mint our coins to read, "In the family we trust." I've had people tell me they're not coming to worship God because they want to spend time with their family.

If we're not careful the family can become an idol. The first commandment says, *You shall have no other gods before me*. That includes our families. The family does not come first, God does. He's the one who created the family, who sustains the family and who provides for the family.

The value of the family is rooted in our role as reflectors of God's glory. 1 Corinthians 10:31 tells us, *Whatever you do, do it all to the glory of God*. This is one of the great themes of Scripture. This world was made to reflect God's glory and it begins with the family.

To live to the glory of God has exciting implications. It means it is not my marriage but God's marriage. It is not my home but God's home. They're not my children but God's children. It's not my family but God's family. It's hard work to have a good family but it's worth the effort when we remember that our families are here to glorify God.

The second reason God created your family is to reveal his character. God loves to use visual aids. When he wants to illustrate that our sins are washed away he gives us baptism. When he wants to symbolize the shed blood and torn body of his Son he gives us red wine and a broken loaf, and when he wants to illustrate the depth and intimacy of his love for us he gives us the family.

Listen to what Paul says to the Ephesian church:

> *Husbands love your wives, just as Christ loved the church and gave himself up for her to make her holy, cleansing her by the washing with water through the word. This is a profound*

> *mystery—but I am talking about Christ and the church. (Ephesians 5:25, 26, 32)*

This means that the way I love my wife should remind my friends of the way Jesus loves his bride, the church. It means that newly married couples are really missionaries demonstrating by their passion for each other the tenderness of Jesus' love for his people. Some go to Oberammergau to see the Passion Play but not everyone can travel that far. God therefore places little passion plays in every community. He creates families whose members, by their behavior toward one another, dramatize the love of God for all to see.

When we recognize that God has created the family to reveal his character we will discover that God's love is a model for marriage in some very practical ways.

God's love is continual. God loves us with an everlasting love. He says, *I will never leave you* and that is why he wants our families to stay together. When they break up, they spoil the illustration. This truth motivates us to work through problems so that we remain a family.

God's love is communicated. God is always telling us that he loves us. It is on almost every page of the Bible. He doesn't just tell us once and leave it at that. So the words, "I love you" must be frequently heard in our homes, not just on Valentine's Day, but every day.

God's love is contagious. When people are around Jesus they catch his love and begin to feel love for others. Zacchaeus is a good example. When he met Jesus he promised to give back all he had stolen from others. By doing this he was passing on the love of God that he had received. So God uses families to pass on the Christian faith, for faith is caught as much as is it taught.

I am thankful that I was raised in a home where love was contagious. My parents told me about the love of God as soon as I was old enough to eat my porridge. Other children could sing, "Jesus loves me this I know, for the Bible tells me so" but I sang, "Jesus loves me this I know, because my mother tells me so." When the German theologian Karl Barth was asked how he could be certain that his great work of Dogmatics was true he smiled and replied, "Because my mother said so."

The family is God's primary missionary society. It provides a means for us to pass on our faith to our children and to allow them to see God's character at work in our lives. I think Pope John Paul II has it right when he says, "The first and fundamental structure for human ecology is the family, in which man receives his first ideas about truth and goodness and learns what it means to love and be loved and thus what it means to be a person."

This reality that God created the family to reveal his character is not to act as a lead weight that pulls us beneath a sea of guilt. The standard is high and none of us will attain it all the time. Sin damaged the first family and it will also affect ours. However, even the way we respond to failure in our families can demonstrate the character of God. Our readiness to forgive other members of our family who have wronged us demonstrates God's forgiveness.

Our willingness to acknowledge, even as parents, when we have failed, can be an occasion when we demonstrate our dependence on the mercy and grace of God.

This wonderful truth that God created our family to reveal his character should ennoble us and cause us to strive to bring our family into conformity with God's purpose. At the same time it reminds us of our daily need for the power of God's Spirit to help us to live up to this holy calling.

The third reason God created your family is to realize his purposes. When God began to work in human history, he chose to do so through families. He worked through Adam's family, and through Noah's family. Hebrews tells us that Noah built the ark *to save his family.* God also worked through Abraham and his family. He told Abraham, *All the peoples of the earth will be blessed through you.* God's laws were directed at families. Four of the Ten Commandments directly concern the family.

God's covenant was passed on through family lines, for he is known as *the God of Abraham, Isaac and Jacob.* Ephesians tells us that God *works out everything in conformity with the purpose of his will.* He is doing that through our families. I find this truth very exciting. It means that our family can be part of God's redemptive purpose. This gives us significance beyond our wildest dreams. We're participating in God's eternal plan. Our family is a reflection of what God is doing in his world.

In Ephesians 3:14-15 we discover something about God and something about our family. The *New American Standard Bible* translates these verses:

> *I bow my knees before the Father, from whom every family in heaven and earth derives its name.*

152

Paul is telling us that there's something significant in every family because God created it. God has placed his imprint on that family. Now, if we don't have a relationship with God we can't achieve his purposes for our family. We can never avail ourselves of the resources that God has to help our family. The goal that God has set for our families is beyond our reach. However, the Holy Spirit can help us as he comes to live within our hearts and our homes.

The good news is that God is in the business of saving families. God does not just call individuals to himself, he calls entire families to follow him. When the Philippian jailer became a believer, his whole family joined him and was baptized. Perhaps you need to come to God as a family, to make a fresh start as husband and wife, to make a new beginning as parents and children, to take a stand for God together.

God has blessed you so you can bless one another in your family. He's patient with you so you can be patient with each other. He's forgiven you so you can forgive each other. He loves you so you can love each other.

Perhaps you're going through a difficult time at the moment. God can help you through it. Maybe the tension in your home is unbearable. God can fill your home with his peace. Perhaps there's no real communication. God can touch your heart and get you speaking to one another again. Perhaps the flame of love is burning dim or has gone out altogether. God can strike another match.

Here's my prayer for your family:

> *Father, we thank you that you created families as the original building block of society. We recognize that Satan's greatest desire is to destroy our families. We ask that you renew our love and our trust for one another. May we be able to change the name of our house to "Bethel," the House of God, because you live there. Thank you for our spouse, our children, and our parents. May our families reflect your glory, reveal your character, and realize your purposes. In Jesus' name, Amen.*

Chapter 37

For Fast Relief—Take Two Tablets

John
March 2000

A few months ago I was listening to a commentator lamenting the fact that the Ten Commandments are no longer posted in our public schools. He equated their absence with the decline of American society, blaming everything from road rage to the Columbine tragedy on the disappearance of the two tablets that Moses brought down from Mount Sinai.

It is easy for evangelical Christians to get fired up at the idea of placing the Ten Commandments in every courtroom, school and public building in the United States. But shouldn't we first start at home? As I was listening to this silver-tongued speaker, I reflected that I have never seen the Ten Commandments displayed in a Christian home. I have spoken in several Christian schools but I have yet to see the Ten Commandments on the walls. I cannot even recall seeing the Ten Commandments in an evangelical church. Now to be fair, the Anglicans are very good about this. Nearly every parish church in England has the Ten Commandments on display somewhere in the sanctuary, but I have never seen them in a Baptist church, including the churches I have served as pastor. That struck me as wrong, so I made arrangements for the Ten Commandments to be hung in the entrance to our church. Because we are people of grace, as well as law, a matching set of the Beatitudes will hang beside it.

The Ten Commandments were originally given by God to Moses as described in Exodus 20. They are repeated in Deuteronomy 5:6-21 as the Hebrew people are about to cross into Canaan. Once they reached the other side of the Jordan River, the Israelites would be in territory where Baal worship was widespread. The commandments are God's clear warning about four common forms of idolatry: the worship of self, power, sex and things.

I believe the Ten Commandments are arrestingly relevant for our own time because they teach us that spiritual obedience must have priority over self; that social compassion must transcend personal lust for power; that moral values are more important than sexual satisfaction and that eternal realities are more satisfying than material things.

The Ten Commandments are also astonishingly comprehensive. They tell us how to have the right attitude toward our Maker (no other gods), toward ourselves (the importance of rest), toward children, employees and even animals (the Sabbath commandment), parents (honor father and mother), our partner in marriage (do not commit adultery) and the right attitude toward those around us (don't covet or give false testimony against your neighbor).

Although the commandments are regarded as antiquated and restrictive prohibitions in our permissive society, they are ignored or rejected at our spiritual and moral peril. Walking along the rugged coastline of central California you sometimes see the sign, "It is dangerous to stray from the path." That sign does not limit our freedom—it secures it. Several people have died because they have chosen to ignore the warnings of the sign. The passage in Deuteronomy 5, which expounds the commandments, also contains the warning, *Do not turn aside to the right or the left. (Deuteronomy 5:32)* Rather, we are to walk in all the ways that the Lord our God commands us. One of the pictures behind the Hebrew word for law (Torah) is that of a direction or a path to walk on.

In June 1995 at a sale at Christie's in New York, the Ten Commandments used in the Charlton Heston movie produced by Cecil B. DeMille sold for $72,000. We too need to value these laws highly. God has given them to us for our protection. Let us thank God that we are free to hang them in our homes and in our churches. But most important of all, they need to be hanging in our hearts.

Chapter 38

Serving the Lord When You Are Grieving

Gretchen
May 2000

Last spring my mother-in-law, Charlotte, suffered a stroke. She never regained consciousness. Although John and I were there within 48 hours we were neither able to speak with her nor see any sign, really, that she knew we were there.

After a day in the hospital there came a moment when I was alone with her. John and his brother Simon had gone for a cup of tea. I felt an overwhelming sorrow at the loss of this women who had been such a powerful example in my life. The tears flooded over me, and as I sat holding her hand I was audibly crying in the way that you only do when you've reached the end of your rope. Just then Charlotte's hand tightened on mine and her thumb began stroking my hand. For many minutes the rhythmic movement continued. They told us that the only part of life Charlotte had was in the lower brainstem—that she was beyond thought and life and anything except respiration. But the Lord permitted this small moment of seemingly deliberate comfort for me as for the last time I felt some spark of life in her.

When you are grieving, the smallest things bring hope. In fact it is precisely this sharpening of focus that the Lord wants us to observe. When we are grieving we notice the created world around us even as people recede into a blurry background. We can have a nearness to God that is unattainable by any other means. We have a power of example through godly suffering that never could be given by less dramatic circumstances.

It is when we pick ourselves up and proclaim the goodness of God when we have every human right to hate him, people listen. They respond. They think that a God who can seem loving in such a situation must be a God to be reckoned with.

There are some practical things that we can do to overcome grief. Many have found help in beginning something new, making a fresh start. If the old patterns, the old music, the old habits bring fresh grief, then it's time to make a deliberate effort to start new traditions that alleviate, rather than agitate our grief.

After the loss of a loved one, some have found comfort in wearing or carrying something that belonged to that person. I began wearing my mother-in-law's ring after her death. She gave it to me three years ago and I had not so much as put it on. She wore it because it reminded her of the original owner, a maiden aunt in the generation above her. I found myself wearing it constantly after Charlotte's death, at least until a jeweler told me that if I wanted it to last for my children I shouldn't wear it out by wearing it daily. I was interested to read in grief literature that I had unconsciously hit upon one of their recommendations—to wear or carry something belonging to the loved one.

Grief has its requirements and its patterns. It cannot be scheduled into a one-week compassionate leave. In some cases, grief is just getting started after a few months when the shock wears off. It is often the worst ten months to a year after the loss. Its timetable cannot be hurried nor can the work of grief be bypassed or hastened. You ignore grief at your peril.

Grief is often circular rather than linear. You think you have passed a certain milestone and won't have to pass it again, but suddenly there it comes looming up again in front of you. Often the same landscape must be traversed many times while coming to terms with the loss of a loved one. C. S. Lewis noted this in his classic book *A Grief Observed*. This can be disconcerting because it may appear that we are slipping back or losing ground.

When you are grieving it is important to remember that your brain is running on half strength or less. Simple decisions become difficult to make. You may find yourself uncharacteristically disorganized, slow or indecisive. However, most of us can run our lives quite adequately with half a brain for at least a period of time. It is marvelous how the Lord can gently use us simply as examples to others of how we handle grief. We have the attention of others in a way that is not normally available. Our words and actions carry weight and power. We have the chance to minister to others simply by grieving in a godly way.

Your life may have been untouched by grief to this point, but eventually all of us will lose a loved one near to us. Legitimate grief also occurs, I believe, when someone moves out of our lives, or a relationship is lost to us by means other than death. I have observed my daughter grieving over the loss of the dear friendship of the McNicol girls following their move to Pennsylvania. We can help those around us who are grieving through change and loss, as well as during the more obvious grief following bereavement.

158

Last summer I was introduced to the Seasons Hospice and to a woman named Nancy who was dying of breast caner. By the time I met Nancy she was in the end stage of her disease. When I first met her she could not speak, or only utter a word or two at a time. The cancer had spread to her brain and interrupted normal thought. Despite this, her eyes were tremendously expressive. At each visit I explained who I was, held her hand, spoke with her briefly and asked her permission to pray. Usually she nodded yes and smiled.

I continued to visit Nancy. I usually rode my bike and so would arrive hot and sweaty. The contrast between my aliveness and mobility and her progressive immobility was painfully great. I spoke to her about the unfairness of me being out in the world and her lying in her bed of pain. The contrast was made even greater when I discovered that Nancy was only about nine years older than me.

One night, to my amazement, I heard her conversing in a high-pitched, frantic voice. I thought someone was in the room but there was no one there—no one except Nancy and the shadowy companions of her mind. She was afraid. She was calling for her brother to rescue her from something only she could see. I talked to her about not needing to fear when Christ was in the room. I prayed again for her and kissed her hand. I rode away with a desperate feeling of not being able to do anything. I have no idea whether my companionship and prayers were welcomed by her.

Nancy died while I was away for two weeks. To watch someone dying little by little is an appalling sight. It brings home the evil nature of the death of the body, and makes us rail at the unfairness of premature loss of life.

Death is evil. It is an evil byproduct of the fall of man. One of the greatest comforts we have in Christ is that death is not the end. For the believer, there is life untouched by pain and disability, by sorrow or wretchedness, in heaven. Losing someone we love very much should give us insight into what it cost God to give up his own Son, not grudgingly or by accident, but willingly, in order to achieve the greater good of redemption for us all.

Chapter 39

A Tail of Two Kitties
John
September 2000

Charles Dickens was right. Life is made up of the best of times and the worst of times. September 12 belonged to the latter. We put our cat to sleep. Actually, Gretchen took her to the vet. I didn't have the courage but masked it by explaining that if the children were to resent us for the rest of their lives, there was no point in ruining their relationships with both parents.

Black Kitty had eked out her nine lives over a period of 20 years. It seemed strange to come home at the end of the day to a catless house. Not that she ever came bounding up to meet me. For the last few years she slept for 23 hours every day. It was what she did the other hour that got her into trouble. In her dotage she became more and more barmy. She couldn't remember the location of her food so we often had to carry her to her bowl. More alarmingly, she couldn't remember the location of the litter box and so she left fragrant reminders of herself all over the house.

She was rapidly ruining all the furniture. One of our less subtle elders commented that the house smelled like a zoo. Another thoughtful member gave us a gallon of odor remover. With the combined efforts of the cat, dog, guinea pig and rabbits I found myself spending more and more time outside in the fresh air.

We carefully planned the funeral. I dug a hole in the woods and made a cross, inscribed with her name and dates. I gathered the children for one last touch of her thick coat and then laid her in the ground and filled in the hole. I suggested that we sing the hymn "All Creatures of Our God and King" but the children gave me that "Daa... d!" look and I realized it would be a solo. Instead, I launched into the eulogy explaining that 20 years ago some dear friends of ours in Los Angeles had a beautiful Siamese cat. One night she got out and met the local tom with the result that ten playful kittens were born. The lady of the house wore long dresses. As she walked by, the kittens would leap for the hem of the skirt and hang on while she went about preparing dinner. It was an extraordinary sight to see half a dozen kittens dangling from her garments like some peculiar fashion statement from PETA. In a fit of generosity Mr. and Mrs. Hadley presented us with two of these kittens. There was no cost for the cats, but we didn't stop to think about the $10,000 we would spend over the next 20 years in food, vet bills and cat sitting.

We had no children at the time so the kittens became a substitute. We had louvered windows that they loved to climb. At times their weight would tip the louvers, trapping them between the screen and the now closed windows. We returned home to find the house filled with anguished mews.

The first item of business was to choose names. We tried Luther and Calvin, Spurgeon and Spinoza, Whitfield and Wesley but it made no difference. The cats came when they wanted to and ignored us the rest of the time. So we gave up on names and simply referred to them as Black Kitty and Grey Kitty. Periodically they would get the "rips" when they would rush around the house for ten minutes chasing each other and tumbling over furniture. No amount of shouting would make them stop. Then suddenly, at some unseen signal, they would come to a screeching halt and act as if nothing had happened.

As a result of being burglarized three times in three months we moved to another house about a mile away. I was worried the cats might return to their old home. I had heard that if you put butter on their paws they would lick it off, associate it with pleasure, and decide to stay at the new location. So out in the backyard I smeared butter all over their feet. This worked well and they immediately rushed into the new house leaving greasy footprints all over the beautiful carpet. Both were spectacular hunters. Each could catch a bird in flight. Lizards had no chance and even the large rats that lived in the palm trees were gamely attacked. When these were caught they were brought inside and presented to us. The problem was that the rats were not always dead. At a delightful dinner party a horrified guest looked over to see a crippled rat, bleeding profusely with intestines trailing, lurching toward her.

On another occasion we came home to find a large rat sitting on a picture frame four feet off the ground. Underneath, Black Kitty was licking her lips in anticipation. The rat had been brought in and somehow escaped the grasp of its tormentor. It had run up the wall for refuge and now was trapped. I felt so sorry for the rodent that I put it in a bucket and released it outside feeling that it had suffered enough.

One day, Black Kitty disappeared and did not return. I went around the neighborhood shouting, "Kitty, Kitty, Kitty," feeling an idiot. Five days later she came shuffling back. She was badly bruised and beaten up and her tail was broken. The vet said he had to remove the tail or it would die and drop off. Until that time the two cats had always slept together and were inseparable. When Black Kitty returned tailless, Grey Kitty did not recognize her sister and would hiss and spit. She clearly felt her elegant tail made her superior, while Black Kitty from that moment on was often mistaken for a Manx cat.

The two cats survived the move to Minnesota in 1989 traveling in the cargo section of the plane. We were house sitting for the Rieglers and so Patti and Marty Gloff kindly said they would look after the cats for six months until our new house was built. We moved in November and the snow came a week later. The cats were mystified by this white stuff and refused to go out in it for the rest of their lives. Grey Kitty, who had survived all the traffic in Los Angeles, managed the extraordinary feat of being run over in front of our house, although in those days only one car a day drove by. This left Black Kitty in charge. We thought she was failing five years ago but then we got our Border Collie, Lacey, and Black Kitty found a new lease on life. She thoroughly enjoyed tormenting the dog, which lived in mortal fear of her. We are convinced this is why she lived so long.

As I shared these thoughts with the children standing around her grave I reflected on all the joy that cat had brought us. In a very real sense she was a gift from God, for God is the giver of every good and perfect gift.

Paul tells us that God has given us all things richly to enjoy. That certainly includes the members of the animal kingdom he brought into being on the fifth day of creation. God has also given us the capacity to love and care for our pets. They comfort those that are lonely. They teach children how to be responsible for another living thing. They forgive immediately and don't hold grudges. They are part of what theologians refer to as "common grace," those gifts from God that are not dependent on our faith, or lack of it, but are simply an evidence of his mercy to all who have eyes to see.

Poor Gretchen was in such a state at the vet's that they sent her a sympathy card informing us that Black Kitty was waiting for her on a rainbow bridge in some sort of feline paradise. However, I don't expect to see Black Kitty in heaven, not because she failed to put up her paw in a Billy Graham Crusade, but because she is not an eternal creature. Only human beings are created in God's image with a soul. We uniquely, of all God's creation, will live forever. We alone are redeemed by the blood of Christ. Black and Grey Kitty were part of this wonderful transient world that is passing away.

So we concluded our memorial service by thanking God for the gift of Black Kitty and the happy memories we have of her sitting on our laps kneading our legs while purring at the top of her lungs. I confess I shed a tear. We go back a long way. I'll miss her. To cheer myself up I began to whistle Cecil Alexander's lovely children's hymn:

All things bright and beautiful,
All creatures great and small,
All things wise and wonderful,
The Lord God made them all.
He gave us eyes to see them,
And lips that we might tell
How great is God almighty,
Who has made all things well.

164

Chapter 40

Walking in Difficult Places

John

September 2000

Next Sunday the leadership of this church is going to ask you to walk in difficult places. It will involve changes and disruptions for all of us because we are now moving to three morning services and three education hours. This means that we are all going to have to change our routines and come to church earlier or later.

Some adult classes will cease to exist. This is a painful transition because some members of these classes have known each other since high school. In January we will no longer have Sunday evening First Alive services.

Some are asking, "Why do we have to do this? So many things in my life are changing that I can't control. I had hoped that at least my church would provide security. Why can't I meet with the people I have grown to love and appreciate? Why does our group have to be disrupted? Why do I have to choose between Adoration Service or Celebration Service worship formats?"

I can understand these questions because I have been asking some of them myself.

Now what I have to do when I am facing a challenge in my life is to put it in a theological context. I try to understand what God thinks of the matter and what he is saying to me. Many of our young people wear bracelets or buttons that say WWJD? What would Jesus do? That is a good reminder to all of us. So this morning I want us to examine the incident found in Matthew's gospel, Chapter 14 verses 22-36.

In this chapter we read about Peter walking in a most unusual and difficult place. He goes walking on the Sea of Galilee during a storm. Now the Sea of Galilee is normally peaceful. It is not really a sea but a lake.

The Sea of Galilee is in the north of Israel. It is about 13 miles long and 7 miles wide. It is 680 feet below sea level. Cool air currents come down from Mount Hermon and collide with the hot air above the lake causing violent storms.

The disciples left Jesus in the evening to cross to Capernaum on the other side of the lake. However, a storm came up and they were unable to make progress. Their boat was small and it appeared it would soon be swamped by the waves.

They were very frightened. It was quite probable that this took place in April and there was a full moon peeping through the clouds. They had been rowing for over six hours and getting nowhere because the wind was against them. Suddenly, walking towards them across the lake, comes Jesus.

Now they weren't men of science, but they did know that people can't walk on water. Therefore they assume that the person was a ghost. They are very much afraid. But Jesus draws near and speaks to them.

Peter is so relieved to see Jesus that he leaps into the lake and begins to walk toward his master. He is doing fine but suddenly he begins to sink. He is wearing his long fisherman's robes. It would be impossible to swim in those garments. It appears that the waves will envelop him and he will be drowned, but at the last moment, Jesus rescues him and puts him back in the boat.

There are four lessons I have found in this narrative. Perhaps you can find more. I believe they can help us as we step out of the security of our boat as a church and as we walk in difficult places as a fellowship.

The first is that the disciples were in their predicament by divine appointment. There was nothing accidental about this. Jesus had sent them into this very situation. The earlier part of this chapter describes the feeding of the 5,000. It had been a wonderful time of encouragement. It was natural that the disciples would like to stay and bask in the glow of this moment but we read:

> *Jesus made the disciples get into the boat and go on ahead of him to the other side. (Matthew 14: 22)*

Reading between the lines we get the idea that the disciples didn't really want to go, but Jesus made them. Verse 23 says: *he had dismissed them.*

They are there on the lake by divine appointment. The eternal Son of God has placed them in that situation because he wants to teach them. He wants to test their faith. He wants to increase their trust.

At First Baptist Church we are in our present predicament by divine appointment. Every week we ask God to guide us. We pray that he will keep us in the center of his will. We ask that he will show us the way he wants us to go.

And we have rejoiced in his blessings. We are grateful for the singles and families he has sent us. It is not great programming or great preaching or great people that have filled this church it is a great Savior. People have come to him and the result is that our children's rooms are filled and our youth rooms are filled and on many Sundays there is not much space in one or the other of our morning services. And so we share something in common with those disciples out on the lake. We are in our predicament by divine appointment.

Not only had Jesus sent his disciples but Jesus also sees his disciples. In Mark's account we are told:

> *He saw the disciples straining at the oars, because the wind was against them. (Mark 6:48)*

I don't know whether Jesus saw the disciples because he was standing on a cliff top or whether he saw them in his mind's eye as he was praying. I think the latter is more likely. Jesus knows all about us. Jesus knew the needs of his disciples on Galilee he knows the needs of his disciples at First Baptist Church.

And knowing their needs he goes to them:

> *During the fourth watch of the night Jesus went out to them, walking on the lake. (Matthew 14:25)*

For Jesus who created the seas it was perfectly easy to walk over their waves. This is encouraging for us. There is nothing created which is not under Christ's control.

Jesus may allow his people to be tossed to and fro by storms of trouble. He may come to their aid later than they wish not drawing near to the fourth watch of the night. Never let us forget that winds and waves and storms are all Christ's servants. They cannot move without Christ's permission:

> *Mightier than the thunder, of the great waters, mightier than the breakers of the sea, the Lord on high is mighty. (Psalm 93:4)*

Why did Jesus walk on the water? To show his disciples that the very thing they feared, the sea, was only a staircase for him to come to them. Often we fear the difficult experiences of life such as surgery or bereavement only to discover that these experiences bring Jesus Christ closer to us. Some time between 3 and 6 a.m. Jesus approached them and calmed them down with these words:

> *Take courage! It is I. Don't be afraid. (Matthew 14:27)*

What a tremendous relief. They realize they were not on their own. They hadn't been abandoned. Jesus was with them. They heard his familiar greeting, *Don't be afraid.*

So it is with us. The Son of God, who knows all about us, comes to us and says, "Take courage. Don't be afraid. I am with you." That changes everything. It is no longer a nightmare but an adventure. We will never find ourselves in a place where Christ cannot find us. The storm is never so severe, the night never so black, and the boat never so frail that we risk danger beyond our Father's care.

Jesus was praying for the disciples while they were on the lake. He is doing the same for us. Jesus Christ is in heaven:

> *making intercession for us. (Romans 8:34)*

Peter left the boat because of the command of Jesus. Good old Peter sees the possibilities. He never wants to miss out on an experience. He might lag behind at times but at least he follows. Here's a chance to try something new. Walking on Water 101. He says, "I want to try that." And Jesus issues a one word invitation, *Come.* Come is a word we often hear from the lips of Jesus:

> *Come unto me all you that are weary and heavy laden and I will give you rest. (Matthew 11:28)   Come, follow me. (Mark 1:17)*

The final appeal of the Bible is:

> *The Spirit and the bride say, 'Come!' Let him who hears say, 'Come!' Whoever is thirsty, let him come. (Revelation 22:17)*

That one word *come* from Jesus was enough to get Peter to jump out of the security of the boat into the adventure of the sea.

We see here the extraordinary power that Jesus can bestow on those who believe in him. Simon Peter leaves the ship and walks on water like his Lord. This shows us what great things our Lord can do for those who hear his voice and follow him. It enables them to do things they would have thought impossible, and carries them through difficulties and trials that otherwise they would never have dared to face.

We need fear nothing if we are on the path of duty. Jesus promised:

> *I tell you the truth, anyone who has faith in me will do what I have been doing. He will do even greater things than these. (John 14:12)*

We too are leaving the security of our present structure. We are going to walk in difficult places because the Lord Jesus has said, *come.* He says "come" and "trust me." He says "come and grow." He says, "come and help me gather in the lost sheep."

So rather apprehensively we are jumping out of the boat and doing something this church has never really done before: holding three morning services, going to elective discovery classes, and starting a café. All this because we have heard the Master say *come*. We are doing it because we want to share that invitation with the people of this community who don't yet know Jesus, who have never experienced his grace, who have no assurance that if they were to die today they would be with him in heaven.

We get into trouble when we focus on the problems. Initially, Peter did very well. Defying the laws of buoyancy, he began to walk on the water and he came toward Jesus. We can imagine his exhilaration and the astonishment of the other disciples as they watched him. No human being had ever done this before. Peter is reveling in being the first one.

Things are going fine as long as Peter has his eyes on Jesus. But then something terrible happens. He takes his eyes off of Jesus and he starts looking at the waves. They are huge, white capped and dangerous. He is an experienced fisherman and suddenly it hits him, "What am I doing? I don't belong here." As he focuses on the problems he begins to sink.

I confess that I can imagine all sorts of problems as we leave the security of our boat. What if nobody comes to one of the three services? What if people stop attending discovery classes altogether because they don't like the changes? What if we can't fit everything into an hour and five minutes? What if my voice doesn't hold up for three services? What if enough people don't volunteer to help in all these new positions that we have created? We can look at these problems and begin to sink. Or we can look at the Lord Jesus and say:

> *I can do all things through Christ who strengthens me.*
> *(Philippians 4:13)*

Peter got in difficulties because he looked at the problems, but he was bright enough to realize that even in his difficulties there was a solution to his sinking feeling. So he cried out, *Lord, save me!* And immediately Jesus reached out his hand and caught him.

Now there are two ways to look at this incident, and our interpretation says something about our personality. Some would say, "Peter should have stayed in the boat. Men were never meant to walk on water. He nearly lost his life by walking in difficult places."

Others would say, "Ah yes, but what an experience Peter had. He could have kept his sandals dry, but he is the only man ever to have walked on water." It is far better to try and fail then never to try at all.

In church life we must be willing to fail. If we don't fail from time to time we are not trying hard enough. If we just stay within the safety of the boat and do those things that we know can be done, our faith will never grow. We need to jump out of the boat understanding that there will be times when we will sink. Perhaps in time we will look back and say, "This experiment didn't work. We'll have to do something else." That's all right. At least we tried. And if we get in difficulties we can always shout, "Lord, save me!" That is a cry that God will always answer. There are some people who struggle in their understanding of what it means to become a Christian. It is really very simple. Becoming a follower of Jesus is simply recognizing our predicament and saying, "Lord, save me!"

From time to time in our Christian lives we find we are sinking and we have to shout, "Lord, save me!" It doesn't mean we were disobedient. Peter was not being disobedient. Jesus had told him to come. Difficulties and obstacles don't mean that we are automatically on the wrong track. They can mean we are on the right one. But we are still sinking and we need to cry out, "Lord, save me!"

Walking in difficult places gives Jesus the opportunity to demonstrate his power. The disciples could have played it safe. They could have stayed on the shore. Peter could have played it safe. He could have stayed in the boat. Had they done so, they would have missed the incomparable privilege of witnessing the power of Jesus. There are a lot of Christians who are bored silly with their faith because they never leave the shore and they never leave the ship. They never place themselves in a position where their faith is tested.

It is one of the reasons I encourage people to join a mission team. You are placed in positions that require reliance on God's power. You are asked to do things on a mission trip that you wouldn't be asked to do if you stayed at home.

I remember sitting in a church in St. Petersburg, Russia. I had arrived there five minutes before the service started and had met the pastor. I was simply there to observe a Russian service of worship. To my amazement, I heard the pastor announce they had a guest of honor who was going to preach and would the Rev. John Steer please step forward and give his message.

I had not anticipated that. I hadn't talked with the interpreter. Things like that don't happen in First Baptist Church. In the 30 seconds it took me to walk from my seat to the pulpit, I prayed harder than I have ever prayed before. And it all worked out fine. I learned something that day about God's power to put words in my mouth in a foreign church.

We are walking into the unknown on Sunday mornings and Sunday evenings. We are walking into the unknown with a building plan that is being developed by our Building Committee.

Later this month we have a consultant coming to meet with our church leadership (and anybody else that is interested) to help us create a strategy for building up God's people and reaching our community for Christ. We have never done anything like this before. That is exciting because it keeps us off balance. It gives us a chance to trust God and to listen to his voice. It is good to walk in difficult places because it gives Jesus the opportunity to demonstrate his power.

We see what he did here in this chapter. First, he called Peter. He says to him, *You of little faith, why did you doubt?* (verse 31) It is silly to doubt when you have got the creator of the world with you…the one who created the sea in the first place…the one who created you, Peter, and has your life in his hands.

It is silly to worry about our church when it is the creation of Jesus. After all he has said:

> *I will build my church and the gates of hell will not prevail against it. (Matthew 16:18)*

Second, he calmed the sea. We read, *The wind died down.* (verse 32) And so dramatic was the change from the storm to the calm that those experienced fishermen in the boat immediately realized who Jesus was, declaring, *Truly you are the Son of God.* (verse 32)

This is the first time they had made that confession of the deity of Jesus Christ. It is only when we see the power of Jesus in our lives, by stepping out in difficult places, that we see the deity of Jesus Christ.

The pinnacle of this passage is the disciples' worship of Jesus. Walking in difficult places in obedience to Christ's command, results in a new experience and understanding of worship.

Walking in difficult places gives Jesus the opportunity to demonstrate his power. He called Peter. He calmed the sea, and he also cured the sick. With the lake now like a millpond, the disciples make their way to

Gennesaret and people brought their sick to him. Matthew tells us, *that all who touched him were healed.* (verse 36)

What a thrill for the disciples to witness those healings. But let us remember that the touch of Jesus has lost none of its ancient power. The reason we are taking our boat across the lake is for people on the other side. For there are a lot of sick people there, and they need to be healed. They are sick of their sin and they are sick of their fears and only Jesus can make them better.

If we are just thinking of ourselves we can stay comfortably in the boat. We have enough room for ourselves and our families. We can enjoy the fellowship we have here and keep everything the same. But we have to go to the other side. We must cross the lake because there are sick people who need the touch of Jesus.

Let us be thinking of them, not of ourselves.

Chapter 41

Fighting Fit at 50

John
October 2000

My thanks to all those who helped me celebrate my half century. Your sympathy cards, tombstones and caskets have been appreciated. I am grateful to my colleagues who all dressed in black and then surprised me in a restaurant, where I thought I was going to discuss church business with the chairman of the Elder Board.

I was overcome with emotion on my birthday morning to discover a cord of wood had been stacked behind my car during the night. Words can't describe the fun I had removing it before I could leave for church.

More excitement was in store when I arrived at my study and found that it was so packed with large boxes, balloons, golden geese and assorted other items. It took me over an hour to reach my desk. My chair had been removed and was discovered in the baptistery, but a wheelchair was thoughtfully put in its place. A large wooden coffin was astride my desk. As it was filled with sand, I could not move it. However, I spent a stimulating day on my feet using the top of the coffin as my writing area.

How I give thanks that I am only 50 once. My brothers, Andrew, from Hanoi, Vietnam, and Simon, from England called to congratulate me on entering geezerhood. They both kept their voices low so as not to unduly alarm me knowing that I have reached the age when loud voices could cause cardiac arrest.

I am sure all who made this a memorable occasion were simply celebrating the fact that 1950 was a most unusual year. It was the year that Mother Teresa began the Sisters of Charity. C. S. Lewis published *The Lion, the Witch and the Wardrobe.* Billy Graham launched *The Hour of Decision* radio program and a three-piece bedroom set at Sears cost $50.

However, as a theologian, I need to go to the scriptures to find out the significance of 50 years. The Bible has a lot to say about this subject. In Exodus 26 we discover that there were 50 loops on the curtain of the tabernacle. Fifty is clearly associated with drapes in scripture. The moral is that 50 is a time to pull yourself together.

Somebody kindly left Numbers 8:25 pinned to my door: *At the age of fifty they must retire.*

However, Numbers 4:35 states: *All the men from thirty to fifty came to serve.* So 50 is not a time to give up but to get going. In Ezekiel we discover that the measurements of the temple were 50 cubits, so 50 therefore is a holy milestone that anyone should be proud to pass.

The most important biblical contribution to our understanding of five decades comes from the book of Leviticus, which states:

> *Consecrate the fiftieth year and proclaim liberty throughout the land. The fiftieth year shall be a jubilee. (Leviticus 25:10)*

The implication is that 50 is an age of glorious freedom. I am discovering this to be true. I have found that I can get away with saying almost anything. People just shake their heads and say, "Poor old soul, he's just confused." So 50 *is* great! I don't feel any different than I did when I was 30 or 20 for that matter. To you the members of my dear congregation I say, "Grow old along with me, the best is yet to be."

Chapter 42

Four Ways God Answers Prayer

John
January 2001

We know that God doesn't always do as we ask but it is amazing how often he does. Again and again we will plead with God for something and receive it. Sometimes we didn't even expect to receive it so it was simply his love, rather than our faith, that moved God to action.

We are like a boy who asks for a mountain bike at Christmas, knowing quite well that it really is too extravagant. Yet, he still receives it because his parents want to please him. We are also like the believers in Jerusalem who were having a prayer meeting because their leader, Peter, had been imprisoned. I am sure they all prayed most fervently and had no doubt at all about God's power to work a miracle to secure his release. Then there was a knock at the door and young Rhoda slipped out to see who it was. It was Peter. Excitedly she ran back to give the news but was told in effect, "Don't be daft Rhoda, it can't be, Peter is in prison." Even when she insisted they still disbelieved her. But there was Peter, free. God had said yes.

God loves to say yes. He loves to give us what we want in order to help us achieve more than our resources will allow. He delights to comfort us in time of sorrows and to replenish our faith in times of doubt. Of course, he does: he loves us, he is our Father.

But sometimes our Father says "no." A few months ago I was speaking to a school assembly. It was the day after there had been a snow day and the school had been closed. I began by asking the students how many of them had prayed for a second snow day? Many raised their hands. I said, "Well God has answered you and his answer is no."

God is a loving Father. Fathers do not give their children everything they want. God is infinitely wiser than us, so his choices are always right. Our understanding is limited but God is omniscient and so there will be times when we ask for something in prayer and God has to say no.

That has certainly been true of my own life too. I can think of things I once wanted quite desperately and therefore prayed for earnestly, but which I now realize would have done me no good at all. My heavenly Father knew better and said no.

A well-known refusal of a prayer request in the Bible concerns the Apostle Paul's thorn in the flesh. Writing to the Christians at Corinth Paul said he had asked God three times to remove this problem, to no avail. After the third "no" Paul realized that there must be a reason even if he couldn't see it. He saw that God wanted him to have this problem to keep him from, *Being puffed up with pride.* Paul stopped asking, and accepted that God knew what he was doing.

Another example of God saying "no" relates to the prayer of Jesus in Gethsemane just before his arrest. The Bible makes it plain that Jesus was in extreme agony of spirit. He had reached his limits. He knew exactly what lay ahead of him: betrayal by one of his close friends, denial by another, and desertion by the rest. There would be the mockery of a trial, whipping, spitting and ridicule followed by a slow and barbaric death. Knowing all this, he asked his father if there was any other way by which he could carry out his task of redemption without having to go through the horror of crucifixion.

> *My Father, if it is possible, may this cup be taken from me.*
> *(Matthew 26:39)*

Yet he immediately added those words of humility and submission,

> *Yet not as I will, but as you will.*

Those words, spoken or unspoken, must always be built into every prayer. In this case God had to say "no" because there was no other way for us to be saved. The whole success of Jesus' rescue mission depended on his accepting the punishment for our sins on the cross.

Teaching us humility is only one of the many reasons that God may have to say "no." We may have to suffer so that we can minister to others who face a similar situation. God may have plans for us that we are not yet ready to receive. Giving us what we ask would get in the way of them.

Sometimes our feeling that God is denying us things is because we are prone to confuse needs with wants. In our acquisitive society few of us are immune to self-indulgence. God promises us daily bread but we are not satisfied with that. We would like a more attractive diet and we usually get it. In a world in which so many are malnourished we need to be reminded to trust our heavenly Father to provide what we need, and thank him on the many occasions when he gives us so much more.

There is another reason why God sometimes must say "no": our sin. We know that we are living a life that is displeasing to God. There may be open rebellion in some part of our life. Though we continue to go to church on Sunday, our prayer life becomes ineffectual. This is not because God is trying to punish us but because our sin has created a barrier between us and God. We cannot pray in the Spirit or in the name of Jesus. Our guilt, whether acknowledged, suppressed or excused, has broken our spiritual contact. We need to repent and forsake the sin before our peace with God is restored.

Sometimes God's answer to our prayer is "wait." We are often in a hurry to see results but God plans for eternity. That means that God often delays giving us what we ask until the moment he knows is right. The Jews prayed for their promised Messiah for centuries before Jesus came. God had not forgotten or stopped listening. He knew exactly what he was going to do and when he was going to do it.

There are other biblical prayers that still await fulfillment. The first is the prayer of Jesus for the unity of his church. Just before his crucifixion he interceded for his followers in these words:

> *I pray . . . that all of them may be one, Father, just as you are*
> *in me and I am in you. (John 17:21)*

Yet 2,000 years later the church is still torn by division. One day, Jesus' prayer will become a reality but in the meantime we must show a great deal of patience and understanding toward our fellow Christians.

The other unfulfilled prayer is found at the conclusion of Revelation. It is the Apostle John's desire that the second coming might not be delayed,

> *Come, Lord Jesus. (Revelation 22:20)*

The expectation of the early church was that the return of Jesus was imminent, but Jesus didn't return and still hasn't. The Apostle Peter had a word for those who were becoming impatient in AD 67. He suggested that the return of Jesus was being mercifully delayed to give people the opportunity to respond to the gospel.

One reason why an answer to our prayers may be delayed is that we are waiting for God to act when, in fact, he is waiting for us. What we must realize is that learning to wait on God and continuing to trust him may be part of the answer to our prayers.

Sometimes God asks us to do it ourselves. If we asked our human father to do something that we are quite capable of doing for ourselves, he would probably say, "Do it yourself." This is not because he is lazy or unhelpful, but because it is in our interest, as well as his, that we should do whatever we can. If we need help he will give it. If we don't know how to do something he will show us. A helpless child and an overindulgent father make a pitiful pair. In the same way our heavenly Father teaches us and helps us but wants us to be capable, willing, and hard-working.

We must never ask God to do what we should be doing ourselves although we will often ask him for guidance in how to do it, and perhaps for the grace and strength to preserve and carry it out.

Very often we need to put feet on our prayers. Let me give you an example. It is good to pray for revival but prayer and action must go hand in hand. There is no revival without prayer but prayer alone is not enough.

It is no use saying that there is nothing we can do but pray. Jesus, in the Great Commission, makes it very plain that the major task of his church is to preach, teach and baptize. If we don't do this it won't be done. As Arthur Pink has pointed out, "The church that does not evangelize will fossilize."

In 1792 William Carey began to stir the conscience of British churches to the need for overseas missions. He was told, "Sit down young man. When God chooses to convert the heathen he will do it without your help." We now know that God won't do it without our help.

There are some prayers that are simply inappropriate. To pray that we pass an exam falls into this category. If we worked hard we will pass. If we haven't, we don't deserve to pass. If God arranged for us to pass when we don't deserve to, it would be unfair on the others taking the exam. Because exams can be stressful, it is perfectly appropriate to pray that we will be relaxed and able to think clearly. That is very different from asking God to manipulate the exam results.

In a similar way I am not sure that we should pray that we will get the job for which we are being interviewed. The job should go to the best candidate, not the one who bends God's ear. If we find ourselves asking God to do what we should do for ourselves, we must expect his answer to be, "Do it yourself."

The Apostle James, in his open letter to all God's people, stressed the need for our faith to be demonstrated by action. He pointed out that faith that does not result in practical activity is not true faith. He demolished the idea of some people being spiritual while others are practical. There are many scriptural examples of prayer being linked to action. We know that the Apostle Paul prayed earnestly for many churches, but how much poorer would those churches had been if he had only prayed.

Sometimes I think God graciously says to us, "mind your own business," when it comes to some of our prayers. He is telling us "that is my affair not yours." This applies to events in the future, which are in God's hands. It covers people suffering from terminal illness. We sometimes tell God we want them healed, or if they are suffering greatly, we would like them to die quickly. Those matters are in God's hands and we should not tell him what to do.

We can pray for his perfect will to be done, and we can pray for the comfort and peace of the dying person but as Job says:

> *The Lord gives and the Lord takes away. Blessed is the name of the Lord. (Job 1:21)*

Sometimes we say God didn't answer. But yes he did. He always does. There is no such thing as unanswered prayer. We may not get what we ask, we often won't. We can be quite sure that God always hears our prayers. We can be equally sure that he deals with them. Our heavenly Father, unlike human fathers, is never too busy. It is inconceivable that God, who is a loving Father, would ever ignore a request from one of his children. God always responds when we pray but it is left to us to discern his response.

Maybe God has something to teach or there is something we must do. Perhaps our prayer was simply selfish. We were concerned with our wants and desires and not with God's will and purposes. Perhaps we were trying to use God as superman instead of asking him to use us. Perhaps we were putting ourselves at the center of our prayers instead of God.

Every prayer should bring us a little closer to God. He knows everything about us, but we constantly need to learn more about him. As we get to understand him better we will avoid treating God as an odd job man. Instead, we will use our prayer time to ask God to direct our lives, refine our natures, increase our knowledge of his truth, and use his power to bring help and healing to those who need it. Prayer is opening our thoughts to God and asking him to replace them with his. When we pray, it is important that we submit ourselves, not just our requests.

Chapter 43

This Is Why We Want to Grow

John

January 2001

As a church, we want to be on the move for God. We want to grow spiritually in grace and numerically as people come to Christ. However, there are consequences to growth. These consequences are not always positive. A recent survey revealed comments like, "Our church is getting too big, I don't know everyone anymore…The corridors are too crowded on Sunday." Some people have felt so uncomfortable with the size of our church that they have left to go to smaller churches.

Frankly, it would be nice to take things easy for a bit and enjoy the benefits of our hard work in the past. I will be honest with you, preaching three times on Sunday morning is a lot more tiring than preaching twice. I really miss greeting people between the services, now that there is so little time between the end of one service and the beginning of the next.

So why do we want to grow? This is an important question and I want to address it because it is vital that all of us understand why we are taking this direction in our planning. Growing will require sacrifices from all of us. We won't be willing to do that unless we are convinced of the necessity of this course of action. I believe there are three primary reasons why we want to grow.

First, because growth brings glory to God. Bringing glory to God is what this church is all about. In fact it is the reason we were created. The Westminster Catechism begins with these words, "Man's chief end is to glorify God and to enjoy him forever." God is glorified when we grow to become more like him. God rejoices when each of us becomes a Christian. God is glad when we obey him. God is pleased when we overcome temptation. God is thrilled when we use our gifts in his services. God is delighted when we witness to others. These are all evidences of spiritual growth.

The opposite scenario is also true. A lazy or uncommitted Christian brings sadness to God's heart. A disobedient Christian brings no joy to his soul. The same is true for a church that is not reaching out to its community, that is smug and satisfied, whose prayer life is declining, whose mission commitment is waning. That church invites the judgment of God, not his joy. Growth is the advance of the Kingdom of God on earth, whether in the life of the individual believer or in the size of God's family.

181

Second, because growth is what Jesus calls us to do. In Peter's confession of faith at Caesarea Philippi, Peter declared that Jesus was the Messiah, the Son of the living God and Jesus replied:

> *On this rock I will build my church, and the gates of Hades will not overcome it. (Matthew 16:18)*

Jesus wants to build his church, not to demolish it. He has promised that one day people from every tongue, tribe and nation will be gathered around his throne in heaven. For that to happen his church must grow, because there are still thousands of cultures without an established church. Jesus' vision of heaven will be incomplete unless his church grows. The lovely truth is that Jesus is growing his church all over the world. Jesus' stories illustrated growth. Remember the little seed that became a big tree, or the parable of the spectacular harvest that yielded a hundred times more than was sown.

The apostolic teaching also encouraged growth. Peter tells us:

> *Grow in the grace and knowledge of our Lord and Savior Jesus Christ. (2 Peter 3:18)*

Jesus is embarrassed when our growth is stunted. That is the clear message of Paul to the Corinthians. He said, we wanted to treat them as adults but they were only babies. Babies are beautiful, but it is a tragedy when they remain infants because their normal growth process is arrested.

So Jesus wants us to throw open the doors of this church and encourage others to come in. That is a very unselfish thing to do. Our natural tendency is to say, "Now that I'm in, let's close the doors."

I know of a church whose sanctuary was full. The Elders thought they should start a second service, but the congregation voted it down. They said "we don't want to become two congregations. We want to keep our church small so that we all know each other."

The fact is, few of us can know more than 60 people well. That church had already reached the stage where they couldn't all know each other. They were afraid of outsiders coming in.

Frankly, I wonder how people like that are going to enjoy heaven, where there will be billions of people standing around the throne. You'd better not be claustrophobic. I also wonder about people who leave a large church to go to a small church. Will they get upset if that small church grows? Will they then leave that church too?

Isn't it awfully arrogant to tell God what he is supposed to do with his church? Shouldn't we allow him to decide the size of the church, making sure that we don't put obstacles in his way?

The fact is, we are not a country club. We are a refugee camp. Country clubs put limits on membership, refugee camps don't. The refugees just keep coming looking for a place of safety and the camp bulges at the seams and spills over. Still the refugees come.

Third, because growth is why the Holy Spirit was given. Think of all the gifts the Holy Spirit gives us. Their purpose is to help us mature in Christ, so we grow up. We are given power to be witnesses in our world. We are given love so that we can care for people unlike ourselves.

We are to love the lost, not be angry that they act like sinners. Of course, they do! That is what they are. When Bartimaeus received his sight, he didn't go around hitting blind people. He was sympathetic. He had been a blind person himself. If we pray and ask God to use us; if we declare our home to be a lighthouse of the grace of God, we will discover that people who are not like us will start to come to First Baptist. We will have Somalians and Cambodians and Hispanics. That will be good because our church will become more like the church of heaven. You see middle class Caucasians will be in the minority in heaven.

We keep asking the Holy Spirit to bring revival and revival is another name for growth. It results in spiritual growth in our own lives and numerical growth when people come to a knowledge of the Savior. They are baptized and join the church. Only the Holy Spirit can make the church grow. Paul understood this. He wrote to the Corinthians:

> *I planted the seed, Apollos watered it, but God made it grow.*
> *So neither he who plants nor he who waters is anything, but*
> *only God, who makes things grow. (1 Corinthians 3:6-7)*

I am delighted that there are many people in our congregation who are allowing the Holy Spirit to use them to be a means of growth in the lives of others. For our part we want to grow as much as God permits us. We want to grow spiritually in grace and numerically as people come to Christ.

In our research, we have discovered that 37 percent of the people in Rochester don't have a church home. There are 100,000 people in the greater Rochester area. That means that 37,000 of them don't belong to any church whatsoever. We would be delighted if they came to our church, but there are lots of good churches in Rochester. We can rejoice when those churches grow as well. We never want to grow at the expense of other churches. We are not interested in stealing sheep from other folds. We want to grow because people who do not know Christ give their lives to him.

We know that followers of Jesus make good students, and good parents and good husbands and good wives. So the best thing we can do to improve life in Rochester is to encourage the citizens of Rochester to find life in Jesus.

So this is why we want to grow. Because growth brings glory to God, because growth is what Jesus calls us to do, and because growth is why the Holy Spirit is given.

Chapter 44

The Victory of Easter

John

April 2001

It is said that there are two things in life that are certain, death and taxes. This year as Easter falls on April 15th, those two things converge on the same day. This is the day on which we are to *render to Caesar the things that are Caesar's and to God the things that are God's.*

Though many have tried, no one has found a legal way of beating the tax system. Today, however, we celebrate the fact that the other certainty of life is beatable. Death not only can be defeated but has already been beaten as Jesus rose from the tomb on the first Easter Sunday morning. That is why we talk about the victory of Easter and the victory that Jesus gives.

Jesus gives us victory over sin. What is the problem with our world, the cause of the breakdown in relationships between countries, people and families? The Bible tells us:

> *All have sinned and fall short of the glory of God. (Romans 3:23)*

We don't take sin very seriously, but God says we should because the prognosis is fatal. The wages of sin is death. Sin is what has messed up our life. Sin is our rebellion against who we are. Sin is the reason we are haunted by dreams we can't fulfill and tortured by requirements we can't keep and driven by goals we can't reach. The Bible doesn't dwell on convincing us that we are sinners. We know that. Rather, it is filled with case histories of people who have been reclaimed because Christ has given victory over sin.

It is interesting to notice the people to whom Jesus appeared after his resurrection. There was Peter who denied him; James, his brother, who depreciated him; and Paul who despised him. These were sinners who met the risen Christ and his victory became theirs. When we walk with Christ we don't have to experience guilt. Four times in God's word the Bible says he forgives our sins, and he remembers them no more. God has thrown our sins into the sea of his forgetfulness and he has put up a sign, "No fishing here."

If Jesus gives us victory over sin it means that our lives do not have to be ruined by it. We can be redeemed from sin and have a new start.

That is why I love being a pastor. I get to see couples whose relationships have been wrecked by sin. They come to Christ for forgiveness and find that their love is deeper than it ever has been before. I see families turn their tension into tenderness when they experience the victory over sin that has been spoiling their home. I see individuals whose guilt is transformed into gladness when the risen Christ enters their lives. Becoming a Christian does not make a life problem-free but it does give us a power to face the problems and it gives us a purpose to our existence.

Jesus also gives us victory over time. Time is relentlessly pushing us toward the grave. There is nothing we can do to stop it, although some try. The town of Le Lavandou on the French Riviera recently passed a law barring any more burials in the town's cemetery because it is full. The law forbids people to die within the town limits if they do not own a cemetery plot. But the law hasn't stopped people from dying. Nineteen people have died without a plot. Their bodies are temporarily housed in the vaults of friends. There is only one law against dying that really works, and that is the law of the resurrection. Paul speaks of this when he writes:

> *The sting of death is sin, and the power of sin is the law. But thanks be to God! He gives us the victory through our Lord Jesus Christ. (1 Corinthians 15:56-57)*

From the day the first couple laid their son in a grave, people have dreaded death. It is the great mysterious monster whose long icy fingers make so many quake with fear. The unanimous witness of history is to the inevitability of death. Each succeeding generation has laid its dead in the grave. The Bible always links death to sin. The Bible says:

> *Sin entered the world through one man, and death through sin, and in this way death came to all men, because all have sinned. (Romans 5:12)*

Death stalks the rich and the poor, the educated and the uneducated. Death is no respecter of race, color, or creed. Its shadow haunts us day and night. We never know when the dreaded moment will come. We attempt to cushion the blow by taking out insurance and we have invented other devices to make our last days comfortable, but the stark reality of death is always there. We ask, "Is there any hope? Is there any way out? Is there a possibility of immortality?" It is not found in the laboratory or the classroom or the hospital, but rather in the empty tomb of Jesus. For many centuries the men and women in Europe looked out upon the sea that we call the Atlantic Ocean and they saw the sun shining upon the glittering surface of the waters. They wondered if there was anything beyond.

Their scholars said that you could sail off the edge of the world. There was nothing out there at all. In fact, inscribed on the coat of arms of the nation of Spain was its national motto: "Ne Plus Ultra." Meaning "there is nothing beyond."

One day Columbus went west off on the shining waters. He sailed off into the sunset, and people waited doubtfully. Finally, after a long time, the sails reappeared and the crowds were exultant. They shouted with joy when Columbus announced that there was a glorious paradise beyond the sea, rich beyond their dreams. The king of Spain changed the motto of his country so that it now reads, "Plus Ultra." Meaning "there is more beyond."

For many centuries innumerable people stood beside the dark hole that we call a grave watching the remains of their loved ones lowered into the earth. They wondered, "Is there anything beyond the dark waters of death?" Then one day a young explorer went west into the setting sun and descended into the blackness of the pit. He sailed off the edge of the world and crashed into hell and people waited doubtfully.

Finally, on the resurrection morning as the sun rose in the east, the Son of God stepped forth from his grave and declared, "There is something beyond. There is a paradise beyond your greatest expectations. And there is a heavenly father waiting with outstretched arms to wipe away every tear from your cheek."

In the great 15th Chapter of Corinthians Paul speaks about this victory over time. He says:

> *We will all be changed—in a flash, in the twinkling of an eye, at the last trumpet. For the trumpet will sound, the dead will be raised imperishable, and we will be changed. For the perishable must clothe itself with the imperishable, and the mortal with immortality.* (verses 51-53)

Because of Christ's victory, time is no longer our enemy but our friend. Instead of moving us toward the grave, it is moving us toward a time when in a perfect body we will live in a perfect place. There will be no more going to bed at night feeling guilty—there won't be anything to feel guilty about! There will be no more going to bed at night feeling hurt because no one will hurt us. We will never have another pain. We will be forever in a home the Word of God calls heaven—all this because of Christ's victory at Easter.

Jesus gives us victory in life. Some people think Christianity is something you get so you won't fry when you die. It is, and that is good. But it is more than that. Jesus gives us the best life we can live now. In the closing verse of the 1 Corinthians 15, Paul summarized the implications of the victory of Easter:

> *Therefore, my dear brothers, stand firm. Let nothing move you. Always give yourselves fully to the work of the Lord, because you know that your labor in the Lord is not in vain. (1 Corinthians 15:58)*

When I was 16 years old I attended a youth retreat with my brother lead by military officers. I think my parents thought we needed more discipline. One of them was a squadron leader in the Royal Air Force. One night he came up to our dormitory and he told us what Christ had done for him. He was one of the pilots in the elite flying formation team called the Red Arrows. He said,

> *Flying is great fun but I have found something even better. It is a relationship with Jesus Christ. It has transformed my life. And boys, it can transform yours.*

That night I gave my life to Christ. Nothing particularly dramatic happened: the earth didn't move and I didn't hear angels, but from that moment on God began to change me. Easter is about a powerful God at work for us and in us. Easter is about confident living forever for those people who link their lives to him. This victory that Jesus gives is real and tangible.

I once had the privilege of meeting Ugandan Bishop Festo Kivengere. He served when Idi Amin was president of Uganda. Idi Amin was in the habit of executing opponents by firing squad. He would command the population to come to a soccer stadium and witness the execution. Festo Kivengere tells of one such event on February 10th, 1973. A silent crowd of about 3,000 had gathered to watch three men be put to death. Festo had permission from the authorities to speak to the men before they died. The men were handcuffed and their feet were chained but when they saw Festo their faces lit up with joy. Before he could say anything, one of them burst out:

> *Bishop, thank you for coming. I wanted to tell you the day I was arrested in my prison cell I asked the Lord Jesus to come*

into my heart. He came in and forgave me all my sins. Heaven is now open and there is nothing between me and my God. Please tell my wife and children that I am going to be with Jesus. Ask them to accept him into their lives as I did.

The other two men told similar stories excitedly raising their hands, which rattled their handcuffs. Shots then rang out and the three men were with Jesus. However, their testimony touched the whole district. There was as upsurge of faith in Christ, reminding us to be joyful even in the face of death.

The victory that Jesus gives us means we can conquer our fears. Paul tells us:

> *For God did not give us a spirit of timidity, but a spirit of power, of love and of self-discipline. (2 Timothy 1:7)*

There is no fear when you walk closely with Christ. As a pastor, I have discovered that people are afraid of two things. They are afraid of dying and they are afraid of living. Jesus says, *don't be afraid, I am with you*. There is nothing you face each day that you and I together can't handle. God has given us a living hope by the resurrection of Jesus Christ from the dead. We can be conscious daily of Christ's victorious power working in us, for us, and through us. We can shout with the Apostle Paul, *Thanks be to God! He gives us the victory through our Lord Jesus Christ.*

The Easter message is not an announcement. It is an offer. Each of us must receive it and come to know Jesus as our Savior and Lord. Easter offers us victory over sin. We never have to feel guilty or afraid again. It offers us victory over time, for when we know Christ we are never really going to die. It offers us victory in life.

The resurrection of Jesus Christ is the primary truth of the Christian faith. It lies at the foundation of the gospel. Without a belief in the resurrection, there can be no salvation. The Bible says:

> *If you confess with your mouth, Jesus is Lord, and believe in your heart that God raised him from the dead, you will be saved. (Romans 10:9)*

Jesus said to Martha outside the tomb of her brother Lazarus:

> *I am the resurrection and the life. He who believes in me will live, even though he dies; and whoever lives and believes in me will never die. Do you believe this? (John 11:25)*

Chapter 45

Growing through Grief
When Everyone's Watching

Gretchen
June 2001

It took me 15 years to look again at the letters we received in the days following the death of our daughter, Kirstie, on May 3, 1986. Reading those cards brought back details I had forgotten: the way we taped them up in countless rows on the walls of our house and the sense of encompassing love we received from God's people…waiting for the mail each day…wanting to be strengthened by the comfort those letters contained.

I had forgotten that so many strangers wrote to us. From churches around the world we received letters that began "you don't know me, but I heard the news from…" and went on to weep with us. I had forgotten how many pastors wrote to tell us of their losses and grief.

When a pastor's family suffers, they are relentlessly in the public eye. How we face grief can strengthen or disillusion our flock. No one wants to become the object lesson for loss, but through our triumphant sorrow we teach far more than years of sermons and Bible studies.

John and I were married when I was 19 and he was 26. The first year of our marriage included John's call to the senior pastorate of Eagle Rock Baptist church in Los Angeles. After eight years, our congregation thought it was high time that we produced a baby. In 1985, our daughter Kirstie was finally born. Like most first-time parents we completely, hopelessly adored our baby.

When Kirstie was almost 16 months old, John and I took her for a bike ride. We rode to the Arroyo Seco in Pasadena—the natural canyon, near the Rose Bowl, that is the channel of the Los Angeles River. There is only a little water in it; it's a concrete, man-made corridor spanned by small bridges leading to bike paths on both sides. We stopped at a bridge to lift our bikes across the fence, taking Kirstie out of her bike seat. We debated briefly where to keep her while lifting the bikes. My side looked safer so I set her next to me on the bridge. It was fenced with a barrier that came up to her shoulders.

We were brand new parents. We didn't know about the startling advances in physical prowess that children make. Our tiny child pulled herself up over a barrier she shouldn't have been able to climb and pitched headfirst to the concrete 15 feet below while my hands were tangled in the bike I was lifting. As I lunged for her I was only a foot or two away from catching her as she fell.

John flung himself over the fence and into the channel while I screamed for help and ran to a nearby man in his car. He drove me to the closest fire station, where they had already mobilized rescue trucks from two stations. By the time the kind stranger returned me to the bridge a rescue helicopter was circling overhead and a crowd of stricken faces had gathered. I too leapt into the channel.

John had moved Kirstie out of the water and stood weeping and praying nearby. He didn't dare pick her up because of her obvious head injury— one side of her head was rapidly swelling and she was unconscious. I lay down on the concrete with my arm about her and began speaking to her. Paramedics soon sprinted down a ladder and began working on her. They cut off her clothes, leaving her naked in the chilly breeze. I didn't know that the hand movements she made, which I thought were signs of life, indicated severe brain damage.

We were only a quarter mile from one of LA's best trauma centers. I rode with her in the ambulance while John was left to deal with the police. We discovered later that we were being investigated for possible child abuse.

When we reached the hospital the team met us at the door and I was adroitly intercepted by a social worker. I was allowed to make some calls. Soon family and friends began to arrive at the hospital. The hours passed. We waited to see her. We hungered for news, not knowing if she was dead or alive.

Finally the chief neurosurgeon met with us, telling us that Kirstie's injuries were so grave that an operation was not possible. A team had put in a shunt to reduce the bleeding and pressure inside her head. Her skull had shattered and formed an enormous subdural hematoma. We asked about her chances. We were told that it didn't look good. When we pressed her, Dr. Egan said, "To a doctor, there are worse things than death. There is very little chance of her recovering any normal function."

Infuriated at being kept from my child for so long, I planted myself on the floor in front of the double doors to intensive care. Everyone who came or went had to walk around me. I begged each one, "When can I see my daughter?"

Four hours after the accident we were allowed to join her. She was on a tall table, constantly attended by a nurse and doctor. Her head was swathed; a pool of blood spread on the pillow behind her from the shunt and her face was grotesquely swollen. I counted eleven tubes in her little body. Blood ran in. Fluid ran out. I took her hand and began to talk to her, and there I stood for the next 15 hours. John and I watched as the numbers showing the pressure inside her head ran up and up and up. We knew that by this time many people were at our church praying for her life. There was a moment about midnight, while this prayer meeting was going on, that the numbers began to drop, and our hearts leaped with hope. But a nurse came in and recalibrated the machine, and the pressure rose unbearably again.

Around 5 a.m. I saw to my amazement that the sky was growing light over the foothills. To my utter astonishment the world was going on with its business. The sun was rising, as it does every day. Life was going on for everyone else. It seemed to me a profound statement that God's creation was bigger than the anguish in my life.

Two days after the accident, a brain function test was done to establish whether there was any blood flow. We had to grasp that the respirator was producing only the illusion of life in our daughter, who was brain dead. It was easy to tell our social worker that we wanted to donate Kirstie's organs in the hope that some other child's life would be spared. Because the transplant wouldn't happen until evening, we had to leave her hooked up to the tubes and apparatus, seemingly warm and alive. For the first time since her accident, I was allowed to take her in my arms to say goodbye.

So we said goodbye, to what appeared to be a living, breathing child, but who we understood was merely a shell or husk. The person we knew as Kirstie was already in the arms of Jesus in heaven, unknowing of her pain or ours.

People always say at death: Time heals. I can tell you that time doesn't heal, but time dulls. More importantly, time gives perspective. By surviving an experience like this, one understands that God is who he is and that he means what he says.

But death also brings fear, because you know how bad loss can be. For a brief period of time I felt invincible, afraid of nothing. After life returned to a degree of predictability and we had other children, the fear returned.

How could I face again losing someone I loved? With the death of a child, something breaks inside that is never mended in this life. Yet that cracked interior is what God fills with himself. Our weakness fills with his strength.

What we learned is, perhaps, little different than the insights of any bereaved parents. Yet to learn it under the unblinking lens of public scrutiny in the ministry raises the stakes somewhat. At its heart is the message you give to your people: faith works.

Suffering deepened our ministry. Our loss of a child profoundly changed our ministry. Prior to this point our lives had been smoothly successful. All sorts of good things had fallen into place for us in ministry, financially, in our happy marriage. Yet Kirstie's death and the church's close-up view of our grief bridged a gap we hadn't even realized existed. People were finally able to relate to us as fellow travelers and sufferers. Now they gave back to us. Many of our older saints had faced loss and had wisdom to share. Children comforted us with their simple faith in heaven. Kirstie's death transformed my teaching when I discovered the faith I'd been talking about had substance. And for all those times since when we've agonized with families over a loved one, our loss has made us empathetic with others who are suffering.

Suffering pulled us together. John and I were knit together in an immensely strong bond. Parents who lose children, especially under circumstances where blame could be given, often are driven to divorce or suicide. We both looked into the abyss during that first year, but by God's grace he used our pain to cement us closer. It was helpful to have such an understanding church. We both took off six weeks, spending a month in England, and then gradually resumed our duties, a life that would have been unthinkable had we not pulled together. People grieve differently. I wanted to hold her toys, smell her clothes, sit in her room. John immersed himself in work and hobbies. Nonetheless we clung to each other like drowning swimmers during the aftermath of her death. The knowledge of what often happens to parents upon the death of a child made us alert to the stresses for others in this situation.

Suffering's lessons aren't wasted. A child lived because Kirstie died. A year later, my pediatrician told me that Kirstie's liver was the only organ they were able to salvage. The young girl who received her liver was, at that time, alive and thriving. In those days transplantation for such young children was rarely done, but Kirstie's death saved a child's life.

194

God doesn't waste our life experiences. Having gone through organ donation made it easier for us to counsel people facing that decision at deathbeds. Years later, John was asked to serve on the board of LifeSource, the organ procurement organization for the upper Midwest. Now in his sixth year with LifeSource, John chairs that board. We've been able to comfort donor families through John's work with LifeSource —a window into the secular world of grief.

Suffering reminded me that God is sovereign. On that Sunday afternoon in the hospital I left Kirstie's room briefly. I went to a room by myself and wrestled with God. I prostrated myself before him in prayer, and I pleaded for the grace to accept his will. I remembered Christ in the Garden of Gethsemane, weeping drops of blood, but obediently doing what would glorify God. I understood in that moment a little bit of what it cost God to voluntarily give up his own Son for us. I never would have given up my daughter voluntarily. It was hard enough giving her up involuntarily. How extraordinary that God should care enough for us to send his son—his only child—to the cross. But I also glimpsed what it cost Christ to obey. And that moment was Gethsemane for me.

If we understand God's sovereignty before the crisis arrives, we will have comfort. Because God is sovereign in the giving and taking of life, we know peace rather than blame in a tragedy. In human terms John and I felt responsible for the loss of a life. But we understood that God is sovereign. The words of Psalm 139 were immensely comforting: *All the days ordained for me were written in your book before one of them came to be.* (verse 16) Although we each had to forgive ourselves, we readily forgave each other, understanding that God was sovereign in the number of days he gave to Kirstie. Agonizing about whether she should have worn her helmet, whether we should have stayed home from the bike ride, wasn't going to make a difference to the number of days God ordained for her before she was born.

This hard-won belief in God's ability to manage our lives convinced us of how important it is to teach God's sovereignty. How else can one bear suffering? Only by trusting in our good Sovereign God does it make sense.

Suffering taught us to receive. We were comforted by hundreds of cards and letters. We were given much more. There was $20,000 given to a memorial fund. We used the money to set up a medical outpost in Haiti. There was the comfort of friends and siblings who dropped everything to be with us—my fellow workers who donated pints of blood—my employers who covered every penny of medical costs, having the bills

195

sent to their office so I wouldn't have to see them. Our faithful church prayed for us day in and day out for years following Kirstie's death. These all loved us in practical and heartfelt ways. Pastors are used to giving. Suffering teaches us to receive.

Suffering taught me to love God's word. People were very kind in what they wrote and said to us. But nothing, nothing at all had power to make sense of our loss except what I read in God's word. I drank up scripture. I dreamed about it. I wore it as armor. What were only words before were now life to me.

Ever since, when I have been called to comfort the suffering, I carry scripture. I have gone bearing my Bible to a mother whose son didn't wake up one morning… to a daughter considering donating her mother's organs… to a friend miscarrying. Often God's word is the only thing that makes sense to a Christian who is suffering.

Suffering taught me to long for heaven. I spent years of my life thinking about heaven. The hardest question I had to answer was: How can Kirstie be happy in heaven if we're not there? After all, we were the most important people in her little life.

I suppose the answer lies in what we wrote on her tombstone: "We love you so much, honeybee; Jesus loves you more." Christian parents must understand that Jesus loves their child even more than they. And children love Jesus back. She is happy in heaven because she is with the one who makes her the happiest.

Heaven is also a place where, increasingly, we long to be because people we love are there. She may not have her parents, but there are her two grandpas, and her granny, and others who yearned over her. Death teaches us to love heaven. As the intervening years have taken three of our four parents, we begin to understand what a relief it is to finally reach heaven, a place of no tears. We must teach those truths to our people to prepare them for the time when they face illness and death.

We accept the fishbowl nature of ministry when we agree to the call. Like doctors at a teaching hospital, we have to learn to do everything, even grieve, under the inquisitive eyes of those we love and serve in order that they might learn. By laying our hearts bare at such a painful time, we permit the Holy Spirit to comfort not only us, but them.

Chapter 46

The Truth Is Out There

John
August 2001

None of us want our lives to be based on a lie. We want our existence to have meaning and significance, and for that to happen it must be based on truth.

When Thomas looked into the face of Jesus and pleaded, *Lord, how can we know the way?* (John 14:5) he was voicing the deepest need of the human soul. We yearn for direction. We long for happiness. Jesus' reply to Thomas provides the answer for all of us. Jesus said:

> *I am the way and the truth and the life. No one comes to the Father except through me. (John 14:6)*

I am the way so that you can be saved. By nature we are lost in a maze of sin. Isaiah tells us:

> *We all, like sheep, have gone astray, each of us has turned to his own way. (Isaiah 53:6)*

Jesus came into this world to seek and to save that which was lost. He is the way for us to be saved. In fact he is the *only way* to be saved. Some people in our pluralistic society find that offensive. They say it is too exclusive. They inform us that all roads lead to God. But that is not what Jesus taught for he goes on to say:

> *No one comes to the Father except through me. (John 14:6)*

Now this is a very clear declaration of what leads us to God and what doesn't. We need to face up to the implications. If we are trusting in anything else to get us to God we are traveling on the wrong pathway. There is only way to God and that is Jesus Christ. To those who would object that is narrow-minded, the gospels respond that the path of truth is always narrow.

C. S. Lewis made the profound point that instead of being angry that there are not many ways to God, we should be grateful that there is at least one. If you want to cross a river you only need one bridge. If you have a disease you only need one cure. The implication that only Jesus is the way to God is what drives our mission efforts. There are two marvelous implications of Jesus being the way for us to be saved. First, the way to God starts right where we are. We don't need to travel to the starting point. We don't need to find God, for God has found us.

197

Second, because Jesus is the way to God, we do not travel alone. A couple of years ago we were visiting some friends in Denver. I had asked for directions to their house but my friend said, "It is hard to find so I will meet you at the freeway exit and I will take you there myself." I was absolutely confident we would arrive because my friend knew the way. After all, he was taking us to his home. So is Jesus, and that is why we don't need to fear getting lost. He says, "I am the way to heaven. You take my hand. I will never leave you." Perhaps we say, "But I am still not certain?" It is a big thing to commit my life to Christ. There are so many groups claiming to be right. So Jesus continues: *I am the truth so that you can be sure.* The Apostle John loves this word "truth." He uses it more than any other gospel writer. For John, truth is the direct expression of God's reality. From the first verse of his gospel John stresses that we see what God looks like in Jesus. When Jesus declared, *I am the truth* he gave expression to one of the most profound concepts in scripture. He is drawing on the idea of the absolute truth about God.

Absolute truth is what Francis Schaeffer used to call, "true truth." Not just truth for you or truth for me, but absolute truth whether you or I believe it or like it: truth that will always endure, truth that will never change.

That is a difficult claim to make in our society because most people don't accept it. Pollster George Barna tells us that 67 percent of all adults do not believe there is such a thing as absolute truth. Seventy-four percent of non-Christians deny the existence of absolute truth and even 52 percent of those claiming to be born-again Christians believe truth is relative. The younger people are the more likely they are to reject the notion of absolute truth. Seventy-two percent of those aged 18 to 25 reject the notion of absolute truth.

This means that as Christians, we will be misunderstood and considered intolerant because our faith is based on the assumption that there is an absolute truth that is knowable. For the Christian, truth is embodied in the person and history of Jesus Christ. We must not be worried or surprised that the world does not know this. The Apostle Paul writes these stunning words in 1 Timothy 3:15:

> *I am writing you these instructions so that . . . you will know how people ought to conduct themselves in God's household, which is the church of the living God, the pillar and foundation of the truth.*

The supporter and protector of God's truth in the world is the church. The reason for this is that the church is the household of God and God is the truth. What he is, and what he says, and what he does, defines the truth. Those who submit to him and listen to him and live his way are the pillars of the truth.

This is one reason why God and his church are so unpopular. We represent absolute claims on people's minds and wills and emotions. If God exists, then we are not God. If God is true, then we cannot desire what is true. It is out of our hands. We have no say in it. No vote.

The universe is not a democracy. It is an absolute monarchy, and people don't like this. So what do they do? Paul tells us in Romans:

> *They exchange the truth of God for a lie, and worshiped and served the created things rather than the Creator who is forever praised. (Romans 1:25)*

Despite our rebellion against God's claim to be absolute truth, we still long for truth. We came from our maker with a desire for truth. When we meet Christ that yearning for truth is fulfilled, for Christ is the personification of truth. His word is the proclamation of truth. As the truth he cannot lead us astray, for that would deny his character. If there were other ways to God he would tell us. If there were other ways of living he would show us.

There are certain things in the Bible that we do not fully understand. This does not mean that they are not true. The problem is not with the Bible but with our lack of comprehension. As our ability to receive truth increases, the veil is lifted so none of us needs to commit intellectual suicide to be a Christian. We don't need to throw away our scientific training in order to follow Christ.

Walter Burke, the former general manager of space projects Mercury and Gemini and vice president of McDonnell Douglas Corporation teaches an adult class in his church. In an interview he declared, "I have found nothing in science or space exploration to compel me to throw away my Bible or to reject my Savior, Jesus Christ in whom I trust. The space age has been a factor in the deepening of my own spiritual life. I read the Bible more now. I get from the Bible what I cannot get from science, the really important things in life."

When Pontus Pilate interrogated Jesus before his crucifixion Jesus told him:

> *Everyone on the side of truth listens to me. (John 18:37)*

To this Pilate asked, *What is truth?* and immediately left Jesus' presence to address those who wanted Christ crucified. Pilate asked, *What is truth?* but would not stay for an answer. He was staring truth in the face, but he could not face up to it.

Ignatius Loyola, in his spiritual exercises written in the Sixteenth Century noted, "For it is not much knowledge that fills and satisfies the soul but an intimate understanding and relish of the truth." Jesus says *I am the truth* so you can be sure.

Jesus says *I am the life* so that you can be strong. This life of ours is quite a challenge and can be terribly brutal. It was for the disciples. Jesus had just told them he was going to die on a cross. They could not imagine living without him. It is into that context of grief and despair that Jesus says *I am the life*.

He is referring to his resurrection, that would prove that he was stronger than death—the greatest enemy we face. Jesus shares his resurrection with us so that we can be strong. It is his resurrection that gains us life and guarantees us life and governs our life and helps us to walk in newness of life.

Jesus offers an abundant life, a triumphant life, a life that can cope with every situation. That is not abstract theology, but practical reality. That sort of life is contagious. It is the kind of life the world longs to have.

Sir Henry Stanley, the man who found David Livingstone in Africa and lived with him for some time, gave this testimony:

> *I went to Africa as prejudiced as the biggest atheist in London, but there came for me a long time of reflection. I saw this solitary old man there and asked myself, 'How on earth does he stop here, is he cracked or what? What is it that inspires him?' For months after we met I found myself wondering at the old man carrying out all that was said in the Bible. Little by little his sympathy for others became contagious. My interest was aroused seeing his gentleness, his zeal and his earnestness. I was converted by him although he had not tried to do it.*

David Livingstone was living in the strength of the resurrection life of Jesus, and it showed.

There is a lovely development of thought in the pages of scripture concerning God's presence with his people. In the Old Testament we read that *God is for us* so David says, *I know God is for me. (Psalm 56:9)*

Later on we find that *God is with us.* For his name is *Emmanuel, God with us.* Finally we discover *God is in us.* For it is *Christ in you, the hope of glory. (Colossians 1:27)*

It is no longer, "The truth is out there." Rather the truth is now in us. For Jesus promised:

> *When he, the Spirit of truth, comes, he will guide you into all truth. (John 16:13)*

So in this extraordinary verse, Jesus tells us, *I am the way the truth and the life.* That claim met Thomas' most basic need and it meets ours too. We are surrounded with lies. Lies about what is important, lies about the origin of life, and lies about the non-existence of moral absolutes. But the truth prevails. This is wonderfully demonstrated in the lives of those living under Communism. They are repeatedly told there is no God. Yet God increasingly becomes more real to them.

Christians in China sing a song called "The Sky With No Fence." It tells of the hopes of the Chinese Christians meeting in secret. They pray for God's mercy to end the persecution. They look forward to the day when they can worship their Lord openly. They long for opportunities to fellowship with Christians of other lands and to bear witness for Jesus to the ends of the world.

The song goes like this:

> *We long for the day when every man sits under his vine,*
> *and every man drinks the fruit of his grapes.*
> *Like the sky with no fence, The good news to the world's ends.*

The good news is that Jesus said *I am the way and the truth and the life. No one comes to the Father except through me.* The implications are profound. *I am the way* so that you can be saved. *I am the truth* so that you can be sure. *I am the life* so that you can be strong.

Chapter 47

Are We Spiritually Ready?

John
September 2001

In the weeks leading up to the church vote on purchasing 60 acres for a new church campus, I heard the question, "Are we spiritually ready to take such a step?" It was raised at an Elder Board meeting, in private conversations and in a comment at the business meeting itself. It is a good question, and one I have spent considerable time pondering. Here are my reflections.

There are spiritual maturity tests that have been created. One might be given to a congregation. The difficulty with these tests is administering them, and what pass mark would be required? In the absence of such test I need to look for other, more general, indicators. I see that our attendance has risen by 16 percent in a year. Our giving has increased by 14 percent. Clearly people are both coming to church and supporting the church. First Baptist Church is on the grow.

There are other signs that indicate both spiritual hunger and concern for the "not yet Christian." The Women's Bible Study had a record attendance at their opening meeting on September 19th with 96 women present in the morning and 58 in the evening. The very next day a brand new program called MOPS was launched. Forty-nine young women were in the building accompanied by 65 youngsters. For me, the encouraging aspect of this is that the idea did not come from the staff or Elders, but from members of the congregation to whom God had given a desire to reach young mothers. I commend Karla Folkerts and her leadership team for making this a reality. Over 50 men have indicated their enthusiasm to be part of a basic training course that involves Bible study, prayer and fellowship. This is the first time we have launched such a program in our church. Clearly God is on the move among our men.

In the first nine months of this year, 140 members of our congregation have participated in long-or short-term mission teams. This is the highest number we have ever sent. Other encouraging signs are the 125 people who gave up their Saturday to attend a worship conference last weekend, the interest in our healing service earlier this year, and the 130 who went to prayer meetings in Elders homes to ask for God's guidance for the land purchase decision.

Sometimes the evidence of the moving of God's Spirit is anecdotal, but I have learned to see individual stories as an indicator of larger trends. On a recent Sunday I was welcoming a visitor to our church who had come from out-of-town to get help at the Mayo Clinic. I invited her home for lunch but explained that she would need to wait for 30 minutes until I was ready to leave. A church member standing nearby heard the comment and immediately jumped in and said, "In that case, come home with us. It will be more convenient." That degree of sensitivity encourages me greatly. On one level I therefore want to say, "yes, we are spiritually ready."

Yet on another level I want to say, "No, of course we are not ready." I think Andy Vaughan's comment at the church meeting was very profound when he said, "If a person says they are spiritually ready, they are probably not." I agree. It is not for us to make that sort of declaration. Certainly when we examine the pages of scripture, we find that God's people invariably did not feel ready for the task to which he assigned them. Moses didn't feel ready to lead the Israelites. Esther did not feel ready to go before the king. Jeremiah didn't feel ready to prophesy, nor did Jonah. Not only did Peter feel unworthy to lead the early church, he clearly wasn't ready. He had just denied Christ and shown the weakness of his faith.

Paul also felt inadequate for the task, referring to himself as, *The least of the apostles.* But as he explained later to the Corinthians:

> *God chose the foolish things of the world to shame the wise;*
> *God chose the weak things of the world to shame the strong.*
> *He chose the lowly things of this world and the despised*
> *things and the things that are not, to nullify the things that*
> *are, so that no one may boast before him. (1 Corinthians*
> *1:27-29)*

The recognition of our weakness is the qualification for our readiness to serve God. The acknowledgment of our powerlessness is the key to our effectiveness.

Very often it is the doing of the task itself that results in our spiritual growth. That is why we believe in mission trips. Many of us set off with rather fleshly motives of simply wanting an enjoyable vacation, but the work we do transforms us and we come back changed people with a renewed desire to serve God.

As we face the monumental task of paying for 60 acres of land and building a new church campus we can say:

> *Not that we are competent in ourselves . . . but our competence comes from God. He has made us competent as ministers of a new covenant. (2 Corinthians 3:5-6)*

With that understanding we rejoice that God has opened wide this door of opportunity for us to extend our territory and possess the land. With no sense of presumption, but rather one of complete dependence, we declare—*We can do everything through Christ who gives us strength.*

Chapter 48

The Day We Were Left Behind

John
May 2002

*After Jesus said this, he was taken up before their very eyes,
and a cloud hid him from their sight. (Acts 1:9)*

May ninth was Ascension Day. We often overlook Ascension Day because it falls on a Thursday, but it is important that we do not miss its significance for our lives. We rejoice in the grand truths of the birth, death and resurrection of Jesus, but the story does not end there. Forty days after Easter, Jesus ascended from the Mount of Olives into heaven. We find the account in Mark 16:19-20. Three facts emerge from these verses to stimulate our faith.

First, the authority of Jesus. *He sat down at the right hand of God.* We need to remember this is the present position of the Lord Jesus. He is not a dying figure on a cross, but the ruling sovereign of the universe. The right hand of the Father is the place of authority and power. In the East, only those greatly favored by a king could sit there. The first Christians understood this and it gave them tremendous courage in dark hours to know that their living Lord was presently interceding for them at their Father's side. Remember when you are burdened this week that Jesus is praying for you and his word is law. His authority is further seen when he sat down. The high priest could never sit down in the Holy of Holies because his work was never done. The fact that Jesus is seated demonstrates the reality of his cry from the cross—*it is finished.*

Second, the actions of the Christians. *Then the disciples went out and preached everywhere.* This was the practical outcome of the Ascension. The disciples filled Jerusalem with the good news that Jesus is Lord. Their enemies tried to stop them, but failed because the Christians had an up-to-date testimony. They had been with Jesus. The last words he said to them had been, *Go into all the world and preach the gospel.* When we understand the present position and power of Jesus we must do something about it.

Third, the advance of Christianity. *The Lord worked with them and confirmed his word by the signs that accompanied it.* Jesus did not just leave a command, he left a power. Ten days after the Ascension came Pentecost, which we celebrate today. This was when the disciples were energized by the Holy Spirit. The result was that the church grew and grew. Today the church is advancing all over the world. We live in exciting days that perhaps are leading to Christ's return.

The old proverb says, "What goes up must come down." This is true of
Jesus. He went up and he will come down. After Jesus had disappeared
into the clouds two angels appeared and gently rebuked the disciples:

> *Men of Galilee why do you stand here looking into the sky?*
> *The same Jesus who has been taken from you into heaven, will*
> *come back in the same way you have seen him go into heaven.*
> *(Acts 1:11)*

Yes, Jesus is coming again to judge the world and claim those who
belong to him. In the meantime he tells us to go and advance his cause.

Chapter 49

Blessed Be the Tie that Blinds
John
January 2002

"I am grateful that my congregation is concerned for my reputation. . ."

One of the greatest joys in being the senior pastor of a generous church is the receipt of lovely and unusual gifts. In honor of George Harrison's death, one of my beloved Elders, who is famous for his eccentric fashion sense, gave me a unique tie on which were head shots of each of the Beatles.

My dear wife begged me not to wear it in public, but seeking to put this gift to good use, I decided to wear it as part of some research I was doing on how congregations respond to unusual neckwear.

Having a Sunday off, I visited a local church in town to hear their new pastor. Fifty-four people out of their congregation of 100 mentioned the tie although not one of them personally greeted me. Apparently they were unable to hate the tie and love the wearer. Three of them did try and cast out an evil spirit from me. They were a bit nonplussed when I explained the tie had been given by one of my Elders, but I think this information just reinforced their prejudices that First Baptist Church is a very liberal fellowship.

Continuing my experiment I decided to wear the tie to our own New Year's Eve service. I was pleased to discover that the majority of First Baptist Church saw me first rather than the tie. Twenty nine people did mention the tie, 25 of them were very envious and wished they had one too. I would have referred to the tie in the service in some way if I could have thought of anything appropriate to say about it that would not have been irreverent or disrespectful to such a holy occasion. However, it may be true that a tie of such dazzling design does not need any explanation as words would simply be gilding the lily. This is perhaps what the hymn writer meant when he wrote Blest Be the Tie That Binds.

An unintended consequence of my research is that wearing the tie may have caused the very generous offering on December 31st that resulted in First Baptist meeting its budget for the year in addition to presenting a check for $50,000 to the Rochester Network for Re-Entry. My suspicion is that visitors to the church on New Years Eve thought that a congregation with a pastor who wears ties like that clearly needs a lot of help and dug deep in their pockets for the closing offering of the year.

Another benefit of the experiment was that it has increased my circle of friends. Total strangers came up to me at both churches and engaged me in conversation. I even had an e-mail from a lady in our church who had eight separate questions about my tie. She has never had so many queries about my theology but I feel this is a first step. This great koinonia resulting from my haberdashery indicates that my neckwear is what the prophet Hosea refers to as *Ties of love (Hosea 11:4).*

As a result of my unusual dress I was put on probation and asked to check in each week at the Welcome Center to have my dress inspected. I scarcely knew how to respond. After all, where would this end? Would my socks and my vest be next? At first I was tongue-tied and then fit to be tied. My stomach was tied all in knots. I felt like the fellow who received Anton Chekhov's letter in 1888 when he wrote, "Your tie is off."

But then I thought if I came by the newly and aptly named Welcome Center they might be tied up with a visitor and so be unable to tie me down to a higher standard of neckwear. I didn't want to think what would happen if one member of the Welcome Center liked my tie but the other disapproved. Would we have a tie breaker?

Being suitably chastened, I resorted to wearing more conservative neckwear such as my blue fly fishing tie. I used to say there were no flies on me but that is no longer true. I always tell my colleagues that we need to be accountable to our congregation so I intend to set the example and make sure that when I ascend the pulpit steps that I cannot say with Isaiah, *Woe is me—I am undone.*

I am grateful that my congregation is concerned for my reputation, appearance and hopefully, my soul. I also rejoice that they have a jolly good sense of humor.

Chapter 50

Stop Reading the Bible

John

June 2002

Recently I read a provocative article by Jonathan Sacks, the Chief Rabbi in Great Britain. It was titled "Stop Reading the Bible." Rabbi Sacks was not suggesting that Christians and Jews cease to read God's word. Reading the Torah is the central part of Sabbath Synagogue services and has been so for more than 2,000 years. Around the world Jews read a particular portion, (known as the parsha) each week during services so as to complete the five books of the Law (Genesis to Deuteronomy) each year.

The Rabbi's point was that "read" is an inadequate word to describe our encounter with the Book of Books. Reading suggests a passive attitude but our approach to scripture must be active. We are not just to read the Bible but rather we are to have a conversation with it. Jews don't just read the Bible, they sing it, argue with it, wrestle with it, listen to it and turn it inside out to find a new insight they have missed before. The reason is that God's word doesn't have a single meaning but rather infinite resonances. Each year as they work through the Hebrew scriptures they find that the Torah is always the same, yet somehow different. What a verse means in 2,002 will not be the same as what it meant in 2,001. The world changes, so each year it forms a different image in the mirror of revelation.

This is clear when we examine the standard Hebrew edition of the Mosaic books. At the top of the page is the biblical text but around it are commentary after commentary, all disagreeing with each another. Each is a voice from a different country and time. Jews preserve and study them all. To engage with the Bible Jewishly is to enter a millennial chat room in which we find ourselves in an enthralling debate between sages from Fifth Century Palestine, Eleventh Century France, Thirteenth Century Spain, and Sixteenth Century Poland. The Bible is a libretto scored for many voices.

Jewish scholar Erich Auerbach observes that the Hebrew Bible cries out for interpretation. It is like radio compared with television. We hear rather then see. We know almost nothing about the appearance of the characters, what they are thinking, or their motives. In Auerbach's phrase, the Bible is "fraught with background." It invites us to supply the details, to elaborate, interpret and engage with the text.

213

There is a sense in which God wants us to be co-authors of his book, for the Bible isn't a book to be read and put down. It is God's invitation to join the conversation between heaven and earth that began at Mount Sinai and has continued ever since. God speaks in such a way as to leave space for us to reply, ask for clarification, argue the case, and get involved. Every generation has left its commentaries, none supplanting the others, but each adding a new layer to the conversation.

I think the Rabbi is right. The best way to make the Bible come alive today is to stop reading it and start conversing with it. That is what keeps our moral sense alive. The Bible declares an unchangable eternal truth. However, the way that truth is applied changes with each generation. In Paul's day the issue was, should Christians eat meat offered to idols? That is not a temptation we face today. However, we do have to make ethical choices about cloning and decide how to allocate human organs for transplantation. From a passage originally addressed to a population who knew nothing about computers, we must make application today for how to run a business or rear our children. As we read scripture there is an encounter between "the now" of the daily news and the perennial "now" of the divine word. Something new always emerges. The ancient text comes to life again. Eternity meets time.

Chapter 51

Reflections on a Family Reunion

John
Summer 2002

One of the temptations of pastoral ministry is to focus so much on others that we neglect our family. As a corrective, Gretchen has planned a family reunion with her three sisters and brother. We are meeting at a fly fishing camp in Colorado. We are determined to get an early start and finally leave Rochester at midday—not bad for the Steers. We drive to Kansas City where Gretchen has booked a motel but when we arrive we discover that they have given our room away. It is late and I feel like pronouncing imprecations on the desk clerk, but since Gretchen made the arrangements I leave it to her. Very patiently she explains our case and shows our paperwork. It is clear that *a gentle word turns away wrath*, because the poor woman apologizes profusely and offers to put us up in another hotel at their expense.

We take the children to a water park called "Oceans of Fun." It is my first time in such a place although, as a Baptist, I expect to feel at home surrounded by all this water. It is an extraordinary experience with thousands of semi-naked people slipping down slides, reclining in inner tubes and enjoying the wave pool. The previous Sunday Gretchen had taught the Joint Heirs adult Sunday school class on the seventh commandment, *You shall not commit adultery*. Adultery begins in the mind and, according to Jesus, can end in the mind. We discuss how this environment was not too conducive to pure thinking. Apart from this, it was great fun.

With all due respect to those who live there, Kansas is a dreary state. Mile after mile of monotonous scenery is broken only by the appalling smell of the stockyards that line the highway. The sole tourist attraction seems to be "The World's Largest Hand Dug Well" which is the pride and joy of Greensburg. On first seeing the signs advertising this man-made wonder we laughed derisively. By the time we arrived, however, we were grateful for any diversion, especially when we discovered that we could also see a meteorite weighing 1,000 pounds discovered in 1949 by H.O. Stockwell. The hand dug well turned out to be better than it sounded. It was begun in 1887 and is a masterpiece of pioneer engineering. Hired on a day-to-day basis, crews of 12 to 50 men dug the well. Other teams quarried and hauled the native stones used for the casings of the well.   When the well was completed in 1888 it was 109 feet deep and 32 feet in diameter having cost $45,000.

We took the stairway to the bottom where the children were delighted to discover coins that had been tossed in by folk who couldn't be bothered to make the trip down.

We visit Royal Gorge, a bizarre blend of absolutely stunning scenery and appalling exploitation. Royal Gorge can be enjoyed on a number of levels. If you have the time and money ($14 admission) you can take in the entire ghastly experience, which includes buying some deer food (for a buck) from a human being dressed as a chipmunk. Or you can do as we did which is drive up to the toll gate, turn around, park, and walk over to the cliffside and take a look for free. The tackiness of the place is exquisite. The owners have done a superb job of destroying the natural beauty, hiding it behind billboards advertising buffalo burgers. What is truly stunning is that nature still manages somehow to awe and inspire in spite of it all. It is amazing to think what it must have been like in the days BC (before commercialization).

We drive through Canon City, the proud home of "Fluff 'em, Buff 'em and Stuff 'em." This firm represents a true milestone in the history of marketing, advertising, promotion and taste. This little business offers one-stop hairstyling, car restoration and taxidermy.

Arriving in Salida, Colorado we pitch our tent in a National Forest Campground at 9,200 feet. Naturally the rain begins as we arrive. Thankfully it doesn't last long, a further evidence of God's mercy. For me, the best bit of camping is the evening campfire. Ever since our honeymoon Gretchen and I have enjoyed sitting by the fire, reading by the light of our Coleman lantern. Apart from Hannah we have all read the fourth Harry Potter book. We discuss its merits and contrast it to the first three in the series.

I have never thought of our yearly camping trips as enjoyable, but they do teach valuable lessons like endurance and hard work. There is certainly no opportunity for idleness. You are either putting up the tent, fetching water, collecting firewood, inflating air mattresses or doing the 101 other chores that are necessary for a successful camp. Sadly, I can't help think of it except as punishment for comforts enjoyed the rest of the year. After all, it was because of their disobedience that God condemned the Israelites to 40 years of camping in the Sinai desert.

We visit St. Elmo, which according to the *New York Times* is the best preserved ghost town in the United States. Gold was discovered here in the 1880's and thousands of miners came in search of their fortune. Some apparently were not well-informed and imagined that all they had to do was back up their cart to the mountainside and fill it with gold. Amazing engineering feats were accomplished in this quest for wealth. All supplies had to be brought up to 10,000 feet by donkey. As Christians, we need the same ardor for both seeking the riches of God's grace and imparting them to others.

Our next stop is Mt. Princeton Hot Springs. This provides the dual purpose of relaxation and cleanliness (which is particularly important, as our campsite has no showers or washing facilities). Gretchen has often commented that my voice carries vast distances. This is helpful when one is in the pulpit but less so when one is talking in private. We were relaxing in one of the pools fed both by water from the hot springs and the mountain stream. As we were sitting in it up to our necks I quizzed the children with biblical questions about water. I asked them if they knew what was buried in the deepest sea? A lady in an adjoining pool heard the question but not Emily's answer. Later she approached Gretchen and said, "I can't leave without knowing what is buried in the sea." Gretchen explained that it was our transgressions and that God placed our sin where it would never be seen again.

There is an atmosphere of jubilation as we break camp. We have decided that this is our last camping trip. In the future we will suffer in hotels like normal folk.

We planned to worship at the Episcopal Church but arrived too late and so went to the Vineyard Christian Fellowship. I remember the early days of the Vineyard movement in California when John Wimber was making waves at Fuller Seminary with his Signs and Wonders courses. Now the Vineyard has become much more of a mainline evangelical church. There was nothing unusual about the service except that it lasted for two hours. We began with 45 minutes of choruses. This was not for the fainthearted. I sat down exhausted halfway through. This was followed by an excellent message on forgiveness. The pastor took 55 minutes, which made me seem short by comparison. There were about 80 in the congregation, mostly young, and dressed in shorts and T-shirts as we were—although perhaps not as dirty as us after three days of camping. The ladies were the most expressive in worship. The men for the most part were passive observers. We were interested to hear the comments of our children. They thought the service was too long and too unstructured. My concern was that there was no reading of scripture during the service. This is a distressing trend I find increasingly common in evangelical churches.

We arrive at Ute Trail River Ranch. It is tucked into the rugged Tarryall Mountains on the banks of the rushing Tarryall River 85 miles southwest of Denver. The ranch is a restored turn-of-the-century fly fishing camp that rekindles the spirit of the way life used to be lived in the Rockies. This is where we are going to have our family reunion. There are six 100-year-old cabins. We have rented five of them for the five families that are coming. Gretchen's family is spread out geographically with three in California, one in Florida and one in Minnesota, so Colorado is a central place. I voted for the fly fishing camp because it gave the men something to do while the sisters talk.

One of the main attractions here is Pike's Peak, the flagship of the Front Range, first spotted in 1806 by Zebulon Pike. The mountain had been known to Ute Indians for years as "the long one." In the 1850's it was a welcome sight to west-bound gold seekers whose covered wagons often bore the motto, "Pike's Peak or Bust." Pike's Peak was also "the purple mountain . . . above the fruited plain" to which Katharine Lee Bates was referring when she wrote "America, the Beautiful." Each July, top race car drivers from around the world compete in the "Pike's Peak Hill Climb" or the "Race to the Sky." There is also an annual foot race to the summit.

There is great rejoicing when, one by one, the other families arrive. At the last presidential election Clinton and Dole were asked to define a family and they couldn't or wouldn't do it, perhaps afraid to alienate some constituency. A family, of course, is those related by blood, marriage or adoption. It is amazing the closeness that this brings. Our family shares few interests or outlooks in common but there is an intimacy brought about by being part of the group. As Christians, we are related to each other by the blood of Christ. We are also related to God and are part of his family through adoption now, and marriage later when Christ comes for his bride, the church.

Jim, the host of the fly fishing camp, gives me my first fly fishing lesson. I practice in an open field. My grandfather was a fly fisherman who made fly rods for a living in Scotland. I hope I have inherited his genes. It is soon apparent that I haven't. I keep wrapping the fly line around the van antenna 25 yards behind me. After several hours of this I finally learn how to lay a cast. I put on my waders and make my way to the nearby stream. I don't catch anything but enjoy recreating, "A River Runs Through It." I have fished all my life but never with a fly rod. This truly is the aristocrat of the sport.

218

My brother-in-law Rick arrives. He has been auditioning for the Cleveland Orchestra and is ecstatic that he has been offered the position of second trombone. He will play under the baton of Christoph Von Dohnányi. It is the fulfillment of a lifelong dream for him and we all rejoice at this wonderful opportunity. He fills the valley with the joyful sound of his instrument. Although he has been playing the trombone for 26 years he still practices for three hours a day in addition to orchestra rehearsals. It is a wonderful illustration of what it takes to excel and master a subject. We can't expect to grow in our Christian life and our understanding of the scriptures without the same sort of diligence.

Jim gives me a lesson on false casting, mending and roll casting. I set off to the river with a Number 2 Carson fly and, to my delight, land two trout, one of which is 16 inches long.

Tonight it is our turn to fix dinner for all the families. The host has the prerogative of choosing the topic of conversation for the meal so I ask each person to describe what they would like to accomplish in the next 10 years. For some it is retirement, for others having children and for the younger ones going away to college. It is good to dream but we need to heed James' admonition,

> *Come now, you who say today or tomorrow we shall go to such and such a city and spend a year there and engage in business and make a profit. Yet you do not know what your life will be like tomorrow. You are just a vapor that appears for a little while and then vanishes away. Instead you ought to say, 'if the Lord wills we shall live and also do this and that.' (James 4:13-15)*

Nicky and I fish the stream together. I come up empty but he hooks a magnificent trout that made the otherwise barren fishing outing all worthwhile.

We are an eclectic lot spiritually. Three of the group profess no faith whatsoever. One was raised in a Reformed Presbyterian Church but is now taking instruction to become a Catholic. Another was raised Lutheran, had a spell of atheism and finally made a spectacular conversion to Roman Catholicism. Two attended an evangelical church for 20 years and found no joy or pleasure in it. They are now members of a Calvinistic Presbyterian fellowship and their faith has come alive. Another was raised Lutheran but now attends an Episcopalian Church and serves on the evangelism committee. Then there are Gretchen and me who have been serving in Baptist churches for over twenty years and yet enjoy the liturgy and worship of almost every church across the Christian spectrum. For years at family gatherings faith was seldom mentioned. Increasingly, as we get older, those of us who are believers find ourselves expressing our trust in Christ.

The discussion tonight asked which character from the Twentieth Century would we like to be? I say Winston Churchill, others chose Gandhi, Mother Theresa and various American Presidents. Gretchen surprises us by declaring she wants to be herself, not because she is famous, but because she is totally content with her life. The group looks a bit surprised. I provide the helpful explanation that she can talk this way because she is married to me. My brother-in-law kicks me under the table. No sense of humor.

Following the evening meal we walk down to the beaver pond and watch ma and pa beaver carefully building a dam of willows in the gathering darkness. It is amazing the amount they can accomplish in one night, lifting heavy stones and dragging mud from the bottom of the pond. One can easily see the origin of the expression, "Busy as a beaver."

We break all Steer records and leave at 5:30 a.m., before the sun has come over the Rockies. It takes 17 hours but we complete the 991 miles back home within the day. We reflect on how our family is becoming increasingly precious to us. We all feel that we have grown closer together and our love for one another has deepened. In these days, when families are scattered over thousands of miles, it is increasingly important to make efforts like this. We return home deeply thankful that "God sets the lonely in families."

Chapter 52

This Blessed Plot, This Earth, This Realm, This England

John
January 2003

> *The title is taken from John of Gaunt's dying prophecy in*
> *William Shakespeare's King Richard II.*

For many years my colleagues had asked me to lead a church history tour of England. I had promised to do so but there was never a convenient occasion for us all to be away. I finally realized that unless I took action I would go to my grave with this promise unkept. With the encouragement of our Elder Board, in January 2003, I took seven members of the pastoral team with me to England. The following are excerpts from my journal.

Steve England, Karen Foster, Cheri Hart, Bill Price, Gary Seaquist, Josh Mulvihill, Dan Farm and I arrived in England for a week of learning about church history, ourselves and the ministry of First Baptist Church. At Gatwick Airport we are met by the representative of the car hire firm. He hands me the keys of an aging diesel van. It is twice the size of anything I've ever driven before. I try not to look terrified. To make matters worse they drive on the wrong side over here! Through angelic oversight we arrive at Windsor Castle, built in 1070 by William the Conqueror and now one of the homes of her majesty, Queen Elizabeth. We visit St. George's Chapel where many British monarchs are buried.

We enjoy a lunch of fish and chips at a local hostelry. Back in the van we make for Stonehenge. We arrived there just before it closed. (How can a circle of stones that was erected 5,000 years ago be closed?) On seeing it Gary Seaquist exclaims, "It's so small." My seven colleagues pay to go in. I refuse on the grounds you can see it just as well over the fence.

We arrive at Redcliffe Missionary Training College in Gloucester and are given a warm welcome by the principal, Simon Steer. The students even carry our bags from the van and place them in our rooms. After a spartan meal Bill, Gary, Karen and I walk the mile into town. We stand at the Cathedral Close and listen to the bell ringers practice. The peals ring out across the city as they have done for 500 years.

We drive to Tewkesbury Abby, where Christians have worshiped for 1,200 years. The local school is about to hold their daily chapel service and the headmaster invites us to join them.

We stand with the children to sing William Williams' great Welsh hymn, "Guide Me, O Thou Great Jehovah" to the stirring strains of the organ. We return to the college in time to join in the weekly chapel service with the students. Steve England then leads us in a helpful discussion on the subject of stewardship.

Over lunch we ask the students where they will be serving God at the end of their course. We then go into the city of Gloucester where we visit Robert Raikes' house. Raikes started the first Sunday School in 1780. He paid his teachers to instruct the urchins of Gloucester to read using the catechism. He was criticized by the established church but by 1786 there were 200,000 children enrolled in Sunday Schools throughout England. We explore Gloucester Cathedral, which has been used in recent years for the filming of the Harry Potter movies. We pay our respects at the statue of Edward Jenner, a local doctor who developed the first vaccine for smallpox in 1796. We paused at the moving memorial to John Hooper, the Bishop of Gloucester, who was burned at the stake by bloody Queen Mary in 1555 because he had embraced the reformed faith. Hooper had been converted by reading a tract written by Ulrich Zwingli of Zurich. We finish our tour at the historic docks of Gloucester and then return to the college for dinner with the students. In the evening Dr. Rob Cook leads us in a very helpful 90-minute seminar on team building and spirituality using our Myers-Briggs profiles. It's amazing to reflect on the amount of unity we have on staff despite the diversity of our personalities.

We leave at 6:30 a.m. for London. Each day begins with a devotion led by a different person. It transforms the monotony of the drive into a holy time. This is followed with a season of prayer. I keep my eyes open as I drive, feeling that God will understand. Dan Farm then provides an insightful presentation on how outsiders view the church, based on some new research by George Barna. The discussion and prayer time are particularly appreciated this morning as it takes us four hours of inching through stop and go traffic to reach London. We arrive at John Wesley's church on the City Road and walk through his house. We then gather in the Foundry Chapel to sing Charles Wesley's great hymn, "And Can It Be?" At John Wesley's grave we give thanks for the lives of these brothers and reflected how they and George Whitfield were used by God to bring about the great awakening in England and America in the Eighteenth Century.

Opposite the church is Bunhill Cemetery where Isaac Watts, John Bunyan, John Owen, Susannah Wesley and other Christian notables are buried. We catch a red double decker bus to St. Paul's where we look at Holman Hunt's painting of "The Light of the World." We enjoy lunch in the crypt of St. Martin's in the Field. It seems strange to be eating apple crumble with the tombstones of the departed under our feet.

The next stop is the National Gallery, where we pay particular attention to the Monets and the Turners, then a brisk walk through St. James' Park to Buckingham Palace. We visit the underground Cabinet Rooms where Winston Churchill ran the Second World War. We then stroll (if one can be said to stroll at my usual pace) through Parliament Square to Westminster Abbey where we enjoy choral evensong sitting in the choir stalls. We walk over Westminster Bridge as Big Ben chimes 6 p.m., reflecting that quite a lot has changed since William Wordsworth wrote his wonderful sonnet "On Westminster Bridge." After a good meal in Whitehall we walk past Downing Street, the residence of the British prime minister, through Trafalgar Square to Piccadilly Circus where there is a statue of Eros. This was erected in memory of Lord Shaftesbury, a notable social reformer in the Nineteenth Century. Like John Wesley, his social concern sprang from his evangelical faith. At least one passenger does not enjoy the ride home. Bill is in the beginning stages of stomach flu.

Both Bill and Cheri are sick today. While they stay behind to recuperate, the rest of us take off for Painswick, a lovely Cotswold village. The parish church is surrounded by 99 carefully trimmed yew trees. We drive on to Bath where we visit the Roman baths, the beautiful Abbey (where Christians have worshipped since Saxon times) and the spectacular Royal Crescent, built by the Eighteenth Century architects John Wood and his son. In 1702 Queen Anne made the trek from London to the mineral springs of Bath, thereby launching a fad that was to make the city the most celebrated spa in England. We discover that the word "spa" comes from the Latin phrase "sanitas per aqua" (health through water). Bath was a favorite retreat for authors like Dickens, Thackeray, Fielding and Jane Austen. Several of Austen's stories are set here. It retains a strong literary tradition to this day.

Returning to Gloucester, I attend evensong in the cathedral. The strains of the choir reaching up to the high vaulted roof, singing Cranmer's Bible-soaked liturgy is a foretaste of heaven. My brother Simon has invited us to his home for the evening. He and Julia provide us with a delicious dinner. Dr. Jonathan Ingleby, one of the professors at Redcliffe, then talks to us about some of the priorities of English evangelicals. He urges us to speak out for the poor and the oppressed and begs us to do all we can to see that America does not go to war with Iraq. This perspective provides much food for discussion. Some of my colleagues are intrigued by the difference in political views among English and American Christians.

We make our way to Bourton on the Water. This lovely Cotswold village lies on the banks of the tiny Windrush River. Its mellow stone houses, its village green, and its bridges have earned it the title of the "Venice of the Cotswolds." We consume a cream tea in a quaint little tearoom with scones smothered in clotted cream and strawberry jam.

Next stop is Warwick Castle, the finest medieval fortress in England. It was started by the first Earl of Warwick, the son of William the Conqueror, in 1088. It is perched on a rocky cliff above the River Avon. Sir Walter Scott described it in 1828 as, "That fairest monument of ancient and chivalrous splendor which yet remains uninjured by time." Peacocks wander freely around the lawns. We enjoy the dungeon, torture chamber and ghost tower and find these rooms more pleasant than did their original occupants. As I wander along the ramparts I tried to imagine the archers with their new secret weapon, the long bow, defending this citadel against the enemy.

Driving the 10 miles to Stratford on Avon, we see the birthplace of William Shakespeare and then watch C.S. Lewis' magnificent play *The Lion, the Witch and the Wardrobe* performed by the Royal Shakespeare Company.

On the way to Oxford Bill Price leads us in an excellent discussion on the place of beauty in the Christian faith. We worship at St. Ebbes, an evangelical Anglican Church with a significant ministry to students. The vicar gives an excellent exposition on Hosea. We have lunch in the home of Stuart and Mee Yan Judge. Stuart is a professor at the Oxford Medical School and Mee Yan is a Ph.D. in sociology with her own consulting business. My colleagues are entertained by Mee Yan's ruthless teasing of me, based upon our friendship of 24 years. In the afternoon we visit The Kilns, C.S. Lewis' home. We then tour a number of the Oxford colleges, including Magdalen, Christ Church and New College. Magdalen is where C.S. Lewis taught. On May Day dawn choristers sing in Latin from its tower. Each college has its own chapel. New College, founded in 1372 by the Bishop of Winchester, boasts a remarkable modern sculpture by Sir Jacob Epstein of Lazarus rising from the dead. Until the 1880's most faculty members at Oxford University were not permitted to marry, and not until 1871 were religious tests abolished to allow Jews, Catholics and Baptists to be admitted as students. Until the 1970's most colleges did not admit women.

The Reverend Spooner, who invented spoonerisms, was warden of New College from 1903-1924. One of his famous rebukes to a student is well known: "Sir, you have tasted two whole worms. You have hissed all my mystery lectures. You have been caught fighting a liar in the quad and I must ask you to leave by the first town drain." (Sir, you have wasted two whole terms. You have missed all my history lectures. You have been caught lighting a fire in the quad and I must ask you to leave by the first down train.) Oxford has turned out some remarkable individuals like John Wycliffe, Roger Bacon, William Penn, John Harvard and Bill Clinton. William of Ockham, who enunciated Ockham's Razor, also studied here. We stood in Wesley's room in Lincoln College where the Holy Club met.

We visited the Martyr's Memorial where Latimer, Ridley and Cranmer were burnt at the stake in 1555. The memorial is just opposite the Eagle and Child, the pub (we did not go inside!) where C.S. Lewis, his brother, Warren, and J.R.R. Tolkien used to discuss their writing over a glass of light refreshment. A plaque on a bridge over the Cherwell celebrates 300 years of Baptist life in Oxford. It was not easy being a Baptist in earlier days. A riotous mob destroyed the church in 1731.

We board the plane at London Airport for our flight back to Minneapolis. The Northwest staff informs us that there is a small problem and our departure will be delayed for one hour. After an hour they tell us it's now a big problem and the plane will not be departing today. We are to be put up by the Hilton Hotel, provided with lunch, dinner and breakfast and then board the same flight tomorrow. We have a whole extra day in England. How good God is!

Chapter 53

Why I Teach
Gretchen
April 2003

One of the most valuable purposes for a holiday in our family life is the chance for both John and me to reflect on the ministry by stepping back momentarily from its demands. We always spend time talking about the present and the future, and discussing the ongoing work of God at First Baptist. For me this often takes the form of a question. Am I doing what I am supposed to be doing, Lord? Where would you have me serve?

During a recent year-long series on the book of Exodus I found myself evaluating my ministry of teaching. My desire in teaching through Exodus was to show the unchanging character of God's love, first through redemption of the Jews, and second through his redemption of us in Christ. I found though, that there was so much factual information in Exodus that it seemed we spent a lot of time acquiring knowledge rather than gaining insight. I perceived that I had come out of the study knowing more but not necessarily being changed by what I was learning.

Perhaps transformation is too lofty a goal for a Bible study. Isn't it good enough that we understand more about God? Although that is a good outcome, it may not be enough. We should come away from any serious encounter with God's word as different people, not just more knowledgeable, but somehow, with our life choices informed by what we've studied. I realize that a large part of that responsibility lies with me as a teacher. I am required to teach with passion ideas that will ignite a response from my audience. But ultimately, it is God who causes transformation. And so we can ask ourselves if we are any different as a result of our studying the Bible. What is God doing in our lives, that is more victorious or advanced from where we were at the beginning of a study?

The New Testament tells us that Moses' face shone as a result of his encounter with God on the Mountain (2 Corinthians. 3:12). It tells us in Acts that it was obvious to everyone that Peter and John had been with Jesus (Acts 4:13). It is my prayer that our study of the Bible would make it clear to all around us that we have been with Christ.

Chapter 54

The John Steer Golf Classic
John
April 2003

I was addressing my ball at the John Steer Golf Classic and trying to visualize a perfect shot. An announcement from the clubhouse disrupted my thoughts. "Will the gentleman on the ladies tee please back up to the men's tee!" I tried to put the interruption out of my mind and lined up my ball once again. Again the announcement came. "Will the gentleman on the ladies tee please back up to the men's tee!" Finally my patience snapped. I put down my driver and yelled out "Would the announcer in the clubhouse please shut up so I can play my *second* shot!"

I am afraid that is the way the whole game went last Saturday. Sadly I didn't win a prize. However, I am getting better at golf. I hit the ball in once and I also broke 70 (that's a lot of clubs). The tournament organizers provided us with a box of three balls, which I succeeded in losing after the first four holes. You will be glad to know I am successfully resisting offers to turn pro.

Chapter 55

Break Up Your Unplowed Ground, it is Time to Seek the Lord

Outdoor service at the future site of Autumn Ridge Church
John
August 2003

I would like to direct your attention to the tractor on the hill. It is being driven by a farmer called Craig Griebenow. As you can see, he has started to plow this land. I want you to think for a moment what Craig is doing and why he is doing it. Use your imagination. Consider the future harvest that is possible because this hard ground is being plowed.

That is an illustration of a spiritual principle that speaks powerfully to us as we gather on the site of our new church building. A month ago our pastoral team sat down to plan this service and I realized there was one text that beautifully related to this situation.

It comes from the Old Testament book of Hosea, who was one of the Minor Prophets:

> Sow for yourselves righteousness, reap the fruit of unfailing love, break up your unplowed ground; for it is time to seek the Lord, until he comes and showers righteousness on you. (Hosea 10:12)

The prophet is speaking to an agricultural people. As he addresses them they perhaps can see, as we can, a farmer plowing his field. Hosea uses this as a picture of what God wants to do in their lives. Similarly the prophet offers us wonderful counsel as we gather on unplowed ground today. I suggest to you that this verse has application for our lives, our church and our future building plans. In this text Hosea presents us with three great opportunities.

First he offers us THE BEST GOAL. Each of us wants a purpose in life. We feel frustrated and empty until we find it. We need something bigger than ourselves to motivate us and keep us going. We have a desire to make a difference and leave the world a better place.

Hosea suggests a solution when he declares, *Sow for yourselves righteousness*. Righteousness means to be right with God and with one another. To sow righteousness means to live a God-directed life. Now sowing righteousness doesn't just happen. It is a deliberate action. Crops don't just appear, they need to be sown. The correct seed must be planted.

231

How do we sow seeds of righteousness? Jesus helps us here. He told several parables about farmers sowing seeds, and he explained that they represented various righteous actions.

Seed represents the word of God. We need to plant the scriptures in our lives. I understand that fall is a great time for planting grass seed. It is also a great time to get into a Bible study group and plant the word of God deep within our souls.

In your newsletter there is information about various Bible study opportunities starting this month. There is a Women's Bible Study, Precepts Upon Precepts, and a Post-abortion Bible Study. There are Bible studies for children, middle schoolers, high schoolers and college students. Next Sunday there are nine different Bible study opportunities. Let's sow for ourselves righteousness.

Jesus also likened seed to faith. He said, *If you have faith the size of a mustard seed...* We plant faith when we embark on an action that requires God's help. Perhaps we apply to join the mission team going to Kosovo, or we sign up to help Somalian immigrants at Friendship Place, or we decide to tell a friend about Jesus. These actions produce a harvest, but the seed must first be sown.

I wonder, as we look at our weekly schedules, if we are sowing righteousness. Are our energies being directed in God-pleasing pursuits?

Hosea realizes that he is getting ahead of himself. Before we sow we need to plow. He encourages us to *Break up your unplowed ground.*

I confess that I have sometimes been lazy as a gardener. I wanted some flowers or some new grass but I didn't want to do the hard work of preparing the soil. I just threw the seeds down. You know the result. Nothing happened. The seeds couldn't take root. They were either eaten by the birds, washed away by the rain, or dried up by the sun as they lay on the top of the hard earth.

The Encyclopedia Britannica says that the plow is the most important agricultural instrument since the beginning of history. The plow is used to turn and break up soil, to bury crop residue, and help to control weeds. This part of the world played an important role in the development of the plow. When the pioneers came, the black prairie soils of the American Midwest challenged the strength of the plows of that day. It was an American mechanic, John Deere, who invented the all-steel one- piece plow. Even with all the improvements in agriculture, farmers must still plow in order to make their ground productive. They break it up to produce a harvest. In Hosea's day, before the advent of machinery, plowing suggested hard work and a certain amount of pain.

When Hosea urges us to break up the unplowed, fallow ground of our lives, he is referring to the process of repentance. The plow of conviction must first break up our hard hearts before the seed of the word can be planted and the gracious rain sent from heaven.

We must turn aside from those actions that prevent us from being spiritually productive. We must weed out those things that are displeasing to God. This can be painful and difficult. It is neither quick nor easy but it is essential if we are to sow for ourselves righteousness.

There are various forms of plows ranging from the moldboard plow to disk plows to rotary plows. Likewise, God uses different ways to break up the hard soil of our hearts. He can shake us up with extraordinary blessings or wake us up with trials and testing.

Let's apply this to our church. Last Sunday at our business meeting we voted to approve the money to prepare this site for building. Soon, large earth-moving equipment will be at work. Truly this unplowed ground will be broken up.

For many years this land has been used to produce a harvest of corn. From now on it will be used to produce a harvest of righteousness. Isn't it exciting to think of the lives that will be transformed on this site in the years to come.

It is great to use our imaginations and think of the thousands who will come to know Christ.

We long that this should be a place where marriages are restored, homes are strengthened, missionaries are sent out, the poor are helped, the immigrant is welcomed, the searching find answers, and the hurting find healing.

Where we are seated is the site of our new sanctuary. Here we will celebrate ancient acts of worship and we will also explore new ways of praising God that are relevant to our day. We will be able to present dramas and musicals and use the performing arts to proclaim the hope of the gospel and the glory of Christ.

Our book center will provide resources for people who want to dig into God's word and find answers to the great ethical challenges of our day. There will be books and materials to guide children and teens and offer practical advice to couples and families.

Isn't this the best goal? Isn't this worth sacrifice and effort? Isn't it worth our giving and our praying? It is not an easy thing to break up this unplowed field and plant a brand new church for the Twenty-first Century.

Some are sad that we are leaving the building that we love. Others have given hundreds of hours preparing for this dream to become a reality. Many are sacrificing to provide the financial resources. It is worth it for it is the best goal. It is exciting to think that God is going to do more than we can ask or imagine.

When the pioneers came to Minnesota in the Nineteenth Century, they cleared away land to farm. For awhile that land was sufficient, but then they needed more space so they cleared more trees. Eventually the Midwest became the breadbasket of the United States, as well as feeding much of the world.

So it is with First Baptist Church. We are presently in our fifth home. This will be the sixth one. We are clearing this land because we have come as far we can in our existing building. We believe that God is not finished with us yet. This is why we are breaking up this unplowed field. This is the best goal.

Hosea also calls us to the best goal at THE BEST TIME. *It is time to seek the Lord.* Now is the very best time. Of course it is. The past is behind us and the future hasn't yet taken place. All we have is the present. Now is the time to seek the Lord.

In reality, there was very little time left for Hosea's hearers. The kingdom fell almost before Hosea had finished speaking. In 722 BC the Assyrian army invaded the land and ten tribes of Israel vanished from the pages of history, graphically showing that righteousness exalts a nation but sin is a reproach to any people.

We don't know how much time we have left, either. This is true both for our own lives and for the time until Jesus Christ returns. That is why we must buy up the opportunity. That is why now is the best time.

The Prophet Isaiah urges us:

> *Seek the Lord while he may be found; call on him while he is near. (Isaiah 55:6)*

Before we embarked on our Imagine a Place fund-raising program, we set aside several months for prayer. As we asked for God's counsel and direction we sensed the message: "now is the time." Now is the best time.

We have seen evidence of that. We were able to purchase this land in a delightful location. If we had waited a few years it wouldn't have been available. We are building when interest rates are at historic lows. We are expanding at a time when our city is enjoying a growth spurt.

Brothers and sisters, it is time to seek the Lord. It is time to seek him for salvation. We traditionally think of the beginning of school as marking the end of the summer. Some of us, as we look at our souls, have to say with Jeremiah:

> *The harvest is past, the summer is ended, and we are not saved. (Jeremiah 8:20)*

Even if we have long delayed, we can still come to Christ. We can still trust him as our Savior. We can still experience his forgiveness. We can make a new start in the power of his spirit. Let us not go through another winter without God.

It is time to seek the Lord. Some of us need to seek him that we might know him better... that we might grow in grace... that we might be conformed to the likeness of Christ. Our souls have become fallow. Our prayer lives have become barren. The fruit of the spirit in our lives is looking like some of the corn and soybeans in southeast Minnesota. It is brown and dry. We need to seek Christ and enjoy his living water, and be refreshed in him.

It is time to seek the Lord. Some of us need to seek the Lord in terms of service. We have sat on the sidelines for too long. We have let others experience the joy and challenge of using their gifts for God. We are never going to make much progress until we allow the Lord to use us.

Finally, Hosea calls us to the best goal at the best time WITH THE BEST OUTCOME.

He speaks of the outcome in two places in our text. He says seek for yourselves righteousness so that we *reap the fruit of unfailing love.* We are enjoying the fruit of the harvest from our gardens right now. My apple trees are laden. Each day I pick an apple and bite into the delicious fruit.

But there is a better harvest. That is the unfailing love of God. The psalmist urges us to, *Taste and see that the Lord is good.* We can't taste the harvest unless we first plow the ground and sow the seed. Hosea tells us it is time to seek the Lord *until he comes and showers righteousness on you.* God promises to share his righteousness with us. He gives us more than we can ever begin to imagine. He grants us what we don't deserve.

Hosea wisely doesn't try to define God's righteousness. It is manifested in such an amazing variety of ways.

We have called this project Imagine a Place because we wanted to use our imaginations to speculate what God will do on this property. In fact, we just can't do it. Whatever we imagine, God will surpass.

I would like you to do something now, if you would. Reach down to the ground and take up some soil. Hold it in your hand. I would suggest to you that this is holy ground. Look at the dirt. See how it is made up of particles of different sizes. They represent the variety of ways that God wants to bless this community through this new church campus.

I have been thrilled as many of you have shared your ideas for this property. Let me tell you some of my own dreams. I imagine a place where mentally and physically challenged individuals can be served and introduced to the Lord Jesus.

Recognizing the community in which we live, I imagine a place for medical ethics, where we grapple with the implications of scientific advances.

With the recent scandals at WorldCom and Enron, I imagine a place where business people can come and discover what it means to be a Christian in the workplace, and how to run their businesses and manage people according to the rules of God's kingdom.

The context of this passage in Hosea Chapter 10 reflects a concern for the poor and the oppressed. The prophet calls the people to break up the fallow grounds of their indifference to care for the needy around them.

Rochester has become a multi-ethnic community. I imagine a place where people come alongside the alien and the stranger and help them to adjust to life in this great nation while introducing them to the one who loves them with an everlasting love. We need to house the homeless and help the hurting, enable the unemployed to find jobs and provide training for those with no skills.

I imagine a place where people discover financial freedom. A large number in this community are in financial bondage because of unwise spending that has resulted in debt. They are having to work two and three jobs, destroying their family lives and causing all sorts of stress. We can help them find contentment.

I imagine a place where those who have retired from the workplace can use their extra time and the skills acquired over a lifetime to further the kingdom, both in this community and around the world. I see a resource center where needs are posted and matched with the skills of retirees. I imagine a place where missions teams are going out every month to serve God both in this country and overseas.

As we gather on this beautiful land that God has given us, enjoying the glory of his creation, the word of God comes to us, *Break up your unplowed ground, for it is time to seek the Lord.*

Before we build we must be broken. Before we move here God must move us. Truly this is the best goal, at the best time, with the best outcome.

Chapter 56

Three Cheers for the IRS

John
August 2003

God bless the Internal Revenue Service! Last month they sent me a check for $1,200. This is part of President Bush's economic plan to jump-start the economy by providing a $400 tax credit for each child under the age of 18. It is the first time my children have turned a profit. It made me wish that Gretchen and I had more offspring. With six children I could have purchased a better car. Amazingly, we didn't have to apply for this bonanza. It simply arrived in the mail, unasked for, but deeply appreciated.

Then, some of my colleagues on the pastoral team had to go and ruin it by asking how I was going to spend this surplus income in a God-honoring way. Why do they have to be theological about everything? What is wrong with just enjoying it, no questions asked? I have lots of ideas of what to do with the money. I need a new lawn mower. There are about ten locomotives I would like for my model train layout. I still haven't taken Gretchen away for our 25 wedding anniversary over a year ago. Then my so-called "friends" reminded me of things I have said in my own sermons. That is playing dirty! I have often preached that God gives us more than we need, not so that we can indulge ourselves but so that we can give to others. The danger is that every time we get a pay raise or receive a generous gift like this one from the IRS, we increase our spending to match our income. The problem with that approach is that it deprives us of happiness: Jesus taught that *It is more blessed to give than to receive. (Acts 20:25)*

So, somewhat reluctantly, I began to think biblically about this unexpected windfall. The president intends it to be an investment in the economy, yet as a Christian I am called to invest my resources in God's kingdom. It has come to me because of my children, and as the money is not in the federal budget, my children will actually be paying for it in the years to come. As Gretchen and I discussed this it suddenly hit us: let's invest the money in the Imagine A Place building campaign. Our new church building will be used to introduce children to Jesus. They will be discipled in the Christian faith and sent out as adults in service all over the world. The building project also will help the economy. It will provide work for many local people and businesses. It is win-win all around, economically and spiritually and we will even get a tax deduction for it at the end of the year!

How are you spending your child tax credit? May I encourage you to invest it in the eternal well-being of your children and that of thousands of others as we together imagine a place where generations to come will know God.

Chapter 57

The Heavens Declare the Glory of God

John

September 2003

Each night at Family Camp about 10 p.m. Gretchen and I took a canoe out on the lake. We paddled in complete darkness to the center of the lake and waited. It wasn't long before Mars appeared in the southeast corner of the sky followed closely by a full moon. It was a spectacular sight and we never tired of it. We continued to enjoy Mars' nightly appearance on our return to Rochester. It was the brightest light in the sky because it was closer to earth, a mere 35 million miles, than it had been for 60,000 years.

Mars has always fascinated us. The ancient Egyptians named it the Red One. The Babylonians preferred Star of Death, while the Greeks called it The Fiery One. It was the Romans who opted for Mars after their own god of war. Star gazers like Ptolemy, Copernicus, Kepler, Galileo and Herschel have puzzled over this small reddish dot that weaves its nightly magic through the zodiac. They drew momentous conclusions. Percival Lowell speculated romantically about how a dying civilization had channelled water across the Martian deserts in an attempt to save itself. H. G. Welles' *War of the Worlds* fed the fascination and he turned the story into a radio broadcast that convinced America of little green men who were coming to get us.

Scripture says that God created the stars on the fourth day. The Psalmist beautifully describes this:

> *By the word of the Lord were the heavens made, their starry host by the breath of his mouth (Psalm 33:6).*

Job refers to the constellations:

> *He is the maker of the Bear and Orion, the Pleiades (Job 9:9).*

We may understand little of the stars but it is clear that God controls them as he uses a star to lead the wise men to Jesus. The Apostle John in his apocalypse uses the mysterious symbolism of stars. Jesus is the morning star. A woman appears with a crown of twelve stars on her head representing the believing community. Local churches are described as stars that Jesus holds in his hands. In Matthew, Jesus tells how his second coming will be marked by stars falling from the sky and the heavenly bodies being shaken.

Scripture records how ancient people were prone to worship the stars because of their distance and mystery. We may feel that we are beyond this, yet we fall into a similar trap when we marvel at the stars but fail to take the next step and honor the one who created them. There has been much written in recent days about Mars and the first movement of Holst's magnificent symphony The Planets has been frequently played on National Public Radio. As we gaze upward let us praise the one who placed Mars in its orbit and has given us the rare opportunity to be alive as it swings so near to our own planet.

It seems almost trite to say that looking at the star is a humbling experience, yet we identify with David when he declares:

> *When I consider your heavens, the work of your fingers, the moon and the stars, which you have set in place, what is man that you are mindful of him? (Psalm 8:3)*

The apostle Paul was an amateur astronomer. Writing to the Corinthian church he describes the various kinds of heavenly bodies noting that one star differs from another in splendor. Certainly in recent days Mars (which of course is a planet rather than a star) has dominated the night sky as it vividly reminds us of the greatness and glory of God who gives us all things richly to enjoy.

Chapter 58

The Implications of Choosing Wisely
Gretchen
July 2004

On our family holiday to England during the summer of 2004 we had an unusual experience. A freak accident caused John to break his scapula (shoulder blade).

It was Father's Day and we were on our way out of the tiny fishing village of Port Isaac, Cornwall, looking forward to an afternoon on the beach playing with John's new cricket set. Our daughter Hannah asked if we could stop at the park. Moments later my husband was in agony with an apparent dislocated shoulder after falling off the parallel bars. We soon discovered that there are no emergency medical services in a place this small. In fact, Port Isaac is called "the remotest village in England" because it is so far from the nearest town nine and one half miles away. Now nine and one half miles may not sound like much, but Cornish roads are extremely narrow. You creep cautiously along, and if you meet someone coming toward you, one of you backs up to a wider spot to allow the other to pass. The nearest hospital was in Bodmin, some 23 miles away. It fell to me to learn how to drive on the wrong side of the road, with the steering on the right side of the car, under conditions where every bump caused John to nearly faint with pain. And the whole way he kept muttering, "How could I have been so stupid?! How could I have been so stupid?!"

That is often how we feel when there has been a disastrous outcome to a choice. I'm not talking about the innocent choice of stopping at the park to play. I didn't fall off the teeter totter or swings, but then, I wasn't showing off on the parallel bars!

Sometimes we feel that life deals us unexpected outcomes, as with an illness or accident. But even with an accident like this one, if we trace back the series of events, we'll see that John made a choice involved in playing on the parallel bars. Usually, though, there's a much clearer relationship between choice and outcome.

To illustrate this, take the subject of purity. If purity is something we desire, then choice is involved early on, as we decide what to wear. I'm from a place (southern California) where people don't wear many clothes in the summer. All that exposed skin has a powerful effect upon sexuality, especially among high school and college students. We inadvertently transmit the message of availability and sexiness by our clothes, even when there is no intention of taking it further.

So if purity's important, think about it when you're getting dressed as well as when you're making those later, irrevocable decisions. One seldom arrives at an unplanned pregnancy or loss of virginity or adultery without having first made a series of choices.

We joke about parents saying "make good choices!" as their adolescent leaves the house. However, making good choices is something we are called to do in Christ. True moral fiber is only provided by a relationship with God, not by personal discipline or willpower. And so the first choice we need to make is the choice to follow God.

By following God, I mean what happens after we come to Christ: the day-in-and-day-out effort to live as though Christ makes a difference to us. To follow Christ means that I put every daily decision through a simple grid: "Will this action honor Christ or dishonor him?" Sometimes the choice isn't really a moral one. For example, Christ isn't dishonored by our decision to go to one college over another. He isn't dishonored if we take a job in insurance instead of banking. But he is dishonored if we stay in a job that has an immoral corporate environment, where we're expected to cook the books or sleep with clients. Fortunately, those jobs are few and far between. Christ doesn't really care about our career choice as long as it is compatible with serving him. He doesn't mind where we go to college as long as we are able to pursue a life of faith in that setting.

I chose to go to a large, secular university, UCLA. I was blissfully happy there even when taking courses that were opposed to my beliefs. In the collegiate environment there is always room for debate as long as you can keep up your end of the argument. I found that the arguments clarified my views rather than destroying them. I also chose to live off campus, so I could stay close to my youth group and church. I knew that I had to remain in the company of other Christians if I was going to tackle opposing worldviews during the week.

The first big choice, therefore, is embracing God and committing to follow him. We don't know the outcome and the implications when we decide to follow God. Only later do we discover that God has been the one drawing us to himself, and that he will lead us in surprising directions. But if you've come to Christ, don't dither about how seriously to follow him. You might be fretting about these questions: Should I be baptized? Should I join the church? Should I begin a ministry? Should I bother to find a Christian group at college? You need to put those choices through the single grid by asking: "Does this honor Christ or dishonor him?" and those decisions will become crystal clear.

Following God is only the starting place for the decisions we make. Another important factor in our choices is selecting life companions. Our companions powerfully affect our ability to walk with Christ. That's why questions such as… should I get close to that person? Should I pull back from my parents a bit? Should I marry that guy?…are so significant.

The simplest way to get an answer for these questions is to put them through the grid: "Does this honor Christ or dishonor him?" Even within our morally-permissible choice, it's difficult to predict the outcome. Whether it is friends or a spouse, the relationship choices we make in early years often determine who will influence our thoughts and actions in later years. That is why it is so incredibly important to become allied with likeminded and godly people.

Choices always have consequences. Sometimes outcomes occur, like John's broken shoulder, that we can't anticipate. But usually we have some idea where our choices are taking us, either toward God, or away from God. The question: "Does this relationship honor Christ or dishonor Christ?" often clarifies larger life choices such as, "Should I marry this man or not?"

One other area of choice I want to mention briefly is the wise use of freedom.

Paul writes in Galatians:

> *It is for freedom that Christ has set us free. Stand firm, then, and do not let yourselves be burdened again by a yoke of slavery (Galatians 5:1).*

It's true that we have extraordinary freedom in Christ. We have the freedom to become like him. We have freedom from the burden of keeping the law. We have freedom from the shackles of sin. But if we hear "freedom" and think "license" we are dead wrong. This freedom exists to help us follow Christ, not so we can grieve him with our poor choices. The fact that we have forgiveness from sin doesn't mean that we can spend our time sinning.

It seems to me that the main temptation during our 20's and 30's is to become sinfully self-directed, not considering what God wants for us, but only what feels good to us. In college one time I spoke with a doctoral teaching assistant about my prospects after graduation. He sighed and with a jaded air said, "Ah yes, I remember those days—the world is your oyster, isn't it?" And indeed it does feel that for the first time in our young lives we have the ability to choose our own course. That course often includes drifting away from God toward promiscuity or materialism. The choice may lead toward something that is not inherently bad, like a career or marriage, but that completely occupies our attention, leaving no time for God. The Bible calls that idolatry— anything that is put ahead of our relationship with God. And, like every choice, those we make early on have consequences for our later lives.

From the ancient perspective of 40-plus years, I want to remind you that being young and single, or even young, married and childless, provides you with an array of choices that is not easily available again in your life. This *is* the time when you can simply pick up and move to Mongolia or Chile and teach English as a second language for a year. This *is* the time when you can throw yourself into relationships of depth and value, when you can serve in your church and volunteer in your community, when you can travel and read books and embrace God fully. Don't defer those things until later. The choices you make now will determine what sort of person you are in your 40s, 50's and 60's. Use your freedom in Christ to become more like Christ.

James writes:

> Why, you do not even know what will happen tomorrow. What is your life? You are a mist that appears for a little while and then vanishes. Instead you ought to say, 'If it is the Lord's will, we will live and do this or that' (James 4:13-24).

All of our choices come down to that one outcome: If it is the Lord's will, we will live and do this or that. So make sure that the "this or that" you choose falls within God's desires for you.

Chapter 59

Sing to One Another in Hymns

John

January 2005

I always enjoy a hymn more if I know the story behind it. Last summer when our family was in England we took the opportunity to visit the homes of three of the great hymn writers. One week we rented a small fisherman's cottage in Brixham, a delightful seaside village in Devon. My son Nicholas and I joined eight other worshippers for Holy Communion one Tuesday morning in the church. The first vicar of the church was Henry Lyte (1793-1847). He was the author of one of my favorite hymns, *Abide With Me*. As a teenager I memorized this and even learned to play it on the piano. Traditionally it is sung before the Cup Final Football Game in Wembly Stadium, the English equivalent of the Super Bowl. Lyte wrote the hymn just before his death. His confidence of Christ's presence with him in the dark valley of the shadow shines though in the final verse:

> *Hold Thou Thy cross before my closing eyes,*
> *Shine through the gloom, and point me to the skies,*
> *Heaven's morning breaks, and earth's vain shadows flee;*
> *In life, in death, O Lord, abide with me.*

One Sunday we drove to the village of Olney in Buckinghamshire, the home of two prolific hymn writers John Newton (1725-1807) and William Cowper, pronounced Cooper (1731-1800). We worshipped in St. Peter and St. Paul Church where Newton was the minister. He is the author of *Amazing Grace* and hundreds of other hymns. He often wrote a hymn especially for a service if there wasn't a suitable one in the hymnbook. My favorite Newton hymn is *How Sweet the Name of Jesus Sounds*. It reflects the strong faith of this man who had been a slave trader. Unlike some poets, Newton wasn't mystical. He was a Calvinist with a practical faith. It took him some time to recognize that slave trading was incompatible with his new-found Christian testimony but once he did he passionately renounced the evil practice of slavery. Newton lived out these words of his own hymn:

> *'Till then I would Thy love proclaim*
> *With every fleeting breath;*
> *And may the music of Thy name*
> *Refresh my soul in death.*

William Cowper was one of England's great poets. He suffered from depression all his life. This resulted in suicide attempts.

247

To keep his friend busy, Newton suggested they compose a hymnbook that became known as *The Olney Hymnal*. Cowper responded well to Newton's love and fellowship but his illness was such that there was a period of three years when Cowper could not attend church, although it was only 100 yards from his front door. Cowper passionately believed the great truths of the gospel, but like so many afflicted by depression he could not accept that they applied to him. His greatest hymn, in my opinion, is *God Moves in A Mysterious Way*. It provides helpful counsel as we reflect on the December, 2004 tragedy in the Indian Ocean. Two of the verses declare:

> *God moves in a mysterious way*
> *His wonders to perform;*
> *He plants His footsteps in the sea,*
> *And rides upon the storm.*

> *Judge not the Lord by feeble sense,*
> *But trust Him for his grace*
> *Behind a frowning providence*
> *He hides a smiling face.*

All three of these hymn writers spoke freely about death, a topic we seldom find in modern praise songs. It is true that they lived in days when the average life expectancy was much shorter. However, they also understood that the Christian life is a preparation for eternity. Even when we are faced with death, Christians can sing because of the triumph of Jesus over the grave. In his hymn, *There Is a Fountain Filled With Blood,* Cowper perhaps reflects his own longing to escape the agony of this life and move on to heaven when he writes:

> *When this poor, lisping, stammering tongue,*
> *Lies silent in the grave,*
> *Then in a nobler, sweeter song*
> *I'll sing Thy power to save.*

I have loved the hymns of these great servants of God all my life, but visiting their homes and churches has given me a new appreciation. Paul tells us that we are to:

> *Sing psalms, hymns and spiritual songs with gratitude in*
> *your hearts to God (Colossians 3:16).*

May God raise up hymn writers from First Baptist Church who will allow us to express our faith in our day as Lyte, Newton and Cowper did in theirs.

Chapter 60

Love is a Many-Splendored Thing

Gretchen
June 2005

I was always fascinated by the use of the word "manifold" to describe the wisdom of God. In Ephesians 3:10 the word translated "manifold" means multi-hued, or many-splendored. Like God's wisdom, God's love is a many-splendored thing, not expressed in just one shade but ranging richly through the spectrum of colors. We tend to corral and limit love by defining it only in terms of specific relationships: husband and wife, child and parent. I would be the first to acknowledge that those relationships are certainly among God's greatest gifts to us in this life.

However, as I grow older, I've observed two interesting trends. The first is that the line between genders becomes obliterated, almost as if we're becoming more like each other (perhaps because we're collectively becoming more like Christ). The second trend is that the affection of friends has become more open and easily acknowledged—even among taciturn Midwesterners! For 15 years in Minnesota our family has celebrated Thanksgiving, Christmas and Easter with friends. This is because our siblings and relatives are far away. These friends, through shared history, have become as dear as family. Perhaps it's just easier to be a friend as we get older and grow in grace.

It seems to me that God gives us a glimpse of heaven through good friendships on earth. After all, there will be no marriage in heaven (Matthew 22:30). One gets the impression that our heavenly releationships will be as good as the best we've experienced here on earth, whether as friends, children, parents, or wives. Could it be that all our relationships in heaven will be as emotionally intimate as the best we've had on earth? In heaven, our shared delight in God, together with the absence of sin, pride, and competition, will make it possible to enjoy what we see only dimly here on earth.

Our culture sometimes implies that the only significant relationships can be those between husband and wife, or parent and child—yet not everyone experiences marriage, or parenthood. Friendship is available to us all. It springs unexpectedly from small groups or shared lives, growing between people who may be quite different, but who share the core love of their lives as believers... Jesus Christ. When Christ wanted to describe the heights of love, he said:

> *This is my commandment, that you love one another as I have loved you. Greater love has no man than this, that a man lay down his life for his friends. (John 15:12-13)*

...not his wife, not his children, but his friends.

Then Jesus said:

> *You are my friends if you do what I command you. (John 15:14)*

Not only has Christ commanded us to love one another, but he's given us the grace to do so through the shared love we have for him. So love freely, my friends. Our good friendships here provide a foretaste of heaven.

Chapter 61

In Grateful Memory of Twitchett (1994-2007)

John

2007

Today I made a sad discovery. Leaving for church I found our rabbit Twitchett lying motionless in his hutch. He had died in the night. Tears welled up in my eyes. He had been a wonderful pet for 13 years. My father bought him for Emily on his last visit to Rochester before he died, so Twitchett was always a very tangible reminder of my dad. We went to Brink's Pet Shop and paid $20 for him, but Twitchett was worth a hundred times that. He was a handsome white and brown Mini Rex with a gentle disposition. In his earlier years Twitchett was feistier but as he aged, he mellowed gracefully. Like many men, the passage of years (or perhaps just a drop in testosterone) turned him into a perfect gentleman.

In the winter he lived in our basement in a large hutch positioned at eyelevel. We passed him every time we entered or left the house, as the basement leads into our garage. I enjoyed taking him carrots, apples or lettuce leaves which he ate enthusiastically as I stroked him. In the summer he lived in a large pen in the garden where we could keep an eye on him from the house. This pen was split into two halves by chicken wire, with Twitchett on one side and his mate on the other. The two would nuzzle each other through the barrier, until one day we discovered that Twitchett had patiently chewed his way through the fence in order to be reunited with his wife.

Twitchett did nothing to hurt the reputation of rabbits for being prolific. He provided his four wives with a variety of litters, gaining the epithet Twitchett: Father of Many. The children raised these adorable bunnies and always hated to part with them. Reluctantly they advertised them in the church newsletter with the irresistible selling point, "raised in a Christian home." I am so glad that Twitchett's progeny are still owned by members of the congregation and community.

I have always loved rabbits. As a boy I bred Dutch rabbits and took them to shows. My first construction project was to build a shed for their cages on which I affixed a large sign that read The Rabitry. I was immensely proud of this until my mother pointed out the spelling mistake. I was delighted when my own children shared my passion for rabbits. Once they were old enough they faithfully cleaned the cages each week and fed the rabbits each day.

Max Gernand kindly provided us with sawdust from his woodworking projects and we purchased sweet smelling bales of alfalfa from Dan Ostergard. Each hutch had a bedroom that we packed with hay, along with comfortable living quarters.

The Bible doesn't have much to say about rabbits. Leviticus provides the obvious information that, *The rabbit, though it chews the cud, does not have a split hoof.* Deuteronomy commands, *You may not eat the rabbit,* which was unnecessary as we had no intention of putting Twitchett in the cooking pot. Yet rabbits are part of God's creation. They are made to reflect his glory. They are given for our enjoyment and Twitchett provided years of that. Rabbits tell us that our God is no minimalist. He over engineers his world as a mark of his magnanimous overflowing grace. We could probably live perfectly satisfactorily without them, but for me at least, rabbits are a gift from our generous God. (I realize that gardeners whose crops are eaten by wild rabbits may disagree!)

Twitchett calmed my spirit. Returning home at 10:30 p.m. after a long Elders meeting with budgets and strategies churning through my mind I would stop at his cage and have a chat with him. The stress would fall away as I looked into the eyes of this docile, trusting creature.

I used to think that animals didn't go to heaven because they don't have souls. However, that probably comes from too much emphasis on the last two chapters of Revelation and too little understanding of the first two chapters of Genesis. Animals were part of God's perfect world before the fall. Death had not entered the world and so animals presumably lived forever. God looked at this world and declared that it was good. By his death and resurrection Jesus defeated the curse of sin. He came not only to restore us humans to our original state of perfection but the whole of his creation, including bunnies, as well.

Therefore I have come to see that heaven is not an insubstantial spirit world only populated with souls, but a tangible material one which contains the best of everything God has made. I have every hope of seeing animals in that paradise that Jesus has gone to prepare for us. I will miss Twitchett more than I can say. He was with us through our children's growing up years. Thankfully, he is survived by Liesbet, his significant other. Liesbet is a lop-eared Belgian doe and I trust that she will be with us for many more years to come.

Chapter 62

A Living Hope

July 2007
John

It's wonderful to be back with you. I missed you enormously when I was away. When we go on vacation, our family enjoys bringing back gifts for friends and family. It might be a piece of china or a bar of Cadbury's chocolate or some tea and biscuits. I wanted to bring you each a gift.

But what could I bring the 1,500 wonderful folk at Autumn Ridge Church without chartering a jumbo jet? Well, I found the perfect present for you. It is the gift of hope. It's a valuable gift because all of us want hope—indeed, all of us need hope.

Now the hope I have for you is not just average hope or ordinary hope. It is A LIVING HOPE.

Peter describes it in his first letter when he writes:

> *Praise be to the God and Father of our Lord Jesus Christ! In his great mercy he has given us new birth into a living hope.* (1 Peter 1: 3)

There is such a thing as dead hope. For example, while recently watching the Wimbledon Tennis Tournament I remembered the time that I thought I might play tennis at Wimbledon. That was a dead hope! But Peter here talks about a living hope, an undying hope, an enduring hope, a hope that continues, a hope that delivers. That is the hope I want to give you.

I bring you hope because it has been much on my mind recently. Our recent vacation abroad was a series of disasters interspersed with hope. Gretchen and I went to visit the Highlands of Scotland for the first time. We took a plane from London to Inverness, a journey that should have taken an hour. As we were preparing to land the pilot informed us that they had lost the hydraulics and so could not brake the plane. Since the runway was not long enough in Inverness they were going to divert to Glasgow, the airport that was just recently bombed. So we went all the way to Glasgow and landed uneventfully, except that the back of the plane caught fire. The passengers got off fine but the ground staff couldn't collect our baggage because of the smoke. When the luggage was eventually retrieved hours later we were told we would be taken the remaining 200 miles to Inverness by bus.

Well, we had enough at this point, so we rented a car, convinced that we could drive there quicker than a bus. Unfortunately, leaving the airport, we took a wrong turn and got stuck in an hour-long traffic jam. We eventually arrived at our little flat on the shore of Loch Broom at midnight, feeling utterly fed-up.

The next day was Sunday, or the Sabbath as they call it in Scotland. We went along to the Free Presbyterian Church and our presence swelled the numbers to 10. The Free Presbyterians are wonderful people. They don't believe in talking to each other in church, rather they go outside to natter. They stand to pray and sit to sing. They use no musical instruments whatsoever and only sing the Psalms. I didn't mind any of that but I did want some encouragement. Indeed, when the pastor began to speak he chose this passage in First Peter and reminded us that we have a living hope. In light of what had happened to us the previous day, when I wasn't sure we were going to be living much longer, I immediately began to feel better. What that pastor did for me that Sunday, I hope I can do for you.

This theme of hope re-occurred at the conference I attended at Spurgeon's Seminary and in every other church service we experienced while we were away. I began to the get the idea that God wanted me to think about hope. Turning this subject of hope over in my mind, I asked three questions that I want you to consider with me.

Where do we go for a living hope? It is an important question for Peter's readers because they are being persecuted. Looking at their situation you might call it hopeless. Peter describes them as *Strangers in the world.* (verse 1) As a result of their suffering, they have been *scattered throughout Pontus, Galatia, Cappadocia, Asia and Bithynia.* (verse 1) In other words, they are not at home—they have been forced to flee. Peter tells them exactly where they must go for a living hope in their hopeless situation. He says you must run to *the God and Father of our Lord Jesus Christ.* (verse 3)

This is good news because if they needed to go to someone with money or influence they were out of luck. They didn't know anybody like that. They did have God, and so do we. Therefore, whatever our situation, however despondent we might feel, we have a God who is here by his spirit, to whom we can run. He will give us hope.

How can we be absolutely certain that this God will give us hope? We can be completely confident because of *God's great mercy.* (verse 3) Mercy is what we don't deserve. We don't deserve a living hope, but God gives it to us anyway.

Perhaps you have heard about the parents of a child who went missing while on vacation in Portugal. She was snatched from her hotel room in Portugal two months ago, and has not been seen since. Her parents have gone to extraordinary lengths to find her. They both have given up their jobs and have traveled around Europe holding press conferences. They have appealed to the kidnapper and asked anybody who might have information to please contact the authorities. The result of their energetic activity is that pictures of the missing girl are everywhere throughout Europe. We saw it plastered all over the town of Ullapool in the north of Scotland, hundreds of miles from Portugal.

All the children of Ullapool have been touched by this tragedy. They have tied yellow ribbons around the railings at the harbor in memory of a girl they've never seen and don't know anything about—but they had heard about her. There was even a photo of this little girl at our rented flat on the off chance that in our travels we might have seen her.

That is a great picture of how our heavenly Father searches for his lost children. His heart is filled with mercy toward us. He will go to any lengths to take us home. Without God we are *without hope. . . in the world*, Paul tells the Ephesians. But with God we have all the hope in the world. So if, like me, you need this living hope, then run to this great God of mercy and ask him for it.

What do we get with this living hope? In other words, what makes this hope so special? We've had many hopes over the years and they have encouraged us for awhile, but sooner or later we forget them or they let us down. Why is this hope different from any other?

The answer is that this hope covers the whole of life, from beginning to end. Indeed, it gives us a new beginning and promises a glorious conclusion. Peter is very clear about this. First he points out that God *has given us a new birth into a living hope.* (verse 3)

A new birth is a new beginning. It comes about when we are born again by the Spirit of God. That is essential to a life of hope. Many of us can't be hopeful because of experiences in the past. We have done things, or have had things done to us, that make it very hard to be hopeful people. God knows this. He said, "It doesn't matter what you have done. I am going to forgive you. I am going to flood you with my presence and fill you with my Spirit. As far as I am concerned everything starts afresh from the moment you become my child."

Not only do we have this new beginning, we have a glorious ending. In his great mercy God has given us a living hope *into an inheritance that can never perish, spoil or fade—kept in heaven for you.* (verse 4)

That was really good news to the readers of this letter because they had lost all their possessions. They either had to leave them behind when they fled the persecution, or their property had been taken from them. Peter comforts them by saying "Don't worry– there is better to come. God has given you an inheritance that you can never lose."

We typically receive an inheritance when someone dies. So who dies here in order for us to get our inheritance? There are two answers to that question.

First, it is Jesus who dies. Peter refers to this when he says that God has given us *a living hope through the resurrection of Jesus from the dead.* (verse 3) The moment that Jesus rose from the dead, his life became ours. We can enjoy it right now.

But there is a sense in which we don't fully receive our inheritance until we die. This is why Peter tells us that *it is kept in heaven for you.* Peter's point to these suffering saints is that the very worst that can happen to them, death, is in fact the very best that can happen to them. It will be by death that they enjoy the inheritance made possible through the death and resurrection of Jesus. We enter into this inheritance because of the death of Jesus, but when the time comes for us to die, that inheritance that has been kept in heaven will be ours in all its fullness and completeness.

I glimpsed some of the glory of this inheritance at London airport a couple of weeks ago. Now I am not normally given to visions at airports so I will explain what I mean.

At the airport I passed the place where departing passengers were saying good-bye to their families. It was a sad scene. In many cases, there were long embraces and tears. Some of the passengers would not see their family and friends for many months, or perhaps years. Saying good-bye to a beloved son or daughter can be desperately difficult.

However, around the corner there was a very different scene. This was the arrival hall. There was a wonderful spirit of expectation in the air. Gretchen and I were first in line waiting for our three children to emerge from the customs area. We had gone to England a week ahead of them. The plan was for the children to follow us. However, due to the spectacular inefficiency of a certain airline, our children had been delayed (essentially abandoned), for two full days at Chicago airport. Meanwhile, their parents were just about having heart attacks wondering what was happening to them.

We had been extremely concerned for them, so their arrival was all the more welcome. As each passenger stepped into the arrival hall, we eagerly scanned their faces. When finally our three children appeared, Gretchen couldn't contain herself. She rushed through the barrier, not caring about security, and flung her arms around them. They were finally home.

It struck me that this scene happens each time a person dies. In the departure hall, we on earth grieve their passing. There are tears as we say goodbye. But just around the corner, in the arrival hall in heaven, the Father can scarcely contain himself. This is the moment he has been waiting for. This is the reason why Jesus died. Our arrival is a cause of great joy in the halls of heaven. This is the inheritance that is ours. It is a moment to anticipate!

There is a measure of comfort in knowing that, as we stand in the departure hall of a funeral service, just around the corner there is a very different scene as God welcomes his children home. As he presents them with their inheritance he says, "I've been keeping this for you. Here it is. This is what you get as a result of being born again."

What should we do with this living hope? Do we just say say, "well this is nice, bear it in mind," or is there some practical application? Peter has two answers for us.

First we are to praise. We're to thank God. We are to worship him for what he has done for us in giving us this unending, enduring hope. This repeatedly emerges in the passage. In verse 3 Peter says, *Praise be to the God and Father of our Lord Jesus Christ.* In verse 6 he adds, *In this you greatly rejoice.* In verse 8, he writes *You are filled with an inexpressible and glorious joy.*

Hopeful people are happy people. If we don't feel like praising today, then we need to reflect on what Peter is saying here and understand the colossal cost and the fantastic consequences of this living hope offered freely to us.

The second thing we should do with this living hope is to persevere—to keep going. *For a little while you may have to suffer grief in all kinds of trials* (verse 6). Peter is reminding these scattered saints that God knows all about their suffering. He is not indifferent to it. He has even permitted it for a great reason:

> *These have come so that your faith . . . may be proved genuine and may result in praise, glory and honor when Jesus Christ is revealed.* (verse 7)

Peter's point is this: people without hope give up. Those with a living hope keep going. They persevere because they know that there is a purpose in their problems and that victory is just around the corner.

On vacation, our family loves to walk on the coastal path. A week ago my son Nicky and I did a 16-mile hike on the north Devon coast. It is often hard-going, but we see splendid scenery. Sometimes you leave the path and find the road blocked by a herd of sheep. This year we ran into a lot of rain and were often drenched with many miles of walking to go. Sometimes we are in remote places where we don't see another human being for hours. We don't give up—we persevere. The reason is that we know what lies ahead. We use an ordinance survey map. These maps show every path and stream, pub and church, road and field. They indicate the contours of every yard of countryside. We can look at these maps and know that in five or six miles we are coming to a marvelous village where we can enjoy a Devon cream tea. Thus, even though our location can seem pretty remote and hopeless, because there's not a building in sight and the rain's lashing down, we keep going. That's the value of an ordinance survey map. It shows you where you are, and where you are going.

As Christians, we have the very same thing in the word of God. It shows us where we are going and it describes this inheritance that can never perish, spoil or fade. The Bible doesn't promise an easy life. On the contrary, it warns of sadness, suffering and sickness, but despite all this Peter can say, *You are receiving the goal of your faith, the salvation of your souls.* (verse 9)

This is why hopeful people can accomplish exceptional tasks. They can persevere in the face of extraordinary difficulties and dangers.

Helmut Thielike was a German pastor in Hamburg at the end of the Second World War when it was clear that Germany was going to be defeated. He wanted to offer hope to his people, so he preached a series on The Lord's Prayer titled The Prayer that Spans the World. When he began the series there were many churches in Hamburg. When he concluded, every church had been destroyed by the allied bombing.

It takes a great grasp of God's hope to be able to say, when your city has been reduced to rubble, *Thy will be done*. Yet that is exactly what God's people can do because they have a living hope. They know where they are going. They have a hope that is possible because of the resurrection of Jesus.

Each country celebrates historical events that bring hope to its people. Our own nation is celebrating one of these this week on the Fourth of July. We remember the Declaration of Independence and how a small band of American colonists were able to take on and defeat one of the great world powers of the day. We draw strength and encouragement from that memory. Looking back helps us to keep going now.

Communities also have memorable moments. We spent a week at the delightful town of Lynmouth in Devon. There are only a few hundred people who live there, but they have one particular event in their history from which they draw hope today. It took place in 1899. There was a terrible storm in the Bristol Channel and a sailing ship called The Forest Hall was in great danger. The ship had both her anchors down but the wind was so strong that it was driving the vessel onto the rocks. It was clear that eventually the anchors would fail.

The lifeboat crew in Lynmouth got the call to rescue the sailors, but the sea was so rough that the lifeboat could not be launched. The lifeboat captain said, "We must take the boat over the mountain and launch it from the harbor on the other side where the water will be calmer." Now you need to know that this hill is one of the steepest in Britain, with a one in four grade. Even today it is treacherous to descend by car. Remarkably, in lashing rain, they put the lifeboat on wheels and began to push it 15 miles overland.

There were only cart tracks in those days, for modern roads hadn't been built. In places, the track wasn't big enough for the lifeboat and so stone walls had to be moved. They persevered despite the enormous difficulties, pushing and pulling that lifeboat up and down one of the steepest hills in England. They arrived at Porlock Harbor at 6:30 the next morning. Exhausted and soaked, they didn't stop, but immediately launched the lifeboat. They rescued the crew of The Forest Hall just before the ship hit the rocks. That community is proud of the feat to this day. They have a display in the town to make sure that it is not forgotten. They even reenacted the event on its centenary.

So, as Christians, we look back on the event that gives us the greatest pride and confidence. It is the resurrection of Jesus that imparts to us our living hope. With Peter we say:

> *Praise be to the God and Father of our Lord Jesus Christ! In his great mercy he has given us new birth into a living hope through the resurrection of Jesus Christ from the dead, and into an inheritance that can never perish, spoil or fade—kept in heaven for you.* (verses 3 and 4)

So God raises his great cup of hope to our lips and urges us to drink deeply. Hope is his gift to us, and I am passing it on to you. Hope is a gift we must not keep to ourselves. When we've received it, we must share it with others. Our church needs to be a place where we are constantly giving out hope—a place open to the Holy Spirit who can fill up God's people with hope, sending them forth with that message to a world that desperately needs it.

I urge you to grasp this hope and enjoy this hope. Our hope is anchored in the past because Jesus rose. Our hope remains in the present for Jesus lives. Our hope is completed in the future because Jesus is coming again.

Father, we thank you that the hope you offer is not a faint hope, or forlorn hope, or a fragile hope, but a fantastic hope, because it is based on the resurrection of Jesus. For if you can raise your son from the dead, you can raise us from despair. If you can pull him out of the tomb, you can pull us out of our troubles. We throw ourselves on your great mercy. We ask that you will cause us to be born again into this living hope.

Chapter 63

Looking Back—Looking Forward

John and Gretchen
August 2007

Two thousand seven has been a year of milestones for our church and for our family. Autumn Ridge Church has been in existence 150 years. Our marriage turned 30 this July... and Gretchen has reached her half century.

Our church celebrated its sesquicentennial with a year of joyful events. We noted our 30th anniversary by sharing the pulpit and talking on the subject of marriage. Gretchen marked her 50th birthday by backpacking in the John Muir wilderness with her four siblings.

Is older better? We hope so, because the future holds great things for us as a congregation. Like the Israelites we can look back and recount God's goodness. In 1912 the new sanctuary of First Baptist Church burned to the ground, but the church went on. In 1980 the congregation built on what was then the outskirts of town, only to outgrow those facilities and move to Autumn Ridge. God has been faithful to us. One of the blessings of being in one place for a long time is the ability to see the great scope of his work.

As the Autumn Ridge Church facility rose from the ground, and the details of construction and financing fell into place, we were constantly reminded: "It's not for us." As strangers flow through our doors and become friends to us and to God through the ministries of this church, we see the truth of that statement. Growth is not usually comfortable, and obedience to God often demands more than we think we can give. But it's not for us. In order to love God and to serve people, we must truly open our doors to the world. Through those doors will enter Christians from the fledgling church in Kosova... newcomers to Rochester looking for a spiritual home... children from Mongolia needing heart operations... former prisoners looking for a new life. We cannot wait to see what God will do with us in the coming years. With Paul we affirm:

> *Now to him who is able to do immeasurably more than all we ask or imagine, according to his power that is at work within us, to him be glory in the church and in Christ Jesus throughout all generations, for ever and ever! Amen. (Ephesians 3:20-21)*

Page 9. Article first published in *SWBC Social Ministries Quarterly*, Fall 1988, under the title "The Anatomy of Grief: How God Restores Our Soul in Times of Loss," by C. John Steer, printed with permission from the publisher.

Page 19. "Mending" by Judith Viorst. From *If I were in Charge of the World and Other Worries* by Judith Viorst. Copyright © 1981 by Judith Viorst. Reprinted with permission of Atheneum Books For Young Readers, an imprint of Simon & Schuster Children's Publishing Division. All rights reserved.

Page 54. Quotation from Roman Catholic theologian John Pawlikowski first printed in *The Challenge of the Holocaust for Christian Theology*, published in 1994 by the Center for Studies on the Holocaust, printed with permission from the publisher.

Page 139. Quote from "Ten Practical Secrets for a Happy Marriage," published in *Learning to Live With the Love of Your Life*, by Dr. Neil Clark Warren.

Welcome to Autumn Ridge Church

Forty centuries ago, Abraham encountered the God of the universe and learned that this God could be known personally. Thirty-three centuries ago the personal encounter was extended to Moses. Thirty centuries ago it was David who taught that intimacy and honesty with God are possible. Twenty centuries ago God entered time to make a personal sacrifice—the rescue of fallen humanity—through the incarnation and crucifixion of Jesus Christ. A bridge back to God has been offered to us all.

It was one and a half centuries ago that a group of pioneers started a church in Rochester, Minnesota to worship God and offer this relationship to others. The congregation, now with a new name and a new $14.3 million facility, remains true to its purpose: Loving God. Serving people. We long to reach families, friends, neighbors and the world with the message that Jesus Christ died to pay for our sins so that each can know God personally. This is an ancient story. It is our story. This is the end of the beginning.

AUTUMN RIDGE CHURCH

Loving God. Serving people.